JOE BUCHER'S crankbait SECRETS

The first complete guide to fishing with crankbaits

BY JOE BUCHER

Published by

 **krause
publications**

700 E. State Street • Iola, WI 54990-0001
Telephone: 715/445-2214

Please call or write for our free catalog of publications.
Our toll-free number to place an order or obtain a free catalog is 800-258-0929
or please use our regular business telephone 715-445-2214
for editorial comment and further information.

Library of Congress Catalog Number: 98-87361
ISBN: 0-87341-729-1
Printed in the United States of America

To my loving wife, Beth:

Without your support, understanding, and dedication, I would not have been able to accomplish the things that I have. You've given up a lot of our time together so that I could research ideas and pursue a career in the fishing business. Thanks for being that special someone who has sacrificed so much for me. You have been my precious wife for 25 years, a fantastic mother to our son, and most of all - my best friend.

table of contents

foreword

I first became aware of Joe Bucher's fishing abilities in the 1970s. As editor of Fishing Facts magazine I'd get a lot of fish photos, but there was something special about this teenager with the ripped jeans. He wasn't send the occasional photo of a nice fish. He was showing off stringers of big bass, lunker walleyes and muskies more than 40 inches long. And all were being pulled from the hard-fished lakes and rivers near Milwaukee! The photos were usually blurry, but it was clear Joe new something about fishing.

Joe and I first became pen pals. We later met at a fishing club meeting where our editor-writer relationship began. Our close personal friendship has grown over the past two decades. As an editor, I could always count on Joe for cutting-edge articles. As he became a well-respected, full-time guide and fished daily, he began to provide Fishing Facts with some of the best and freshest material the magazine had ever published. I enjoyed editing Joe's articles because I often learned something from them.

Although many years have passed, I still remember ground-breaking articles he wrote about catching walleyes out of wood and various weed-fishing situations. He had some great musky articles that covered everything from fishing weeds at night to trolling open water for suspended fish. He could write about, and catch, anything from lunker bass to giant crappies.

While there was no aspect of fishing that Joe overlooked, a lot of his articles were about crankbaits. I still remember first reading about Joe using deep-diving plugs to catch walleyes and musky, day or night, in wood, weeds or suspended over open water. Most musky anglers regard Bucher's DepthRaider as the ultimate musky crankbait. There is no doubt Joe knows crankbaits. This book reveals many of the secrets he's picked up from years of on-the-water experience.

Spence Petros

Hall of Fame Angler

foreword

When Joe told me he was writing a book on crankbaits, I knew it would be outstanding. And it is.

I was first introduced to fishing nearly 50 years ago, when a small percentage of the anglers caught most of the fish. This ratio has changed dramatically in recent years thanks to improved angler education. That's something we can thank Joe for. He was one of the pioneers in teaching people how to catch more and bigger fish.

While he is most recognized in the field of musky fishing, his contributions to the understanding of how to catch bass, walleye and countless other gamefish, cannot be overstated. His expertise encompasses not only techniques, but strategies and tools. His Buchertail line of fishing products has become the standard upon which in the industry describes excellence.

In the 20 years we have been friends, his innovations in the field of fishing have continued to inspire me. Joe's actions on the water exemplify that there is always a better way. His results speak for themselves.

Unfortunately, most fishermen who have reached a reasonable level of expertise ignore much of the information presented by Joe and other educators. By doing so, they never achieve the highest level of performance that Joe shows when he offers a bait to the fish.

I hope you will READ and BELIEVE the information between the covers of this book. Doing so will increase your fishing success dramatically.

Tom Gelb

Field Editor, Musky Hunter magazine

introduction

To say I have an affinity for crankbaits would be an understatement. Even though I've developed a reputation as a versatile, all-season, all-species angler, I have to admit that I am partial to crankbaits. In fact, some would label me "crazy" about this lure category. I have at least a dozen large tackle boxes loaded to the brim with crankbaits of all sizes shapes and colors. I love crankbaits, and have lots of them. But most importantly, I've learned how to fish them.

That's what this book is all about — helping you learn about crankbaits. Not only how to fish them, but also the inside scoop on what really makes a crankbait tick. I'm talking about recognizing specific design features, and being able to understand why a particular crankbait does what it does. Once you know what makes a crankbait tick, choosing the right lure for any fishing situation becomes a lot easier. Knowledge breeds success with any fishing technique, and the subject of crankbaits is no different. The more you know, the more success you're going to have. I've often used the phrase "The more you learn, the luckier you get."

Contrary to popular belief, crankbaits are not mindless lures. Even though the term crankbait implies simply "cranking" a bait, there is actually much more to fishing these lures than that. Once you know the real scoop, and you definitely will after reading this book, crankbaits will probably become your main weapon. It just happens naturally, because you'll start catching more big fish on these lures than ever before. The more you learn about these fascinating lures, the more fish you catch, and consequently, the more you tend to rely on them. I know this will happen to you because it happened to me in just this way.

As will be revealed inside the pages of this book, my success with crankbaits started with one lure. I then learned everything I could about that lure before moving on to another. Each lure became a building block in the coliseum of crankbait fishing. Much of my evolution as an angler came along with my newfound knowledge of these lures. Along the way, I learned of the great differences among the crankbaits I fished. Some were floating divers, while others were sinkers. Some had big diving lips, while others had tiny ones. Some were long, thin-bodied baits, while others were short and fat. Some were plastic, others wood. A few were even metal. To say that all of these lures were basically the same would be a grave error. Yet it is one many anglers make.

My experience shows there are vast differences in some crankbaits. That's why I separated them into several categories and designated a chapter for each inside this book. For example, how could any angler even consider using the same approach with a floating balsa minnow bait like the Rapala and a lipless rattling plug such as the RatLtrap? Furthermore, how could you even think of working a sinking, metal blade bait like Luhr Jensen's Rippletail the same way you would work a floating diver such as the DepthRaider? All four of these lures are technically crankbaits, yet they're all very different. They all have their own personalities.

Depending on the fishing situation, each of these lure categories can be of equal importance. So much depends on the location of the fish, at what depth they're holding and what kind of mood they're in. When conditions are right for one of these specific crankbait categories, that lure will get hot. In the process, lots of fish will be taken and confidence will grow accordingly.

It's always important to keep an open mind about crankbait styles, and resist falling into the trap of fishing just one type of crankbait. None of the crankbait categories can be overlooked. In the large scheme of things, each is a tool designed for a certain job. When the job calls for that tool, you'll need to know what tool (lure) to choose, and how to properly use it. That's why I wrote this book.

I'm convinced that better than 95% of the anglers who own crankbaits do not know how to fish them. Even if this guess is wrong, I'll bet it isn't off by much. Most of these lures do nothing more than collect dust or rust. Many were originally purchased because of a strong ad campaign, or they simply "looked good" to the gullible buyer. All of these lures are actually good baits, but they need to be fished correctly in the right time and place. Knowing how to fish them correctly, and being able to recognize the right time and place is also what this book is all about.

I also made certain to include the basics of crankbait fishing when putting together this book. You'll learn about tackle combinations, line choices, and lure tuning. Outfitting the lure with the right rod & reel combo can make a huge difference in overall performance. The line, more specifically the line diameter, is one of the more critical factors in crankbait performance. It's so important, that I've devoted an entire chapter to it. Tuning a crankbait is another basic task not to be overlooked. An improperly tuned crankbait not only doesn't track straight, it doesn't catch fish. Tuning is worthy of its own chapter, as well.

Some of my favorite situation/presentations are the highlights of the tactics section. This includes crankin' weed flats, weed lines, wood, hard bottom, current, and open water. These techniques were discovered and developed through countless hours on the water. I like to call this on-the-job research. I learned how to fish crankbaits while I was a full-time fishing guide. It took years. The techniques are now considered classics in the world of crankbait fishing.

I also thought you'd enjoy two unusual chapters that push the envelop in crankbait fishing: cold-water crankin' and night crankin'. Few anglers try crankbaits in cold water. Most people never even consider that they might actually work. The chapter on cold-water fishing blows the lid off the old, established school of thought that artificial lures don't work in cold water. The cold-water blueprint for success is actually quite simple: **SPEED CONTROL + DEPTH CONTROL = FISH**. That equation works no matter what the water temperature.

Finally, I reveal some of my best-kept secrets in the chapter on night crankin'. Nighttime fishing has been a lifelong pursuit of mine. I began night fishing for bass as a teenager, and continued to chase walleyes after dark later on. But I'm probably most well-known for popularizing night fishing for muskies. The mighty musky was once considered a fish that didn't feed after dark. This chapter not only reveals that they do regularly feed at night, but it also shows crankbaits to be the best lure for them. Find out how my friends, guiding customers, and I dominated Wisconsin's big musky catches throughout the 1980s and on into the 1990s with this amazingly productive tactic.

No matter what your favorite fish species, it's a good bet that crankbaits will catch 'em at some time throughout the season. Remember, as you read this book, knowledge is your key to success with the crankbait. The more you learn about your lures, the more success you're going to have with them. Understanding the basic functions of various crankbaits is a start. Then you must learn how to use them in different situations.

You've heard it said before, "You must see the big picture." It's the same with crankbaits. There are a variety of fishing conditions that present themselves on any given outing. To achieve any level of success you need to locate the fish and choose the right lure to reach the fish and trigger a strike. Hopefully, this book will help you accomplish these goals as you learn more about the world of crankbaits.

fundamentals

chapter 1

The Roots Of A Crankbait

The term "crankbait" was actually coined by bass tournament anglers back in the late 1960s, and generally referred to any hard-bodied lure that had a natural, built-in action when retrieved. Before that time, such lures were referred to as plugs, wobblers, vibrating lures, and divers. In fact, the word "plugs" was as much the accepted terminology in this category of lures back in the 40s, 50s, and 60s as "crankbaits" is today. However, plugs also included top-water lures to some fishermen. Nowadays, the word crankbait does not include surface lures. The term "crankbait" only refers to a subsurface lure today.

What bass fishermen originally called a "crankbait" back in the days of Jimi Hendrix has now become a generic category including any hard-bodied lure made out of wood, plastic, foam, or any other market-acceptable material, that has a built-in action. Crankbaits can float or sink. Some are designed to run deep, others run shallow. A crankbait may or may not have a diving bill. For example, the famous Rapala is a floating lure with a diving bill. Another well-known bass lure, the RatLTrap, is a sinking lure that has no

diving bill, but it's also considered a crankbait. The Rapala falls into the crankbait sub-category called "minnow baits" while the RatLTrap fits into an equally popular crankbait sub-category called "lipless crankbaits." We'll decipher these many sub-categories in detail later.

The common denominator for all crankbaits is a built-in wiggling, wobbling action. As soon as any of these baits are retrieved or "cranked" it will automatically wiggle and wobble. Obviously, "cranking" a bait through the water spawned the term. Arguably, one could suggest that all spinners and any other lure that has an automatic action could be called a crankbait, but thankfully pro anglers and lure manufacturers have separated these other lures into specific categories. Right now the crankbait category encompasses an incredibly wide selection of lures with many sub-categories. Adding any unusual product to this category might only confuse all parties involved. As long as the lure is has a hard body with a built-in wobbling action, it must and should be considered a crankbait.

Later in this book I'll go into great detail on how

to fish all the various types, but for now let's take a look at the evolution of the crankbait to better understand what these lures are all about. As you will see, the crankbait category has been predominant in the evolution of lures. Various forms of the crankbait have existed since artificial baits were first used.

Where it all began, no one really knows, but lure collectors have traced the first crankbaits back into the early 1900s. There wasn't much lure marketing going on back then, so many of the originals were simply hand-made by some angler strictly for personal use. The lures did have a built-in action of some kind, and therefore must be considered crankbaits. Eventually, lure companies sprang up: Firms like Heddon, Pflueger, Shakespeare, Creek Chub, South Bend, Arbogast, and Bomber became legendary among anglers. The Heddon Company pioneered many of the great lure designs and innovations that are still popular today. Many of Heddon's original lure innovations are still considered classic manufacturing principles. Their diving lip configurations, hardware usage, body shapes, and painting schemes can still be found in many of today's lures.

In my opinion, the folks at Heddon were some of the greatest lure innovators in history. Many of their early designs are still being sold today. Lures such as the Zara Spook, Crazy Crawler, and Tiny Torpedo are older than I am, and are still immensely popular sellers that still catch fish. Heddon's Zara Spook is probably even more popular today than when it was first produced. Heddon's engineering genius was unmatched in those early marketing days, and it still commands the respect of other lure manufacturers today.

Here's a selection of the some of the original old-time classic crankbaits. Note the diving lips on theses lures were carved right out of the body. Lures included here are the (from top to bottom): Heddon King, Lazy Ike, Shakespeare Mouse, Creek Chub Mouse, and Helin Flatfish.

Lipless crankbaits are generally thin-bodied, sinking lures with no built-in or attached diving lip. They feature a very tight vibrating action. Here are some of the more well-known models (from left to right): Bayou Boogie, Rattlin' Rap, RatLtrap, Sugar Shad, Cordell Spot, and Mann's Razorback.

Heddon and their competitors discovered long ago the secret of a diving bill. They realized diving lips were the key to making a lure dive and wiggle. Initially, diving lips were carved right out of the body on such lures as the South Bend Bass Oreno, Shakespeare Mouse, Creek Chub Darter, Helin Flatfish, and the Lazy Ike. The goal was to get make the body wiggle and carving a lip apparently seemed like the easiest and best way to do it. The Bass Oreno, Mouse, Darter and similar lures had soft, smooth swimming motions that really caught fish of all species, and still do today.

Interestingly, these original old-time lure lip designs were put to use on more recent phenomenona such as the J-Plug, a highly productive Great Lakes salmon/trout trolling lure. Many very popular musky lures also borrowed the frontal designs from these

classics. The Bobbie Bait, Smitty Bait, Seeker, Stalker, and Burt baits all have either that Bass Oreno or Darter head design on them. All of these lures have similar actions to those originals of yesteryear.

The original Flatfish and Lazy Ike were some of the first lures to feature an improved vibration and body wiggle with a built-in design; not employing any additional attached diving lips. Both lures had a unique banana-like configuration and a line-tie attachment somewhere on the upper head side of the lure. This banana shape created a built-in diving lip. It also resulted in a tremendous resistance and strong vibration when cranked. I remember a time when these two lures, the Lazy Ike and Flatfish, were super hot sellers and fantastic fish-catchers. Today, the Lazy Ike is no longer available, and few Flatfish grace the trays of tackle boxes. Yet the design is a classic and many of today's more popular lures have simply rediscovered the workability of this great crankbait design. Contemporary lures like the Believer and Swim Whiz are examples of newer baits utilizing that same banana-shaped configuration.

Another style of crankbait that relies totally on the shape of the lure to create the action is the lipless crankbait, like the RatLTrap. Some of today's anglers might think that this design is relatively new, but lipless crankbaits have actually been around for quite awhile. They have some interesting roots. While many consider the RatLTrap to be the original, early 1960s books show lipless crankbaits such as the Pico Perch, Bayou Boogie, Heddon Sonic, Heddon Sonar, Mitey Minnow and Gay Blade to be the true pioneers. Some of these lures were made of metal, some of wood, and some of plastic. No matter, they all featured the same unique concept — a sinking, tight vibrating, high speed lure with minimal resistance. This subcategory of the crankbait still remains extremely popular as both a seller and fish-catcher. The RatLTrap and similar lures are some of the hottest selling on the market. And they seem to be catching plenty of big fish. The versatility of this lure remains its best asset. It can be fished at virtually any depth, and for almost any gamefish species.

By the way, the desired action of the RatLTrap is quite different from most of the older lure designs like the Creek Chub Darter, Bass Oreno, Lazy Ike, and

Metal-lipped crankbaits were the rage of the 1950s, 60s and early 70s. They paved the way for many future diving lip concepts. Some of the more popular early versions include (from top to bottom): Heddon Vamp, Heddon jointed Vamp, Pflueger Mustang, Creek Chub Pikey Minnow.

Flatfish. The older lures were fat-bodied floaters. The lipless crankers, on the other hand, are thin-bodied sinking lures with a very tight vibration.

Eventually, attaching metal lips of various configurations became the rage. The introduction of the attached metal lip was significant in that it enabled lure manufacturers to create an entire family of lures from one body design simply by adding different lips to them. Running depth was also vastly increased by the new metal lip attachments. The angle, size and design of the lip could easily be altered to accomplish various tasks. This triggered a huge introduction of plugs from a wide group of manufacturers. Heddon highlighted the River Runt and Vamp series. Creek Chub championed its famous world record catchers, the Wiggle Fish and Pike Minnow. Fred Arbogast featured the Arbogaster and Mudbug. Bomber broke it open with its original big lipped Bomber crankbait. Many more lure designs from a host of manufacturers followed.

It was during this era of the metal-lipped lure that many of today's crankbait concepts were born. This is when lip angles, lip size, lip configuration, and many other specific aspects of crankbait action, running depth, and overall performance took hold. Undoubtedly, there will always be improvements made in lure materials and in lure characteristics, but the metal-lip era was definitely an important one. Not surprisingly, lures such as the Mudbug and Bomber are still sold and used today. Their fish-catching ability hasn't deteriorated one bit.

Sometime in the early 1970s, clear plastic lips became the thing. The clear lip concept probably originated with the original Rapala lures, which were already popular in the 1960s. Cosmetically, these lures looked far more natural than some earlier baits. This was especially true in more subtle minnow bait lures like the Rapala. Obviously, a Rapala with a metal lip wasn't going to cut it. The plastic lip was an integral

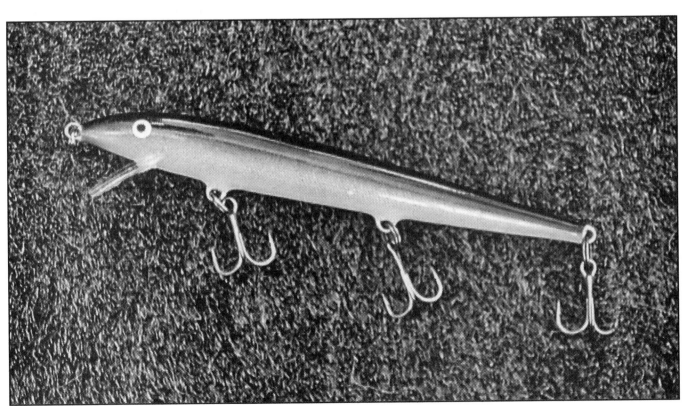

The Rapala really came on to the scene in the U.S. sometime in the early to mid-1960s. This was one of the first crankbaits to feature a plastic lip. This spawned an entirely new generation of plastic-lipped lures.

part of this lure's success as a seller. It wasn't so much that these lures were better fish-catchers, but they definitely were catching more fishermen. Eventually the popularity of the Rapala became the catalyst of a whole new generation of crankbaits. These are the lures you see on today's tackle store shelves.

Realism became the goal and the marketing platform. Clear plastic lips simply looked more realistic than old metal versions. Metal-lipped crankbaits and lipless crankbaits still caught plenty of fish, but the market wanted clear-lipped baits. By the 1980s, manufacturing advances produced crankbaits that looked very realistic. Cosmetically detracting metal lips were loosing their appeal. Invisible, clear lexan lips were now the rage. Eventually, the entire lure was molded from clear plastic. Clear plastic butyrate, ABS, and other plastic materials were molded with ultra clear masked lips that produced a superbly natural-looking product. Best of all, they not only caught fish but were far more durable. This created a new level of manufacturing competition for higher quality crankbaits.

Today these innovative trends continue. The computer age has provided lure companies with some exciting new manufacturing capabilities. This not only includes state-of-the-art design, but also superior finishing techniques. However, never underestimate the true fish-catching power of all crankbait designs young and old. The longevity of Heddon's products as fish-catchers proves beyond a doubt that great lures easily withstand the tests of time. Crankbaits of all shapes, sizes, colors, and actions are simply going to catch gamefish of all species. The key will always be in choosing the right crankbait for the right situation. As always, you need "...the right tool for the job." The seasoned crankbait fisherman assesses his present fishing condition, and chooses the correct crankbait accordingly. In the following chapters, we'll learn more about how to accomplish just this.

chapter 2

Crankbait Dynamics

With the myriad of crankbaits available today, it's important to learn what makes a crankbait tick before purchasing lures. It's even more important to learn about crankbaits before snapping one on the end of your line. A lot of money is wasted each year when anglers purchase lures that do not fit any particular angling need. Many of these lures are bought simply because they look good. It's not that the lure purchased won't catch some fish, it's more that the angler has no idea where and how to use it. Furthermore, he or she hasn't the foggiest notion of what tackle is needed in order to get the most out of this plug. Understanding the dynamics of the lure is basic, but essential. In other words, if the angler doesn't understand how the crankbait functions, and what it's capable of, it's doubtful that this lure will be a consistent fish-catcher for him.

One thing I've learned through years as a consultant for various lure manufacturers and through the design of my own line of crankbaits, is there are certain dynamics that make a crankbait function properly. Every aspect of a crankbait's design has some purpose in mind. This includes such factors as: 1) body shape, 2) body length, 3) diving lip size, shape, and angle, 4) overall buoyancy, 5) line tie placement, and 6) hook selection. The best-made lures, those that have withstood the test of time, have been well thought out by both engineer and angler. They've gone through a lengthy prototype process during which many things have been taken into consideration. Let's examine each of these features more closely, and you'll begin to understand just what makes a crankbait tick.

Crankbait body shape can have a strong affect on many aspects of a crankbait's personality. Fat-bodied lures displace more water, generally are more buoyant, and consequently run shallower with the same comparative diving lip on them. Thin profile lures slice through water with minimal resistance. Conversely, thin-bodied crankbaits are less buoyant and run deeper with the same diving lip. Contrary to accepted opinion, the diving lip is not the only determining factor on maximum running depth. More appropriately, the diving lip determines the action. It's the body shape and it's resulting buoyancy that makes a lure run deeper or shallower.

Buoyant baits are generally preferred for fishing around any kind of cover such as weeds and wood. The increased buoyancy of a fat-bodied crankbait usually results in a tail up/nose down action, as well. This means that most of the collisions that are bound to occur while working a crankbait through cover will strike the diving bill area. Fat-bodied, buoyant crankbaits, with their tail-up nature, will back themselves right out of cover when the line is released. The strong buoyant nature of these lures makes them a shoo-in for shallow water cover situations.

Lures of less buoyancy are the normal choice for deep crankin' around minimal cover and clean bottoms. The lack of buoyancy is the lure's best asset for attaining depth.. A thin profile crankbait with less buoyancy is therefore tailor-made to track deeper and stay deep. Thin profile crankbaits have less of a tendency to run tail up/nose down. They move through the water almost horizontally. While this does not bode well for any applications over weeds or heavy brush, since the hooks are likely to catch on cover more often, they can still be worked over such spots if the cover is of a consistent depth. The trick is to choose a thin-bodied crankbait that runs a perfect depth to skim just above the cover.

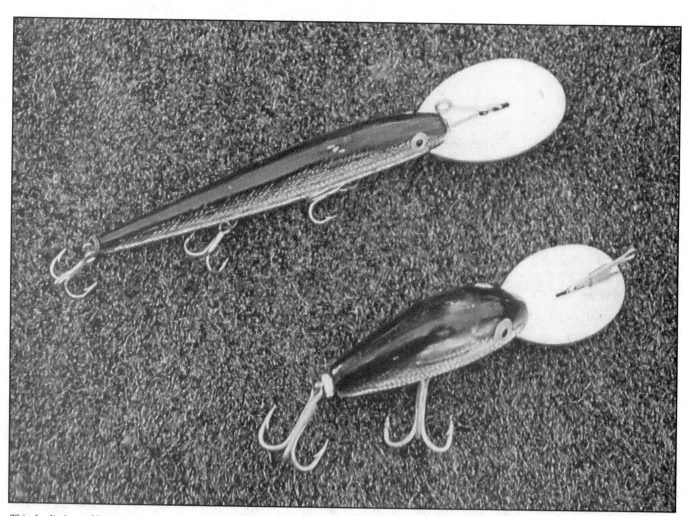

Thin-bodied crankbaits are generally less buoyant and run deeper than a fat-bodied lure with the same comparative diving bill. Long, thin-bodied crankbaits are preferred whenever gamefish are on a heavy minnow diet of perch, shiners, or some thin-bodied shad species. They are exceptional choices in clearer water and excel when a less buoyant lure is preferred. A fat-bodied crankbait gets the nod wherever gamefish are chomping on crawdads or fat-bodied minnow forage. They appear to be better dark-water choices—excelling in cover.

Because fat-bodied crankbaits displace more water, they create more vibration and cast a bigger silhouette. This makes them the preferred choice for dark water and night fishing. Whenever you're faced with turbid water conditions, larger profile, fat-bodied crankbaits are sure to be more effective. Night fishing creates almost the same scenario. Big, fat-bodied baits with a larger silhouette and improved water displacement are likely to be superior night fishing lures because it is easier for gamefish to find these lures in low visibility conditions.

More vibration and larger silhouette can work against you in clear water situations, however. Sight feeding fish are the general rule when visibility is good, no matter what the light conditions. Clear water sight-feeders generally prefer thinner profile plugs. The attractant here is a natural look that's less obvious. Large profile, fat-bodied lures might be a repellent here. A slim lure with smoother, tighter action might be more desirable. Whenever any kind of gamefish appears to be bait shy go with a smaller, slimmer profile

crankbait to compensate. This usually turns the tide in your favor.

Overall body length on any crankbait style is another noteworthy factor. That is why lure manufacturers often provide a size selection. Longer baits also

Plastic lures hold up well to the punishment dished out by pike and muskies.

Fat-bodied crankbaits are usually more buoyant since they displace more water. They also create more vibration and cast a bigger silhouette. Fat-bodied crankbaits are productive whenever fish are foraging on crawdads or fatter profile baitfish such as shad, bluegill or crappie. They are great choices for dark water, and whenever you're crankin' in heavy cover.

create more profile, displace more water, and create more buoyancy. The biggest thing longer baits create is a bigger baitfish look. Longer baits also require more hooks; three trebles instead of two. Longer baits are generally preferred when gamefish are feeding on long-bodied minnow forage. Longer baits also seem to catch bigger fish in open water. Anytime you're forced to fish for suspended fish, whether it's walleyes, bass or muskies, longer baits are usually superior.

However, short-bodied crankbaits have their time and place, too. As a caster, you'll usually find that short-bodied crankbaits travel on a cast more accurately. The makes them a superior choice for any

pinpoint casting situations around cover. Long bodied lures, on the other hand, tend to catch wind on a cast and sail unpredictably off course. A lot of miscue casts can be frustrating when fishing around cover with long bait. The stronger the wind, the more of a problem this creates.

Short-bodied baits are also preferred by gamefish when they're on eating a lot of crustaceans. Smallmouth bass, for example, feed heavily on crawdads during all warm water seasons on most waters. Short-bodied crankbaits more closely resemble crawdads than do long ones. In this case, like so many others, it's not so much that the lure has to perfectly replicate the crawdad as it is to be in the same size and shape profile. The fish are conditioned to react positively to short-bodied prey. Give them anything that's close and, bingo, you've got a bass on.

The subject of diving lips is another factor, a major one, in the overall performance of the crankbait. The shape, size, and angle from the body greatly impacts action, running depth, tracking speed, and other characteristics. Some mistakenly believe that diving lip length is the only criteria that affects running depth. How that diving lip is anchored on the lure, combined with the location of the line tie are also critical factors. Utilizing only one standard diving lip, the running depth and action are greatly influenced by where the lip is positioned on the lure body. Where the line tie is positioned on the diving lip further affects the action and running depth.

On one side of the spectrum, a diving bill that protrudes straight off the lure at nearly 0 degrees should provide the maximum dive and the tightest action (1a). Exaggerated in an opposite sense, the further down a diving lip angles off the body towards 90 degrees (1b), the less it will dive and wider the wobbling action. A lip that is anchored somewhere between the two (1c), should have a medium running depth with a medium wobble. This basic rule of thumb on diving lip positioning enables the astute crankbait angler to quickly identify the running depth and

Oversized, fat-bodied crankbaits are excellent night-fishing lures since they cast a larger silhouette and displace a lot of water. This makes it easier for any night-feeding gamefish to find these lures in such low visibility conditions.

action of a crankbait before you even purchase it.

There is another variable that needs to be considered. It's line tie positioning. The closer the line tie is positioned to the lure itself, the larger the digging/diving surface of the lip and, to some extent, the deeper the lure will dive. Looking at Description Two, without changing the angle of the diving lip from 0 degrees for maximum dive and tightest wiggle, the diving depth and action can still be altered by the placement of the line tie. A line tie placed close to the lure body at 2a will run much deeper than at 2b or 2 c. (See illustration on p.17) The line tie placement might enhance or destroy a lure's wiggle depending upon the individual lure and diving bill design. Only through experimentation will you know for sure. Once you've passed a lure's maximum "tightness" in action, it has no action at all. A line tie positioned at 2a might do just that.

The lure might indeed run real deep, but it probably won't wiggle at all. Experimenting a little at a time, the line tie will need to be repositioned toward the front of the lip, somewhere between 2a and 2c until a wiggle begins to occur. Once that "sweat spot" is found, you have attained maximum depth with the tightest possible wiggle. As the size and shape of this lip is altered, so may the "sweat spot". The best product design engineers have discovered these bill basics and toyed with them constantly. Few anglers realize the work that goes into successful prototyping of lures

Short, fat-bodied crankbaits are very productive on bass since they have such an affinity for crawdads. All short-bodied crankbaits have some resemblance to a scurrying crawdad and therefore bass react positively to them in nearly all waters.

Large diving bills that protrude off the lure body at nearly 0 degrees (top lure) provide maximum depth and the tightest possible action. The farther down a diving bill angles off the body towards a right angle of 90 degrees (bottom lure), the less it will dive, the shallower it will run, and the wider its wobbling action.

before their introduction.

The latest innovation on large diving bills was the addition of a raised ridge on the very end of the diving bill (see photo p.18), to enhance its digging/diving capacity. This unique innovation first showed up on Mann's 20+ and 30+ series in the late 1980s, and has since been used by several other manufacturers. The system does work. It creates an angle overtop the 0 degree mark at the end of the diving lip, tilting the lure's dive plane a bit more, and thus increasing the overall running depth.

Another aspect of the diving lip spectrum is the actual shape of the bill. An incredibly wide variety of lip shapes exist today, and no doubt many more will pop up tomorrow. Some are rounded, others are more squared. Some come to a point in the center, while others have a unique cup shape to them. And still others have a triangular lip. All of these shapes do impact the

action on a crankbait, as well as the lure's ability to bounce over the bottom or careen off cover.

Squared lips catch more water surface and therefore generally run the deepest when compared equally in size and basic shape. However, squared lips have minimum side roll and will not roll off a rock, weed clump or stump. Squared lips drive the lure straight ahead like a tank with the steering locked in forward. A great design for attaining maximum depth, but not the most desirable for cover crankin'.

Rounded lips catch a bit less water than squared ones, slightly reducing depth attainability and slightly softening or widening the wobble. Rounded lips will roll out of snags much better than squared ones, however, making them the preferred choice of many manufacturers. The rounded lip also looks cosmetically pleasing on lures, making it an additional plus for manufacturers.

Crankbait General Applications

Buoyancy Level	Function	Performance	Application
high floater	fast rising semi-weedless	tail up/nose down backs out of snags	thick cover (weeds, wood) warm water aggressive fish
weak floater	slow rising	tail up/nose down	moderate cover rocks, grass
suspender	neutral buoyancy	horizontal track holds in place/pause	clean bottom cold water reluctant fish
sinker	sinks	sinking countdown	clean bottom deep water fast retrieves speed triggering shallow

The farther down a diving bill angles off the body towards a right angle (90 degrees) the less it will dive, the shallower it will run, and the wider the wobbling action.

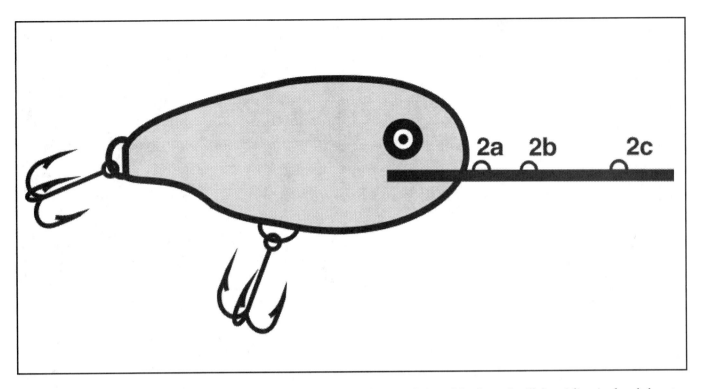

The closer a line-tie is positioned to the lure itself, the larger the digging/diving surface, and the deeper it will dive. A line tie placed closest to the lure body at 2a will run much deeper than at 2c, for example. It will also "tighten" the lure's action, As you move farther away from the lure body (towards 2c) you decrease the running depth and loosen the wobbling action. The ideal line-tie placement, in this instance, is where you can attain the maximum depth with the tightest wiggle. This is called the "sweet spot".

Triangular crankbait lip designs have been around for a long time, and are still popular because they do an outstanding job of careening off cover, yet they still create an excellent action on almost any lure body. Initially the older lure manufacturers used metal versions of the triangular lip on such lures as the Cisco Kid, but newer manufacturers have incorporated this same proven lip design on several plastic lures large and small. The great thing about the triangular diving bill is that it naturally rolls to one side or the other to careen off cover. As long as the outside surface of the triangular lip is wide, and the lure has good buoyancy, any crankbait with a triangular lip edge should do well in any bottom-bouncing, cover-colliding situation. There are no real drawbacks to this lip design, if you're looking for a cover crank.

Buoyancy is a final factor that must be considered in the crankbait equation. Floating, sinking and suspending baits have their time and place, but it's impor-tant to thoroughly understand the pros and cons of each. In a nutshell, buoyancy is most desired in shallow cover. The thicker the cover, the more buoyancy is desired. Buoyancy adds a weedless quality to a crankbait. As stated earlier, buoyant crankbaits have a built-in tendency to run tail up/nose down. Any cover that is encountered is then likely to make initial contact with the lure's diving bill area. The hooks are somewhat guarded by the lure body. A tactful release of line tension usually enables a buoyant bait to back itself away from cover, and the debris that has collected on the diving bill usually falls free from the lure at this point.

Buoyant baits are least desired when an angler wants to attain and maintain maximum depth at slow speeds. Buoyancy resists depth and the diving nature of the plug. Therefore buoyant baits are not the best choices for deep crankin'; particularly in cold water. A less buoyant crankbait will dive deeper at slower speeds

Mann's 20+ and 30+ series crankbaits were the first to incorporate a raised ridge at the very end of the diving bill. This enhanced the lure's diving capacity. It actually creates a digging angle overtop the 0 degree mark, tilting the lure's diving plane a bit more. The result is a slight increase in overall running depth.

and maintain depth at slower retrieves. Sinking or suspending-type crankbaits are better choices for clean bottoms, and colder water temps. Suspenders are particularly good when you want to crank a lure and twitch it longer next to deep cover.

Many of today's best bass pros have rediscovered the old art of jerking a long minnow style crankbait like the Rapala or Rogue next to cover of some sort. But now they've taken this old technique to another level by adding stick-on lead tape to the underside of their favorite plugs in order to slow down or completely neutralize the minnow bait's buoyancy. This same concept has also been applied to just about any other style of crankbait, deep- or shallow-running. The goal here is to keep the lure in a hot fish zone longer. In many cases, this hot fish zone is somewhat deeper than the norm. Buoyant minnow baits simply run too high to be effective here, and they float up too quickly. By adding weight, these lures could be worked at greater

depths and at slower speeds. Whenever you're trying to trigger cover-tight fish in deeper cover, suspender crankbaits do have their advantages for sure.

Sinking crankbaits have some very unique versatility aspects to them that apply surprisingly to both deep and shallow water situations. When great depths are desired, obviously the sinking crankbait is the way to go, if you're a caster. Instead of trying to conventionally crank down a big lipped floater to great depths, the idea here is to simply cast the lure out and let it sink to the bottom. Depth is then easily maintained with a slow retrieve. This system requires a level sinking crankbait and a knowledge of "sink rate." Sink rate is nothing more than knowing how fast your lure actually sinking.

For example, if the lure sinks to the bottom at 16 feet in approximately 16 seconds, you have a lure with a sink rate of 1 foot per second. This kind of ratio is most desired since it makes depth calculation simple: All you do is count the seconds and you know the

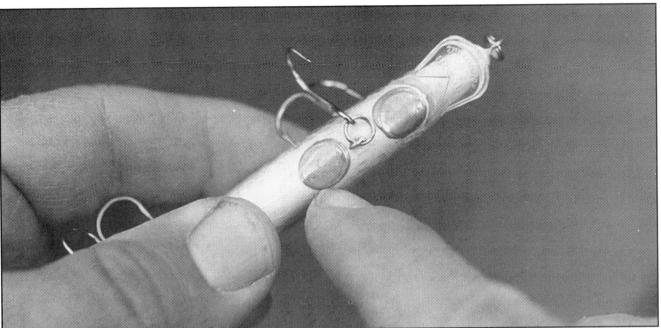

Adding stick-on lead tape to the underside of a favorite crankbait is a popular modification for slowing down or even totally neutralizing buoyancy. Storm's Suspend-A-Dot lead tape can be purchased at most sporting goods stores.

How you position your boat to a fishing spot is largely determined by the layout and the topography. Some spots require a perpendicular presentation while others demand a more parallel approach.

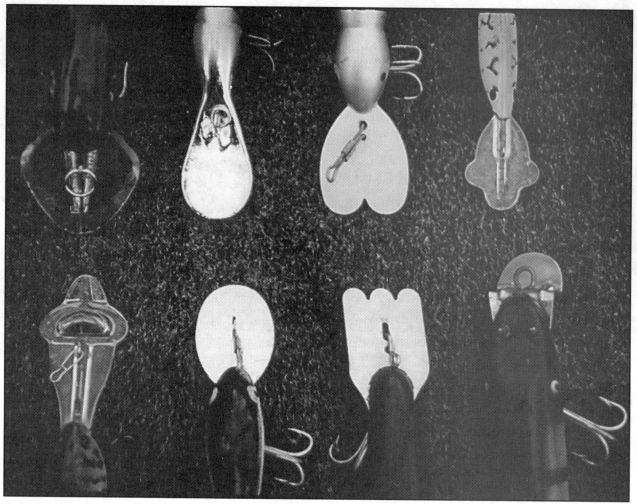

An incredibly wide variety of lip shapes exists on today's crankbaits. All of these shapes do effect the lure's action and its ability to bounce bottom and career off cover.

depth. Countdown crankbaits are exceptional producers for deep-water gamefish on hard bottoms. This technique is particularly good in the fall when most freshwater gamefish gravitate to deep hard bottom structure.

But it can be equally effective any time gamefish are deep and near a clean, hard bottom. Whenever you're faced with fish hugging tight to deep hard bottom, a countdown crankbait is viable option.

Suspended fish are also very catchable with a sinking crankbait. Once again, knowledge of the lure's sink rate, along with an idea of the approximate depth the suspended fish are holding is crucial. I have found that countdown, sinking crankbaits are particularly productive on fish suspended along a summer ther-

mocline. Once you know the depth of the thermocline and the relative position of the fish, experiment with various countdown depths until you score. For example, if you're seeing a lot of marks on your sonar unit at 22 feet suspended over deeper water, try counting the lure down to 20, then 21, then 22 then 23 on successive probing casts. Eventually, you'll hit on the productive number.

Another application for the sinking crankbait is to create additional speed triggering action over shallow water fish. In this instance, the sinking crankbait forces you to speed up in order to maintain a shallow track. As you slow down your retrieve with a sinking crankbait it runs deeper. You need to speed up to make a sinker run

Crankbait Body Shapes

Body Shape Profile	Function	Application
fat, wide	displace more water more buoyant cast larger silhouette resemble crawdads/bluegills wide bodied baitfish	cover (weeds, wood, etc) dark, turbid water color shallow water situations night fishing sound feeders
thin, elongated	low buoyancy displace far less water natural minnow resemblance	clean bottoms clear water suspended fish deep water situations sight feeders

Walleyes will take crankbaits any time of the year, no matter the water color or weather conditions. Crankbaits always catch walleyes.

shallow. This is a superbly effective tactic with sinking lipless crankbaits such as the RatLTrap. Hundreds of fish are caught each season by casting a sinking, lipless crankbait over shallow weeds, and cranking at high speed. The bait is literally zinging by these fish with a high vibrating action. Any weeds that are encountered require a hard ripping action in order to free the lure from the cover. This entire method is aggressive to say the least. Strikes are vicious, and the technique works well in both cold and warm waters, dark and clear. While this tactic was perfected on bass, it works with equal efficiency on walleyes and pike. We'll get into more detail on this and other techniques later on.

As you can see, there are lots of things to consider when choosing a crankbait for a fishing situation. The more you comprehend the dynamics of the lures in your tackle box, the better you'll be at choosing the right tool for the job. Understanding body shapes and sizes, diving bill shape, size and angle, and the lure's buoyancy basics helps a great deal. It makes every crankbait in your box a more specific tool, designed

perfectly for that one situation. The more you learn about the dynamics of these lures, the easier this choice becomes.

A round-lipped crankbait is particularly good around rocks, gravel, shale, sand and other hard bottoms. These baits tend to roll themselves laterally out of snags while maintaining the general action of the plug.

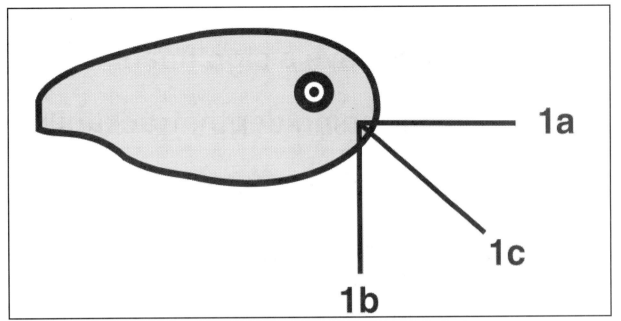

Diving lip angle or positioning in reference to the lure body greatly effects both action and running depth. The exact same diving lip, positioned at various angles, produces dramatically different results. For example, angle or position 1a provides maximum dive and the tightest possible wobbling action. Conversely, 1b should produce the widest wobble (action) and the shallowest dive. 1c is a compromise of both, producing a wide wobble and moderately deep dive.

Short, fat-bodied crankbaits represent crawdads in many respects. Crawdads are, of course, one of the favorite foods of smallmouth bass.

All these factors have a significant impact on the action, running depth, trackability, and fish attraction of any crankbait design.

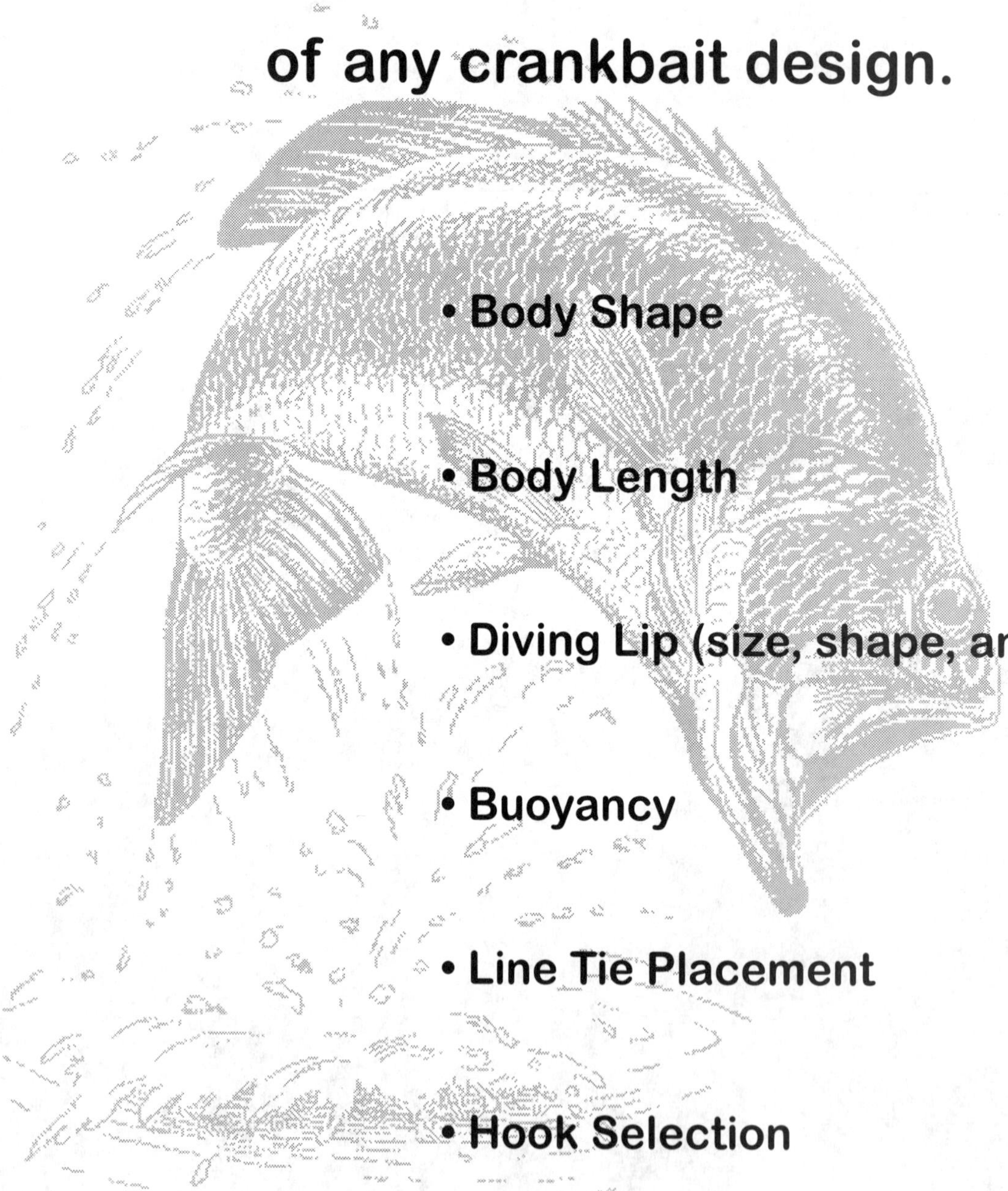

- Body Shape

- Body Length

- Diving Lip (size, shape, and angle)

- Buoyancy

- Line Tie Placement

- Hook Selection

chapter 3

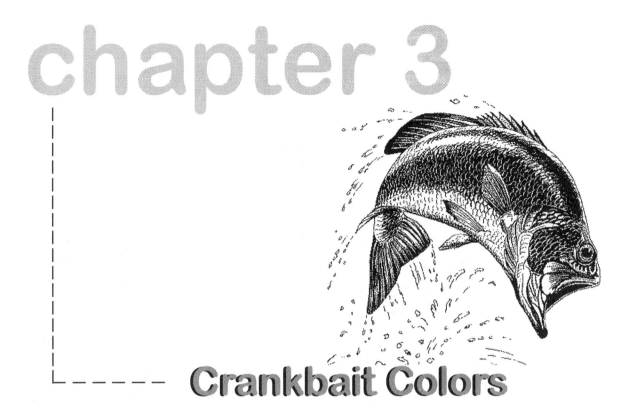

Crankbait Colors

I could relate hundreds of experiences throughout my fishing days where a specific color really made the difference in the amount of fish caught. Yet the one that quickly comes to mind involves a recent summer walleye trolling trip with my good friend, Tom Keenan. Tom and I were about to film a episode for my television show depicting all the factors that go into successful planer board trolling for open water suspended walleyes. However, an hour into the excursion with no strikes, lead us both to consider switching gears. We hadn't had a single strike on a lake loaded with suspended summer walleyes that we'd had no problem catching in the past.

Before "pulling the plug" on this tactic, we decided to experiment with a normal process of elimination routine that involved: 1) switching lures, 2) changing depths, 3) changing speeds, 4) trying different areas. None of these attempts made any difference. We were now two hours into the trip without a strike. What's even more frustrating is that we could see the fish on our sonar equipment. We basically knew where these fish were and how deep they were holding from

previously successful trips, along with our up-to-date info from the sonar. Yet, up to this point, they just wouldn't bite.

Admittedly, I was ready to try something else. I'd had enough of these finicky walleyes. The day before, I'd caught some nice smallmouth bass on the same lake in some man-made fish cribs off a nearby point. My urge to switch gears grew stronger by the minute as I nodded toward the point and said, "I can feel those cribs calling to us, Tom. Those smallies can't wait for us much longer. Let's bag this walleye thing and head for that point." Tom was close to acknowledging defeat, but suggested trying one more pass. "This time, let's try some chromes on them. It probably won't make any difference, but it won't take more than few minutes to try them."

Tom had just gotten some new wild chrome colors from the folks at Storm Lures. He had a whole bag of new Thundersticks in color patterns I'd never seen before. This included a unique lime green back with specs on it. We cranked in, re-rigged lines with various new chrome colors, and made one more pass across our most promising area. While Tom watched the lines and worked the boat, I began getting our bass tackle ready. After all, I was convinced that this ploy wasn't going anywhere.

Just as I finished tying the knot on the first bass outfit, Tom yelled "Joe, fish on!" Stunned by the sudden turn of events, I dropped the bass rod, and took over the boat controls while Tom cranked in our first customer, a 24-inch walleye. "Well, we finally got one, Joe", Tom proudly bragged. "They might want that weird green spec pattern." I was about to discredit his theory when a second rod went off. "I've got this one!" I demanded. As I cranked the walleye into netting range, I immediately saw the only other green spec Thunderstick we had rigged buried in this walleye's jaw. I immediately came to the same conclusion. "You got any more of these?"

Of course, we couldn't get those green spec pattern Thundersticks back out fast enough. Tom started peeling apart the packaged lures, as I cranked in various lines. Subsequent trolling passes produced fish after fish. All of them coming on the four green spec pattern Thundersticks we had out. None of the 27 walleyes we caught in the next few hours came on the two other color patterns we had out. We

had indeed found an unusually strong color preference on that day.

The color of a lure, and how it affects both fish and fishermen, is one of the most intriguing aspects of

Almost all gamefish show a preference for one color over another at some time. It's up to the angler to experiment with various patterns and hues in order to find out if there is indeed a such a preference.

the sport. The color that fishermen choose isn't always the one that the fish prefer. Generally speaking, fishermen often choose certain lure colors over others because of looks or reputation. Why a fish bites a certain color over another has certainly been the controversial subject of many articles over the past 30 years or so. Some biologists, as well as anglers, claim that certain colors have a stronger strike trigger than others. The strike triggering qualities of certain colors also seems to vary within different gamefish species, as well as time of year, and water clarity.

In this opening story, that new green spec chrome pattern was super hot. I have to tell you honestly that I've never seen it perform to that level again. But it has now become a mainstay color in my walleye trolling arsenal. Yet this same color pattern has not been that productive on bass or muskies. Just walleyes. That's why I made the comment that strike triggering qualities of colors vary with different gamefish species. Time of the year and a lake's water clarity also appear to have something to do with this.

The old philosophy on colors is to closely "match the hatch" – choosing a color that closely resembles the target gamefish's most preferred forage at that time. While this may sound good in theory, there are always some problems associated with this method of color choice. For one, the average angler has very little real first-hand knowledge as to what exactly the fish are feeding on at any given time. One has to actually see his target species eat a specific forage, kill the fish and

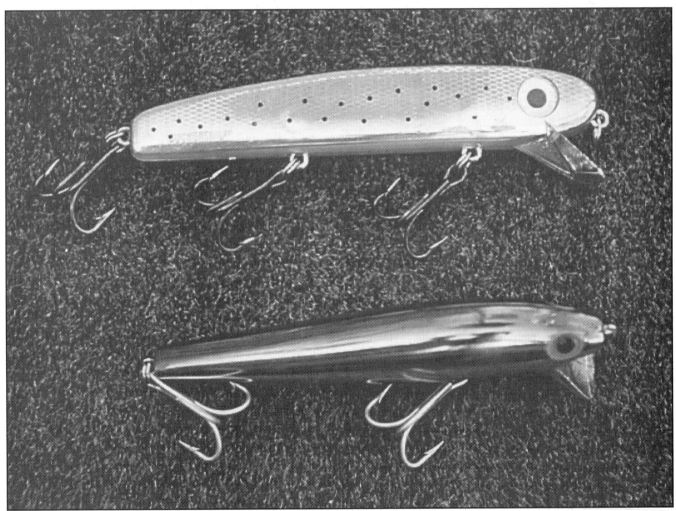

Chrome patterns are outstanding fish-catchers for all kinds of gamefish. They seem to really excel whenever fish want excessive flash. These same fish are often tough to catch on more natural subdued tones.

Color patterns that closely "match the hatch" of natural baitfish species are nearly always the best way to start. Here's a selection of some of the more popular patterns available today.

examined its stomach contents, or see the fish disgorge some kind of forage at boatside or in a livewell. So, while I somewhat agree with this strategy, it is, more often than not, built primarily on assumption rather than fact.

A lot of anglers like to choose a color that simply stands out more. The thought is to make the lure stand out in a crowd. Being "one of the Jone's" here (matching the hatch) is a bad idea since the target fish already has plenty of natural baitfish to choose from. Quite often this strategy is very productive, especially in dark water situations. Gamefish like northern pike seem particularly vulnerable to this approach. Give the nasty northern a lure it can easily see, one with high flash and gaudy coloring, and pike are sure to jump all over it. Walleyes can often be fooled with the same secret as we witnessed in the opening story. How many gamefish of all species fall to bright chartreuse color patterns? If you're talking about "matching the hatch," nothing is

remotely natural about the a gaudy color like this.

Another popular approach is to simply choose a color of confidence. I have to admit that I end up utilizing this strategy more than any other. Success breeds color confidence. Even though I have boxes of crankbaits in all shapes, sizes, and colors, I tend to rely on one or two colors when I'm unsure of a situation. Admittedly, this often creates a false confidence since it's hard to catch fish on an unproved color if you don't try it. That's why it's important to test a variety of colors on a hot fishing situation in order to determine if there is indeed a preferred color. More often than not, the reason you caught fish on one color more than another is because you give that color more water time. Testing colors in the line of fire is the only way to know for sure if a color preference exists.

Why an angler fishes with a certain color over another may have its origin in an entirely different nature. Marketing masters know that most anglers,

Chrome patterns work exceptionally well on walleyes. Spence Petros caught this big walleye with a chrome pattern diver over a shallow rock hump.

inexperienced and veteran, usually purchase a color that simply looks good. The colors that most appeal to anglers are consequently the best sellers, and therefore are usually the best fish-catchers since they get more water time. Tackle manufacturers have taken advantage of this buying trend time and time again, and retailers take this purchasing habit all the way to the bank. Simply put, the most successful tackle manufacturers make great-looking colors that catch lots of fishermen. The end result is these colors get used more and consequently catch more fish.

In addition, I can tell you with all honesty that some of the best fish-catching colors I've ever designed for my own lure company were poor sellers. I still use many of these patterns regularly and have documented their supremacy in many instances. To say these were "confidence colors" would be an understatement. I'm convinced that if these colors were used enmass anglers would catch more fish per hour using them. But that will never happen. Most of these colors have absolutely no sex appeal. They don't win any beauty contests. They just catch fish.

The ever-popular "firetiger" crankbait pattern is a perennial best seller on almost every tackle shelf no matter what the species, no matter what the region. One quick glance at any such tackle shelf will tell you why. The firetiger pattern stands out more than any other color. This masterfully painted and marketed, hi-vis color pattern, artfully blending fluorescent chartreuse, lime, and orange, simply jumps out at the

The ever-popular "firetiger" color pattern is a perennial best seller in most tackle stores. It is as good a "fisherman-catcher" as it is a "fish-catcher" due to its highly attractive color schemes. Admittedly, there are times when it is a superstar performer on the water.

Foil patterns closely resemble natural minnows. They have been great sellers as well as outstanding fish-catchers for over three decades.

consumer. The resulting sales jump out as well. Whether firetiger is as good a fish-catcher as it is a fishermen-catcher is open to debate. There are times when firetiger catches its share of fish for sure. But there are other less popular colors that are often superior fish-catchers.

Experienced anglers are more inclined to match the hatch, choosing crankbait colors that closely resemble the particular forage fish their target fish is feeding on. Let's take the basic bass angler and decipher his/her stereotypical color thought process. Bass anglers are high on crawdad colors, which include blends of brown, orange, green and chartreuse, for many bottom-bouncing situations. Crawdads are favored food of both largemouth and smallmouth during the spring, summer, and fall. So it stands to reason that crankbaits with these color patterns would work well in these situations. Bass also feed regularly on shad, shiners, and other flashy minnows; particularly in and around weed cover. Natural minnow patterns with pearl, chrome, and foil sides are in high demand here.

The top-selling bass crankbait color patterns are therefore crawdad and shad.

As water color darkens, the general rule of thumb, no matter what the fish species, is to bring out the color. This is where loud, overbearing colors such as firetiger seem most appropriate. The key here is not so much to match the hatch as it is to stand out, making it easier for the fish to find the bait. Bright, flashy chrome patterns seem to work well here, too. So do those gaudy colors such as bright orange and hot pink that have no natural look to them at all. The entire philosophy of making a color stand out in turbid water seems to work well for all fish species. Firetiger and other crazy unnatural colors that are easy to see, give the fish a better turbid-water target. This strategy works equally well on muskies, pike, walleyes, and bass. So, I guess the answer is yes – firetiger is really a good fish-catcher. Fish it in turbid water for any species and you're likely to do well.

Generally speaking, really clear water conditions demand a more natural, subtler color pattern. Toning down the color in clear water is a good general rule of thumb, although I've seen plenty of exceptions. Close replications of resident baitfish patterns are almost sure winners. It's tough to beat subtle shad or cisco patterns in clear water reservoirs for all species. If shad or ciscoes are present and the water is clear, natural shad patterns featuring translucent silvery/white bodies are sure winners for everything from trout to bass, walleyes to muskies. I've always thought that gamefish get "baitfish color conditioned" in waters of this nature and respond aggressively to white/silver/chrome/blue. These are the dominant colors of the baitfish present in these kinds of waters. Rarely will you go wrong with this approach. Watch for this obvious preference for white-bellied, white flash baits. It can really be strong on some waters.

Clear waters with ample weed growth usually have another dominant forage fish whose color triggers the same aggressive response – perch. Many waters north of the Mason-Dixon Line have a perch forage base. The farther north you go, the more important the perch becomes. Walleyes, pike, muskies, and even

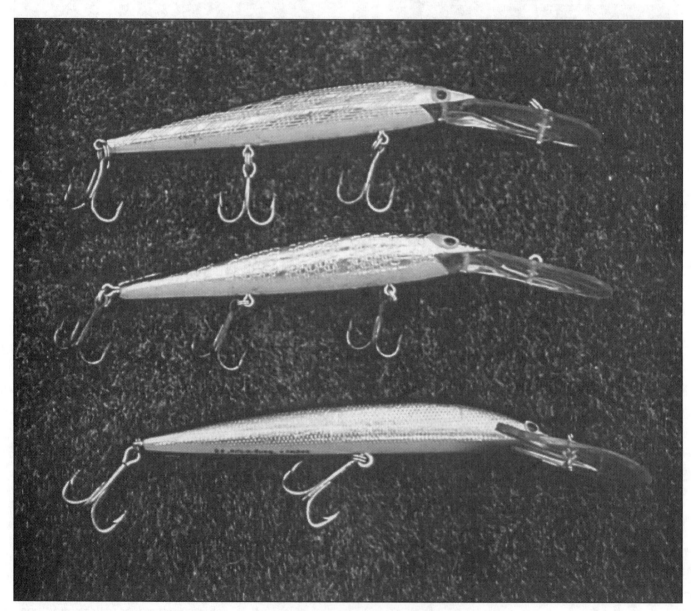

Close replications of silvery white baitfish are tough to beat in many clear water reservoirs. If shad or ciscoes are present in the waters you fish, don't hesitate to check for a preference that leans more to lure patterns with white/silver/chrome/blue.

smallmouth bass use perch as a large part of their diet throughout most of the season in many northern waters. This is of paramount importance in color selection. One must always consider perch patterns when fishing waters of the north. This means leaning heavily on green with some yellow and orange accents.

Unlike the shad/cisco connection, which features white/ silver/chrome/blue, the perch has a dominant green hue. The best crankbait colors in perch waters usually have some green in them. A natural perch pattern contains dominant green combined with yellow, orange, and some white. Another strong triggering image in waters where perch are the dominant food source seems to be vertical stripes on lures. Gamefish will hit lures with vertical stripes over most other lures in waters that hold plenty of perch. Even lure colors of chrome, and silver or gold foil are more productive if they have stripes. The stripes are another one of those positive conditioned response factors. You simply can't go wrong most of the time with a striped lure in perch dominated waters.

Water clarity should dictate the contrast of a perch pattern crankbait. In really clear waters, a natural perch pattern will probably be your best bet. If you're trolling open water for walleyes, a chromed perch pattern might be even better since walleyes appear to really like chrome flash.

Conversely, darker water perch patterns need some fluorescent backgrounds. Firetiger is a good perch pattern in dark water since it is green dominant and it contains vertical stripes. A hot perch pattern featuring the natural stripes and scales of a perch combined with

Lures that have a "dominant green" hue are sure to be the hot ticket in shallow waters that contain perch. Another strong triggering image in perch forage waters seems to be lures that contain vertical stripes. The classic firetiger pattern (shown) has all these attributes.

fluorescent green, chartreuse and orange backgrounds can be absolutely deadly in this situation.

Seasonal color preferences are worth noting, as well. For some odd reason, fish appear to respond better to certain colors depending on water temperature. For example, bass tournament anglers discovered long ago the secret of red for cold water bass in the spring. Crawfish patterns that have strong red dominance are usually the best early spring, cold water producers. I totally agree with this finding. While I've tried to dispute it, a deep red crawfish pattern is simply the best overall bass producer in the spring. It's so much more productive than other colors at this time of year, that I've grown to rely on it almost totally before the water temp climbs above 55 degrees. This is especially true for smallmouths, and largemouths appear to have an equal affinity for red in cold spring waters.

I assume the reason these fish are drawn to red in the spring has something to do with the first appearances of crawdads, but again, this is only an assumption. This red craw pattern seems to be strongest in bass, which feed heavily on crawdads early, but it also seems to work well on other species, too. I've caught a number of muskies on red crawdad cranks during the early spring, and a load of walleyes, too, but these species are not as crazy about red as bass are.

Chrome lures with a blue back are exceptional cold-water producers, too; particularly in the fall. Lipless rattling crankbaits like the popular RatLTrap and similar models are fish catchin' machines in this color pattern during cold water, but large-lipped diving crankbaits sporting the same blue/chrome pattern can do equal damage. Truth be told, I've caught some of my biggest late fall muskies on deep divers in the blue/chrome pattern. Some of the biggest fish I've encountered in cold clear waters of late autumn, I'm

Red crawdad patterns are super spring bass-catchers. They are equally productive on both largemouths and smallies.

Gaudy, flashy colors produce exceptional results on visual feeders such as northern pike. Pike seem to like lures that stand out in the water.

Walleyes will often take brightly colored crankbaits. Whenever walleye action appears slow, try switching to a color with more flash and boldness. It often makes a difference.

talking right before ice up, have fallen to blue/chrome. If you're a fan of the fall, it's important to remember that as the water dips down into the mid to low 40s, nothing beats blue/chrome in clear water. If the water has a slight "turnover stain" to it, gold chrome with a green back is no slouch either. Never underestimate chrome in the fall. It's a cold water killer.

The color blue is worth noting. While blue is hardly natural, even though some open water baitfish such as shad and cisco have some translucent blue hues in them, blue has proven to be dynamite in cold water. It's a pretty good spring color too, but not nearly as deadly as it is the fall. Why fall fish are so turned on to

blue-backed crankbaits is somewhat inexplicable, but the proof bears out, particularly when water temps dip below 45 degrees. I've caught every species of freshwater fish on blue backed crankbaits in the late fall, when the water is ultra cold. This includes muskies, walleyes, and lakers.

When I was still guiding full time, I really spent some time testing colors on cold water fish in the late fall. This was especially true on late fall trolling outings for big walleyes, lake trout, and muskies. I'd often troll six lines or more with various patterns out initially to test for any color preferences. When you're catching big numbers of fish daily, weekly, and seasonally, a

Crankbait Colors and Why

Color	Dominant Hue	Function	Water Color	Application
firetiger	green/chartruese	hi flash	stained, turbid	perch base
shad	white/pearl	flash	stained, clear	shad/white minnows
chrome	silvery chrome	hi flash	clear, stain, turbid	cold water killer
natural perch	green/yellow	match/hatch	stained, clear	all purpose/perch
silver foils	silvery	flash/hatch	stained, clear	all purpose/minnow
gold foils	brassy/gold	flash/hatch	stained, clear	all purpose/minnow
black shadow	black	silhouette	turbid/day all-night	turbid waters, night
night shiner	black	silhouette	turbid	rivers, turbid waters
red tiger	hot orange/red	hi-vis/gaud	turbid, deep stain	rivers, turbid res.
blue smelt	white/blue	flash/hatch	clear	cold water
red craw	deep red		Stained, clear	spring, cold water
clown	chartruese/chrome	hi flash	stained, turbid	all purpose
nat. craw	brown	match/hatch	stained, clear	crawdad base/bass
crappie	pearl/white	match/hatch	clear/stained	crappie base
sucker	white/gold/black	match/hatch	all waters	white forage base
red sucker	deep red		Clear, stain	red reaction fish
redhorse	yellow/orange/brn	match/hatch	stained	carp/redhorse forage
cht pikey	chartruese/or	hi flash	stained, turbid	perch base
gold chrome	gold chrome	hi flash	stained, turbid	stained/turnover
rainbow trout	white/pearl	match/hatch	clear	trout base lakes
rainbow dace	green/pink/chrome	flash/hatch	clear	cold water
chrome perch	green/gold	flash/hatch	stained	cold water
parrot	chartruese/blue	flash	stained	bass/walleyes
bone	white	flash	stained, turbid	bass-reservoir

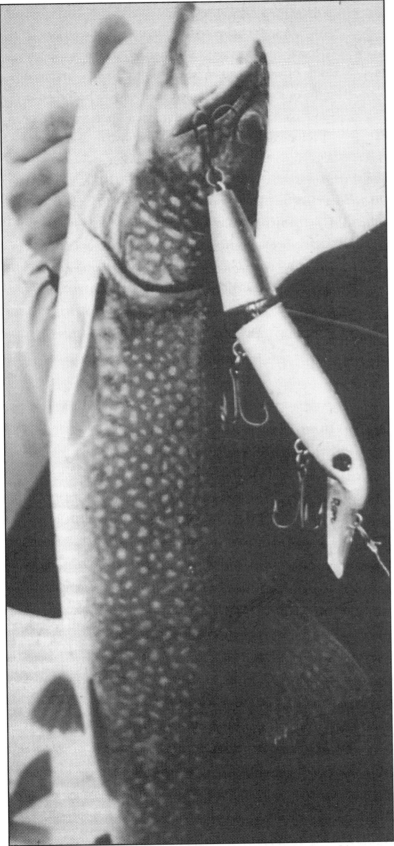

The white lure with a blue back is another killer in gin-clear waters. It's particularly good when the water is very cold, both early and late in the year. This lake trout couldn't resist it.

musky, and several walleyes over the 8-pound mark on one specific lure. The lure was a white DepthRaider crankbait with a blue back. Back then it was one of my secret cold weather colors. My good friend Tom Gelb has also taken some huge fish on this same color combo during the cold water periods. The blue/white lure is generally a poor seller, but a great fish-catcher of big, trophy-class fish in cold water.

The only way to legitimately test fish for color preferences is to run various lure colors over them. This is best done over a high confidence area that you know has fish present. One of the best times to check for color preferences is when the fish are really biting. When I was still guiding full-time, I'd do this on an almost daily basis. My basic policy was always to give my customers the proven lure, and then I'd play with a lot of off-beat colors in order to check to see if there were any real color preferences occurring. This provided me with a daily testing ground for color prefer-ences, as well as many other factors. It was a golden opportunity to learn a lot about how fish reacted to various colors. I learned a great deal from these tests.

Heavy fishing pressure can alter the productivity of certain colors over time. Usually, louder, gaudier colors like firetiger, or overly flashy tones with chrome seem to loose their effectiveness in heavily fished waters, while subdued hues become more attractive. In fact, semi-transparent color patterns often establish themselves as primary fish-catchers in heavily fished waters. Any lure color pattern that gets too popular tends to get overfished. This over-exposes the color to the fish popula-tion, diluting its impact at triggering strikes. Whenever you see this occurring, give trans-parent colors a try. The see-through look just might be what is needed to keep the fish biting under intense fishing pressure.

Foil patterns, made popular years ago on minnow baits such as the Rapala, are still very productive today. Silver foil with a white belly has been good on both minnow baits and diving crankbaits for bass and walleyes in clearer waters. Black back and silver has been more productive in warmer water temps, blue back and silver better in colder water. Gold foil has been an outstanding color for me for largemouths, smallmouths and walleyes in coffee-stained lakes no matter what the season, but they've been particularly good in later spring with water temperatures over 55 degrees. A gold foil crankbait is also nearly always better with an orange belly in combination. You'll cast a lot of crankbaits before you find one that outperforms black back/gold foil sides/orange belly in stained water. It's one of my confidence baits for bass.

Choosing the right color on a crankbait can depend upon a number of things: The targeted species, time of year, weather, water color, fishing pressure, and type of lure you're fishing can all have a bearing on your choice. However, nothing beats pure confidence in a color. Once you've caught a few fish on a certain color, it's easy to get hooked on it. Rarely will confidence steer you wrong in this regard. Believing in a bait makes you fish it more often and at a different pace. The result is usually more fish in the boat. Never stop experimenting with colors. Check for color preferences when fish are hot, and refine it when fishing gets tough. Always keep an open mind about trying new color patterns. More often than not, it won't make a huge difference, but there will be those instances where it makes or breaks a trip.

Big fish really seem to like blue chrome patterns in cold water. Musky master Tom Gelb took this magnum musky on a blue chrome color right before a snow storm in November while fishing with the author.

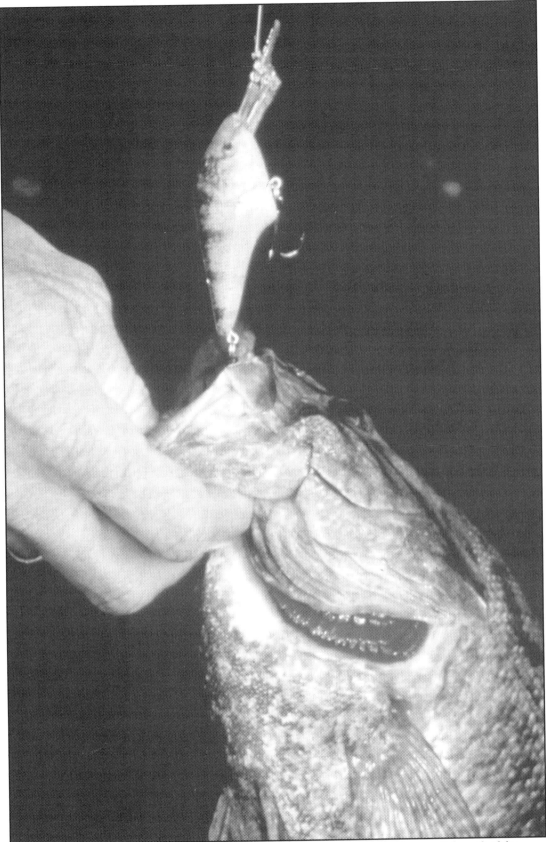

Perch are the preferred minnow forage, at some time of the year, for most warm-water gamefish north of the Mason-Dixon Line. A perch pattern crankbait is one of the most universal of all colors on crankbaits. It matters little what species you're after.

chapter 4

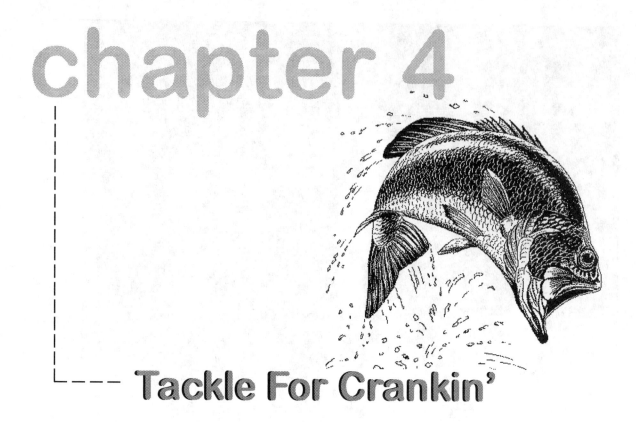

Tackle For Crankin'

Crankbait fishing has certainly been around for several generations and tons of gamefish have been taken on a variety of plugs. There is also a wide selection of rod/reel/line combinations to be considered. Recently some of the best crankbait fishermen have taken the time to analyze what rod/reel/line combinations seem to work best with these vibrating lures. Species-specific crankbait anglers have gone so far as to create specialized rod/reel/line systems to accommodate the needs unique to their favorite species of fish and their most popular lure. It's important to understand that these needs might vary greatly from one species to the next, as well as from one specialized technique to the next.

To more clearly illustrate the tremendous variances that can exist in crankin' tackle combinations depending upon the species and situation, let's examine two polar opposite species and the most popular crankin' system for each. You'll see clearly what I mean. On one side of the court there's the walleye tournament scene and its tremendously popular open-water trolling techniques. This primarily involves planer-board trolling with crankbaits. The preferred crankin' stick for the walleye troller is generally an 8 ½-foot rod that's somewhat parabolic. On the other side of the spectrum, you have the equally fanatical musky hunter casting heavy (2- to 4-ounce) crankbaits. A very specialized heavy-action rod is needed to pitch these larger lures efficiently, and set the hook when a fish strikes. Both of these rods are called crankin' sticks, but they're hardly close to being the same. While both techniques are considered contemporary crankin' tactics, they are obviously on opposite sides of the rod/reel/line spectrum.

Right out of the blocks, it's obvious that trolling demands an entirely different style of rod than casting. Trolling small crankbaits is also an entirely different deal than casting big crankbaits. Even though they're both crankin' tactics per se, they're completely different in every sense of bait presentation sense. A typical open-water trolling rod for walleye crankbaits is at least 8 to 8 ½ feet long with a soft, parabolic bend. The main functions of the open water walleye crankin' rod is to first create spread, getting the rod tips as far away from

Tackle combinations for crankin' vary a great deal depending upon the size of the lure being used. The functions of both the rod and reel also come into play after a big fish is hooked. A deep rod bend is desired to prevent hook shake.

the side of the boat as possible. The second function is to keep soft, steady tension on the lure so hooked fish can't get off, and light wire hooks don't bend out during battle.

The preferred walleye trolling reel for crankbaits has a large capacity spool to encompass 200 yards of line or more, and it should contain some sort of built-in line metering system so precise line measurement is always possible. The best line for open water walleye trolling with crankbaits is a durable, but thin gauge 10- to 15-pound test. The durability is needed to withstand constant abuse of attaching planer boards and snap-on weights. It must be thin so it will allow the lures to attain maximum running depths. Would this kind of crankin' tackle suit musky fishing situations very well? Would the bass tournament guy be at all interested in this kind of crankin' stick? Obviously not.

Casting big crankbaits over weed cover for muskies is in another league. So is bass crankin'. Musky crankin' is actually a beefed-up hybrid of bass crankin'. The musky crankin' stick is quite a bit stiffer, and the lures are sizably larger and heavier. A typical crankin' rod for muskies is a medium/heavy action 6 ½- to 7-footer, with a thick, heavy butt section tapering quickly towards the tip. Musky crankin' sticks need loads of power and response in the butt section, but enough tip to bend in order to keep steady pressure on a hooked fish. The main functions of the musky crankin' stick are to first –easily cast the heavy weight 2 to 4 ounce crankbait without buckling, and second – to responsively rip and tear the crankbait through cover. The musky crankin' stick must also have tremendous hook-setting power in order to drive large-diameter hooks into the tough jaw of a musky, yet maintain

The ideal crankbait trolling reel needs large line capacity and a built-in line metering system. This enables precise line measurement for accurate depth control.

enough rod tip bend so the fish can't tear off or shake loose.

The typical musky crankin' reel has medium line capacity, capable of containing no less than 60 yards of 30- to 50-pound class mono or braided line. The most desirable musky crankin' reels also have lower gear ratios for minimal drag resistance while crankin' big lipped divers. They also need excellent drag systems for battling big fish, and a good centrifugal cast control for minimal backlash problems. Continuous anti-reverse is another big asset of the best musky crankin' reels to promote reel gear longevity.

The bass crankin' stick is again different from the walleye or musky outfit. Hundreds of tournament anglers have honed various rod actions in order to come up with a perfect stick for their applications. Since I do a great deal of bassin' with crankbaits, I do fully

understand their needs. The best bass crankin' sticks are 7 ½ feet long, very lightweight, and carry a medium-light action. Unlike a bass flipping stick, which sports a quick-reacting medium heavy action, needed to power bass quickly out of thick cover, the bass crankin' stick action is best described as slow-reacting.

In this instance, the softer action, slow-reacting rod gives bass a chance to take the lure better, and reduces hook shake on the jump. Long, soft-action rods keep a much more even pressure on the fish which really aids the angler when trying to keep a jumping fish hooked. This is especially important when fishing with smaller crankbaits sporting thin wire treble hooks. It seems to really stand out when fishing lipless crankbaits and any other high-leverage lure that fish seem to have an easy time throwing on the jump. The medium-light action 7 ½-footer provides this much-needed advantage and more. Bass anglers have found these long, soft-action rods also throw smaller, lightweight lures better.

The best bass reel for crankin' varies a bit with the style of crankbait used. While trolling for walleyes anglers need line capacity and a line metering system. Musky hunters need power plus large line capacity. The bass angler needs neither of these. A perfect bass crankin' reel is a small profile baitcaster with a slightly lower gear ratio; somewhere in the 4 to 1 range. The smaller profile makes it easier to cast the outfit for countless hours, while the lower gear ratio reduces drag against both the reel and angler from the heavy-lipped divers. A higher geared reel in the 6 to 1 range might still be preferred for low-drag, high speed lures like lipless crankbaits, however. This is one of the reasons why bass anglers have so many outfits.

There are also many anglers north of the Mason-Dixon line who cast crankbaits for walleyes during the spring and fall. Most of the time, the crankbaits being tossed for walleyes are small, and the lines being used are light – usually less than 10-pound test. Of course, small, lightweight crankbaits and ultra thin lines don't perform well on any baitcasting outfit. That's why the vast majority of walleye crankers prefer spinning gear. A good spinning rod for walleye crankin' is generally a medium to medium-light action 6 ½ to 7 ½ footer. The preferred reel is a small 6- to 7-ounce spinning reel with a gear ratio of at least 5 to 1. Overall weight of the rod/reel outfit is a concern here. Lightweight outfits make it much easier to cast these lures for hours without fatigue.

As you can see by these examples, there is no way that one rod fits all in the crankbait world unless you strictly chase one species of fish. Even then, you'll probably need several outfits. That is why I've devoted an entire chapter to it. There are simply too many unique situations in the world of fishing today. While you might be able to take a wide variety of gamefish species on crankbaits, the specific method, lure size, terrain, and individual fish species all require some

specialized tackle. Much like the serious golfer carries a bag full of various clubs for shots of different lengths and different greens, the versatile crankbait fisherman needs to be rigged with a number of outfits for different species-specific situations.

Even the one-fish purist needs several outfits to accommodate various lure sizes and individual fishing situations. Using the wrong rod, reel, and line can hamper the overall performance and success with any crankin' tactic. Let's take an even closer look at a few of the most popular crankin' tactics and really concentrate on proper outfitting for each.

Situation One:
Casting For Bass With Conventional Crankbaits

Basic Tackle: Medium to medium-light action 7 ½ ft. rod, low-geared 4:1 baitcasting reel.

Bass fishermen, in general, are sultans of specialization, and their need for a technique-targeted crankin' stick has been met by an entire industry of rod and reel manufacturers. Unlike the musky, pike, and walleye fisheries, the entire bass fishing business is tournament driven. A percentage of walleye anglers are up on tournaments and the tournament atmosphere, but not like the bass industry as a whole. The reason I mentioned this is it has a huge impact on how products get introduced and accepted into the marketplace. Generally speaking, if the bass tournament professionals aren't using it and promoting it, you won't find it in a tackle store.

If a bass pro wins a tournament on a specific lure, rod, reel, line and technique, that gets a lot of notice right away. It creates an almost instantaneous leap-frog effect with other tournament pros quickly jumping onto the bandwagon – trying out the same lure, rod, reel, line and technique. Within short order, the word spreads like wildfire. The marketeers then jump with both feet into the fire introducing a host of products that relate to this technique, utilizing the endorsement of the winning tournament pro who developed or popularized it. This has pushed the production of some outstanding lures as well as the outfits used to cast and work them.

The world of specialized bass crankin' is another classic example of this whole thing being set in motion by tournament influence. Bass were being caught on crankbaits, and tournaments were being won on crankbaits for a number of years before any one angler decided to use some unique tackle for this tactic, but eventually a few noted anglers did. Two bass anglers come to mind when I think of crankbait tackle specialization: Paul Elias and Rick Clunn. These two guys, throughout the last two decades, have made tremendous contributions to the evolution of crankbaits, and crankin' tackle for bass. Both anglers won a series of tournaments on crankbaits and then the press exposed the details of their crankin' needs.

Paul Elias was certainly not the first to win a bass tournament on a crankbait, but his first big win on crankbaits revitalized the struggling crankbait sales market in the late 1980s. Paul's tactic of "kneelin' and reelin'" with an extra long rod, thin line, a low-geared reel, and an extra large billed deep diver triggered a revival in crankbait sales that has maintained itself since. This included specialized tackle matchups for his odd method. Lots of manufacturers began building big-lipped divers, longer crankin' sticks, and low geared reels in order to capitalize on the renewed interest. In turn, this helped to create a whole new breed of crankin' specialists and further refined the tackle used for them.

It should be noted, however that Paul was not actually the first to "kneel and reel". That technique was first discovered by an angler named Bill Adcock of Baton Rouge, Louisiana, back in the 1960s. Bill was a phenomenal crankbait fisherman and deserves mention in this book along with several other

A long rod serves several valuable purposes in trolling. One of these is keeping fish hooked after the strike.

crankin' pioneers. Bill Adcock caught stringers of big bass by "kneelin' and reelin'" but his success occurred prior to the bass tournament tornado of the later 1960s. Therefore the press had no interest. Bill Adcock never attained any notoriety outside of his hometown, but several lure manufacturers did retain Adcock's services for lure design. He was one of the crankin' pioneers.

Paul Elias did popularized the kneel & reel technique with his tournament wins. More than kneelin' and reelin', Paul Elias's crankin' success on bass spawned many new ideas in tackle specialization for crankin', most notably the need for a low-geared baitcasting reel. The lower geared reel had more overall gear power and created less drag when retrieving high-resistance, big-lipped divers. Reel manufacturers created some specialized "crankin' reels" featuring the slower retrieve and increased gear power. These reels featured gear ratios as low as 3 to 1 instead of the newer industry standard 5 to 1 high-speed versions. Since then, bass anglers have settled on 4 to 1 ratios as the accepted reel of choice for deep crankin' with big-lipped divers.

One of the most successful bass tournament anglers in history, Rick Clunn, was instrumental in the development of the long rod for crankin'. Rick was also not the first angler to ever win a tournament on a crankbait, but his thoughts on a specific crankbait rod changed the entire rod market for this lure. Being one of the greatest all-time tournament anglers, Clunn was not so much concerned with the performance of a rod for casting and working the lure, but more so on hooking and holding fish after they hit the plug. He surmised that the high percentage of bass that jump and throw certain highly productive crankbaits could be reduced substantially by utilizing a longer, slower, less responsive rod. The end result was a flurry of such rods from various manufacturers, and the specialized "crankin' stick" was born for bassin'.

Today's most popular bass crankin' stick is a 7 ½ footer that's lightweight, but relatively slow in rod tip action. This slow, parabolic medium to medium-light rod action enables one to cast a wide range of small to medium-sized lures that run shallow, mid-range, and deep. While it doesn't respond quickly to strikes, the fish has a tough time getting off once hooked. As Clunn suggested, the slower reacting rod actually lets the bass (and any other gamefish) take the lure deeper on the strike before there's a reaction from the angler on the other end. The result is a more solid hook-up initially on the fish, and a constant deep bending pressure on the rod itself preventing any possible slack line during jumps or thrashes. This rod is now a mainstay in any bass tournament boat.

Situation Two: Trolling Open Water Walleyes With Crankbaits

Basic Tackle: 8- to 10-foot soft action baitcast style trolling rod. Large capacity baitcast trolling reel with line meter.

Walleye fishing has certainly gone through a major renaissance in the last decade. A sport that was once dominated by jigs and live bait rigs and bottom-oriented techniques is now quite different by comparison. Bottom-oriented live bait techniques now only account for a fraction of the walleye fishing format. A fast-paced tournament mentality has overtaken the traditionalists. Along with that, the discovery of new walleye fishing frontiers in open water has changed the way anglers think about getting bait to the fish. Borrowing a page from Great Lakes salmon trollers, the new breed of walleye warriors outfit their boats with rod holders, planer boards, long rods, line-counter reels, and a huge selection of crankbaits. The whole focus is maximum water coverage in an effort to locate and catch fish suspended in open water.

No live bait tactic can provide the simplicity, the efficiency, nor the speed that trolling crankbaits in open water does. Open water trolling with crankbaits is simple to do, it's exceptionally effective at covering precise depths with a trouble-free, maintenance-free method. Best of all, open water trolling with crankbaits features maximum water coverage. This is the most critical element to success with open water trolling no matter what the species. You have to be able to locate these "needle in a haystack" schools of open water walleyes. This method makes it possible to do so. But the right tackle is critical.

Comparatively, you can see that this crankbait system is in another world when compared to casting for bass or muskies. While both systems feature crankbaits, the rod & reel combination for each isn't even remotely similar. The demands for each a crankbait system are totally different. In one instance you're casting (bass), in the other you're trolling (walleyes), but that's just the beginning of the differences in these crankin' tactics. The productive lures are different, the terrain that attracts each fish is different, and the tactics required are simply on opposite sides of the planet.

As far as I know, the true pioneers of open water crankbait trolling for walleyes were noted walleye tournament pros, Gary Parsons an Keith Kavajecz. While many Lake Michigan charters were certainly trolling crankbaits over open water with planer boards far before Gary and Keith, these two guys honed the system for suspended walleyes. They perfected the use of an attached in-line planer board, instead of the more standard Great Lakes mast system, and were the first to develop specialized rod & reel combinations that are considered normal walleye crankbait trolling gear today.

Gary and Keith experimented with a wide range of spinning and baitcasting rods & reels initially, but eventually settled on tackle similar to what Lake Michigan charter captains use for the salmonoids. Two of the staples of this system of crankbait fishing in-

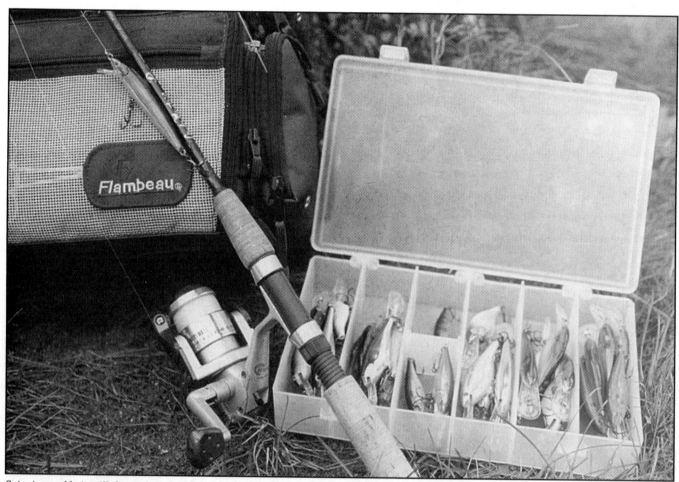

Spinning tackle is still the preferred way to go for smaller, mini-sized crankbaits. Softer action rods are generally preferred here since they are more forgiving against line breakage, plus the tend to cast very light, wind-buoyant lures better.

cluded a long 8- to 10-foot baitcast style rod and a large capacity baitcast trolling reel with a line meter. As we've already discussed to some degree, extra long rods helped maintain spread and organization with multiple lines out, as well as being a great aid in fighting fish. The metered reels were critical in duplicating productivity. Both items are now standards in any contemporary walleye boat.

The extra long rods made it easier to keep lures away from the boat and separated from each other. Positioning longer rods inside rod holders up or down, inside or outside, and a trouble-free spread is accomplished. When you consider that a typical open water walleye cranker trolls with at least six rods, this factor does become quite significant. Remaining tangle-free is always an issue no matter what the fishing technique, but when you're talkin' open water crankbait trolling with an army of rods, things can quickly get out of hand if you're not careful. Long rods help a great deal here. So do the in-line boards.

The extra long rod is also a welcome aid in fish fighting, as well as providing the superior ability to lift the planer board out of the water quickly during the fish battling process. Since the preferred method of in-line planer board fishing is to tightly fasten the board to the line so the fish can't break it free, and

detaching the board as you crank it in during the battle, the extra long rod provides additional lift to get the board up and out of the water more quickly. Anyone

Tackle combinations for crankin' vary with lure size and the structure being fished. Bait casting gear is preferred for larger lures and cover applications where heavy lines are needed.

who's done any amount of this kind of crankbait fishing will agree that the water drag these boards put on the rod is tremendous. Being able to get them out of the water eliminates this.

A large-capacity trolling reel of the baitcast style with a line metering device is also a staple of the walleye crankbait troller. As I will cover, in more detail in upcoming chapters, the length of line between the crankbait and the rod tip, or in this instance between crankbait and planer board, greatly affects the running depth of the lure. Being able to troll lures at a precise depth range is the key to making contact with more walleyes. Being able to quickly duplicate the productive line length and it's corresponding running depth with six or more lines is paramount to the performance of this system. A line-counter reel is an essential part of this technique.

Situation Three:
Casting Big Crankbaits For Muskies & Pike

Basic Tackle: 6 ½-to 7 ½-foot medium-heavy action baitcasting rod. Strongly geared, medium line capacity baitcaster.

Musky fishing was a sport dominated by spinners, top-water lures and wooden jerkbaits for the better part of its conventional existence. Crankbait fishing was rarely considered an option. It was left only to a tiny percentage of desperadoes. On top of that, the selection of musky-sized crankbaits was slim for years. While eastern U.S. did have a number of successful crankbait trollers, the bulk of the musky world — over 98% — were casters. They cast shallow water with spinners, jerkbaits, and top-water. Casting crankbaits was simply not an acceptable technique for the most part.

Looking back, this still seems odd to me since the majority of the world record class muskies being caught during the 1940s and '50s were taken on some of the classic early big crankbaits such as the Creek Chub Pikie Minnow, Heddon Vamp, and similar plugs. The bigger fish were obviously coming from deeper water,

and crankbaits were catching them. Yet the masses still refused to acknowledge this preferring to cast a bucktail, top-water lure or jerkbait instead. It was as if all muskies caught on crankbaits were flukes.

All of that tradition slowly began to change in the late 1960s and into the early 1970s. Some of the best northern Wisconsin musky guides begrudgingly started casting crankbaits on a regular basis. Lures like the Cisco Kid, Pikie Minnow, and a newcomer, the Bagley DB series, became standards. As musky guides fished later into the fall, the traditional lures became less productive. Musky guides during this era eventually learned that as water temps cooled through autumn, crankbait success really improved. Crankbaits were slowly gaining acceptance with the casting crowd, but it wasn't happening overnight.

By the mid- to late-1970s, articles of many sorts began to appear in various fishing publications on crankbait fishing for muskies. The early pages of Fishing Facts Magazine, in particular, educated a whole new breed of anglers on the value of casting deep divers along weed edges and over hard bottom humps for untapped muskies. I was one of those readers who took this information and ran with it.

In the mid-1980s, I began development of the original DepthRaider crankbait series. Along the way, we (my guiding customers, friends, and I) caught a bunch of big fish on them. It's worth noting that this occurred during all seasons; spring, summer, and fall. It has been said by many of today's musky masters that this really spurred the crankbait's acceptance in the musky market. Our eventual introduction of the DepthRaider in 1988 completely changed big crankbait marketing and acceptance in the musky world. Many other crankbait introductions were to follow. New rods and reels to work these bigger baits were needed. In 1983, I developed the first musky crankin' stick for Cabela's. Musky crankin' sticks are now offered by most major rod manufacturers.

Today, musky crankin' is a mainstay method for all seasons, and we've educated a new generation on how to fish them. We'll deal with this in more detail later on, but for now, let's take a look at the ultimate musky crankin' stick which is a far cry from that original "pool cue" musky rod.. The conventional pool cue musky rods in the 5 ½- to 6-foot range simply didn't cut it for crankbait fishing. A crankin' stick for muskies must have power for hooksets, but also needs length for fish-fighting, casting, and lure manipulation.

Rod power can never be underestimated in musky fishing. It is essential for both hook setting and lure manipulation through weed cover. Power ripping weeds off lures is only possible with a responsive, powerful butt section. Instant power and solid impact is necessary in order to move a large lure in the jaws of a big musky as well as drive large diameter hooks into its mouth. A soft action rod simply won't accomplish this with any degree of regularity. Yet, the rod tip must still bend so that it doesn't rip the hooks loose. In other words,

there's a fine line between too much power and too little in a musky crankin' stick. You need the length, and the power, but you also need some bend.

Length is the least understood aspect in a musky crankin' stick. Length, at least 6 ½ feet, is needed to properly work the crankbait in a figure 8 at boatside. Without length, you can not work lures correctly in a figure 8. The figure 8, of course, is one of the most deadly parts of the musky retrieve with any lure, but it is absolutely essential with crankbaits since such a high percentage of fish follow a lure to boatside. Longer rods make better figure 8 patterns with your lures at boatside. They also make it easier to hold on to a big fish that hits with a mere foot or so of line out. A shorter 6 ½ foot rod with stiffness and power is superior in feel, and for cleaning debris off the crankbait, but it falls a bit short in figure 8 effectiveness as well as fish-fighting ability. The ultra long 7 ½-footer has less

Giant crankbaits have a time and a place. They are most productive on muskies and pike, but do occasionally take big bass and walleyes, too.

overall feel and control, but it's far superior on the figure 8 and will save you many muskies that strike a short line.

The best compromise seems to be 7 feet. With ample stiffness and power in the lower 60% of the rod, a 7-footer that's designed with the proper blank stiffness, will still provide plenty of feel and overall control, yet provide enough length to easily execute a large figure 8. The difference between a 6 ½ and 7-footer is quickly evident in both its ability to work the figure 8 and its fish-battling benefits. The 7-footer provides a bit more bend, resulting in less fish lost. While both are adequate, I prefer the 7-footer simply because it is superior on the figure 8.

The sheer weight and thrashing power of a big musky tends to tear large holes around the hook in the fish's mouth. The lack of a bend in the conventional short "pool cue" musky rod promotes putting too much pressure on the fish in order to keep the rod bent and prevent hook shake-off. What quickly happens is a big fish is lost after a few thrashes with the shorter rod. Add a bit more tip bend to the musky crankin' stick, a 7-footer, and hook-hole-tear is reduced substantially. Less pressure is automatically

exerted on the fish with a 7-footer that allows for some tip bend, and the result is a higher percentage of boated fish.

Rod and reel combinations for crankbait fishing vary a bit with the species you are after and the lure size you choose. Generally clear water means smaller baits lighter lines and spinning gear.

Actually, I do use both the 7- and 7 ½-footer an equal amount for musky crankin'. I'll opt for the beefier 7-footer with deep divers in around any weed cover; especially larger crankbaits in the 3-ounce range or more. But the 7 ½-footer gets the nod whenever I'm running smaller crankbaits or shallower divers in less demanding cover. I'll also usually replace the hooks on my shallow divers with a premium thin-wire style when using 7 ½-foot crankin' sticks. This makes it a snap to hook big fish, and you'll rarely put enough pressure on this kind of hook to bend it with a 7 ½-footer that has a fast taper, and some tip action. The additional bend of the fast action 7 ½-footer also greatly reduces hook-hole-tear. The end result is an enviably high percentage of well-hooked fish. This is particularly important when you've got a 50-incher thrashing on the other end. Long rods keep 'em on until they can be safely netted.

The ideal baitcasting reel for musky crankin' is medium-sized for hand comfort, but strongly geared for crankin' performance. I am personally not a big fan of the older, traditional, round-reel baitcasters like the Ambassadeur 6500C for this kind of musky fishing. These reels tend to be uncomfortable over the long haul, they lack substantial gear power, and the lack of a continual anti-reverse reduces their overall smoothness and crankin' strength a great deal. Even though they continue to be the industry's most popular musky reel, I feel they are no better than an average choice for crankin' muskies.

Smaller profile baitcasters with a more comfortable gripping surface, and a continuous anti-reverse, which substantially improves smoothness and gear strength, are the preferred choice. My all-time favorite for years was a now-discontinued reel called the Trophy SS200. It had all of these features, but was a poor seller and never gained wide acceptance with the retailers who still to this day prefer to sell the average musky customer a traditional round reel. Shimano's Calcutta series is, as of this writing, one of the best products available in this class. It is relatively comfortable, but it is exceptionally smooth and strong. It has the tightest continuous anti-reverse system around, and the best overall engineering. It's price, however, reflects these qualities. They carry the most hefty price tag in the market.

Situation Four:
Casting Small, Mini-Cranks For Walleye, Trout and Bass
Basic Tackle: 6- to 7- foot light action spinning

Here's a method of crankbait fishing that is probably attempted by more anglers than all other methods combined, yet it gets the least amount of press. Nearly everyone who fishes for bass, walleyes, and trout has, at one time or another, thrown a small crankbait with a spinning rod. Nearly every tackle box is full of such lures, and nearly everyone who fishes owns at least one spinning outfit. Enough said.

There's no great secrets to expound upon here, but there are a few things worth noting. For one, stiffer action spinning rods are more accurate, but less versatile. A factor worth noting if you're target-casting small plugs. Stiffer action spinning rods also work crankbaits through weeds much better. The additional power and response of the stiffer stick explodes weeds off more cleanly, resulting in a more debris-free lure. Finally, the stiff action rod is more sensitive. You'll feel the subtle lure vibrations of small crankbaits much better on the stiffer spinning rod. This increases your ability to adjust speeds, work the lure more effectively over weeds and other cover, and actually feel strikes.

However, soft action rods are more forgiving. You're much more apt to break-off with a stiff action spinning rod when utilizing light-weight lines. Anytime you're forced to fish with line weights under 8-pound test, the softer action rod is worth considering. This is an important consideration in gin-clear waters, and/or where some additional depth is desired with a small crankbait. The difference in running depth, for example, with a #5 Shad Rap on 4 lb. test versus 8 lb. is substantial. Your overall running depth with this lure alone will be decreased by as much as 2 feet by using the 8 lb.

over the 4 lb. There might be some situations where this is critical to your success.

Soft action rods will also cast ultra-light lures farther than stiff ones will. The more wind resistant the lure is, the more critical it becomes to use a long, soft action rod. If you're struggling to get distance with a favored little crankbait, switch to a longer, soft-action rod and see what a difference it makes. I'm a big fan of a light action 7-footer for this situation. A light action 7-footer, combined with 4 lb. line, will usually cast the smallest, most wind-resistant crankbaits with ease. I wouldn't hesitate to go even longer in some cases.

I also feel a lot more confident battling a big fish on such tackle. It's rare to break a line, no matter how big the fish is, with long, light action spinning rods. I've landed muskies up to 33 pounds on such gear, as well as smallmouths up to 8 ½ pounds, largemouths over 10 pounds, and northern pike near 20 pounds. Fish of these sizes are scary customers on short spinning rods, light lines, and stiffer actions. But providing there's not an abundance of cover nearby, you'll have no problem whipping down the biggest gamefish in the system with a longer, soft action spinning rod as long as you take your time. It took me almost an hour to catch that 33-pounder on a light action spinning outfit back in '78. To this day, I consider this incident one of my greatest angling feats. The long, light action rod helped a great deal.

Baitcasting gear works exceptionally well with larger crankbaits and heavier gauge lines of 10-pound test or more. This kind of tackle is recommended when cover is an issue.

Summary

There is no single outfit that best suits the crankbait fisherman. So much depends upon the species being targeted, the water being fished, the depth the fish are at, the cover they're hiding in and the size of the lures being used. Also, the method of crankbait fishing being utilized has a tremendous bearing on the tackle needs. Trolling small crankbaits requires completely different setups than casting large ones. Trolling, in general, demands a different stick than casting. There is no such thing as an all-purpose crankin' rod.

Crankin' tackle is sure to continue evolving as more anglers experiment with crankbaits under a variety of conditions. I fully expect better reels to be developed. I also think we can improve rod actions featuring lighter overall weight as well as superior components. Line diameter as well as durability continues to improve each and every season. The crankin' tackle used today will probably always work, but don't be surprised to find a far better selection of specialized crankin' sticks in the future.

Reel needs for crankin' are in much the same boat. While a low-geared, small baitcaster might work great for casting and crankin' standard deep-divers, it would be a poor overall choice for smaller plugs. A spinning reel is the better bet here. Yet neither the spinning reel nor the small baitcaster would service the troller very well where line capacity and metering are key concerns. A large capacity reel is nearly always better for trolling. Trolling reels, overall, are very poor performers when utilized in any casting application. They're too big, too bulky, and they don't have the design features needed to make smooth, trouble-free casts.

The best policy is to have a variety of outfits specifically suited for the crankin' purpose in mind. The more methods you master, the more species of fish you chase, the more outfits you're going to need. If you're a multi-species, multi-method angler, this obviously means you're going to have quite an investment in tackle. While some non-fishing wives might frown at this thought, the crazed crankbait fisherman is excited by the thought. After all, the more toys, the happier the boy! Right?

chapter 5

The Line Factor

"How deep does that lure run?" This is the most-asked question of a crankbait manufacturer at any consumer show. Lord knows I've been asked this question no less than 1,000 times, and my answer is always the same – "it depends." There is not a simple answer to this question since a number of variables can affect the potential running depth of any crankbait; particularly floating/divers. As we've already discussed in some detail in previous chapters, a number of factors determine the running depth of a crankbait. Speed of retrieve is certainly one of them. However, line diameter and length of line (cast length) are the most critical.

In an exaggerated sense, imagine attaching the deepest-diving crankbait in your tackle box to your wife's clothes line. Let out 50 feet of that clothes line, attach it to the back end of your boat and begin a straight trolling pass. How deep do you think this lure is going to dive with that thick diameter rope? Obviously, not very deep at all. Conversely, attach that same crankbait to an equal length (50 feet) of 2-pound test monofilament and make the same trolling pass again.

Do you think this lure will dive any deeper? You bet it will.

Now, of course you'd never fish a crankbait on a thick clothes line, nor the ultra-thin 2-pound test, but the basic idea here is to understand line drag. Plainly put, the thicker the diameter of the line you choose to fish on any given crankbait, the shallower that lure will run. Thicker diameter lines simply capture more water, and therefore create more drag. This resistance or line drag pulls the lure up, reducing its overall diving range. I just cited an exaggerated example, utilizing a clothes line vs. 2-pound test, but subtle variances in depth diving performance exist in real fishing situations with various line tests on your present outfits.

Basically, if you want to increase the running depth of your lure, you'll need to drop down a notch or two in line size. On the flip side, if you need a lure to run a bit shallower, use a heavier weight line. Subtle diving differences of one to two feet are possible by switching lines. In fact, they're quite common. For example, a typical bass/walleye crankbait that dives to

Joe Bucher (right) and his father Joe Bucher Sr. really played havoc on shallow-water walleyes with crankbaits for many years. When most anglers were working jigs and live bait for this seemingly passive fish, Joe and his dad would prove time and time again that crankbaits would trigger larger walleyes on a regular basis.

8 feet with 10-pound test, will likely dive to 10 feet with 6- to 8-pound line. That same bait will probably only hit 7 feet with 12-pound test. The only way to know for sure is to try various line sizes with this lure until the perfect running depth is obtained.

Frankly, I always find it kind of odd that some anglers want a lure to dive as deep as possible. This is not always desirable. A lure that dives too deep over tall weeds is going to plow. A lure that dives too deep over a shallow cresting rock hump is more likely to snag up in rock crevices. A lure that dives too deep along a stained water weed line will hang up too much. Ideally, you want a lure that dives just barely deep enough. That is always more desirable in my book. I want a crankbait to "tick" the weed tops, the rock tops, and weed line fringes. This makes it much easier to

keep it working cleanly.

Heavy lines can also work in your favor for other specific fishing situations. Top-water lures usually work much better on heavy gauge lines. The added drag here keeps the line up, reducing the line sinkage and making it easier to keep a lure up on the surface. In a sense, the thicker line improves the lure's buoyancy. This same philosophy works with shallow-running subsurface lures like spinnerbaits and bucktails as well as crankbaits. If your primary targets are shallow, and you want a slower spinner presentation that still keeps the spinnerbait shallow, heavy line is an asset here. Heavy line will also reduce the lure's descent or sink rate. This is something that jig fishermen need to consider all the time. Rig a jig on a heavy line and the sink rate or sinking speed decreases noticeably. This also comes

The tackle you choose for crankbait casting or trolling depends on a number of factors: size of lure, depth and, to some extent, the species of fish you are after. Spinning tackle is best suited for smaller crankbaits and lighter lines, especially when fishing in clear water.

into play when using a sinking count-down style crankbait. Your sink rate with a count-down will surely be noticeably faster with thinner gauge line than with a thick one.

When it comes to crankbaits, heavy gauge lines can have many huge advantages. One of my favorites is making a real deep diver run shallower to match a specific situation. Many examples could be cited here, but let's look at one that happened just recently. The last year that my dad was alive, 1997, we found some walleyes up on a grassy flat cruising the tops right before dark. We were able to stay on this productive pattern for over a month. The mean depth of this flat was about 8 feet, but the tops of the grass were only about 3 feet from the surface. Dad and I found the walleyes were hot for a perch # 7 Shad Rap that typically runs about 5 ½ to 6 feet down on 8- to 10-pound test.

Dad and I were catching plenty of walleyes overall, but we were having a lot of trouble keeping that # 7 Shad Rap from "grassing up." We tried a few other lures, but it was quite obvious that these walleyes had a real affinity for this particular bait. As the days went by,

the grass bed began to mature more and more. This meant even taller grass and a tougher time keeping the lure clean. My dad was particularly frustrated on these later trips with the troublesome grass tops collecting on his crankbait's hooks. He was fouling on nearly every cast, greatly reducing his overall fish-catching potential.

To make matters even more challenging, the fish-catching window was small anyway — about an hour — right between sunset and total darkness. So any wasted casts were really hurting production. We tried switching to a variety of other shallower-running lures, but the walleyes didn't want 'em. They wanted that # 7 Shad Rap, and that was that.

Finally, I suggested running a couple of rods with 12- to 14-pound test in order to reduce running depth. My dad was reluctant at first, worrying that the thicker line would ruin the lure's action and discourage strikes. I was concerned about this too, but thought it was a least worth a try. Anyway, we tried it, and it worked! We ran the same baits on 12-pound test, a heavier, thicker line, and it reduced the overall running depth by about a foot. This was just enough to eliminate the majority of the grass problems. Thankfully, the wall-

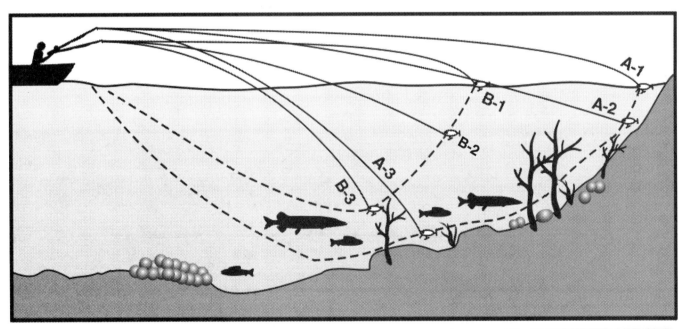

The underwater travel path of a crankbait varies with casting length. A short cast produces a V-shape, while a longer cast is apt to create a more U-shaped angle. Short casts simply don't allow the lure to reach maximum diving potential before the line distance becomes too short.

eyes weren't discouraged by the slightly thicker line. We caught just as many, and had a lot more fun.

Here again, there was nothing more than a subtle change in tackle – a jump up in line diameter– that made the difference. Once we had the perfect line size, we could run that Shad Rap perfectly over the grass tops nine casts out of 10. Because our lures were grassed up a lot less, we caught a lot more walleyes. Our production picked up every night afterwards. Incidentally, we also shortened up our casts quite a bit, too. This further reduced grass problems.

Basically, this is one of the most basic fundamentals of being a good crankbait fisherman. Having the knowledge to adapt your tackle, most specifically the line, to the conditions at hand, in order to make the lure run the right depth is essential to success. This is only possible by first understanding the concept of what makes a lure run deep. The true crankbait pros know these simple secrets and make the whole system work wonderfully. The less experienced rarely catch on, miring in frustration instead, vainly attempting to work the lure effectively over a spot like the grassbed I described. The end result is lots of grass, but few fish.

Of course, thinner gauge lines also have their place in crankbait fishing, and their purpose is often just the opposite. Thin lines cut through the water like a razor, making the lure dive to its maximum depth potential. Combine this with a longer cast and the potential maximum depth increases even more. Let's take that same grassbed scenario, only make everything deeper. In this case, the flat is 16 feet deep, but the grass tops are no higher than 8 feet from the surface. Now this little crankbait is going to run way too high on the 14- to 17-pound test. You need more depth.

If that lure appears to be hitting around 5 ½ to 6 feet with the 10-pound line, dropping down to 6-pound test may be necessary in order hit those 8-foot tops. If that doesn't do it, you might need to drop down to 4-pound and increase your cast length in order to further increase running depth. The closer you get to those grass tops, the more fish you're probably going to catch. A close attention to tackle detail is critical, and in this case, the line diameter is the key element. The astute crankbait fisherman always considers the line diameter and the way it affects running depth. The simple formula is to analyze how deep you need your

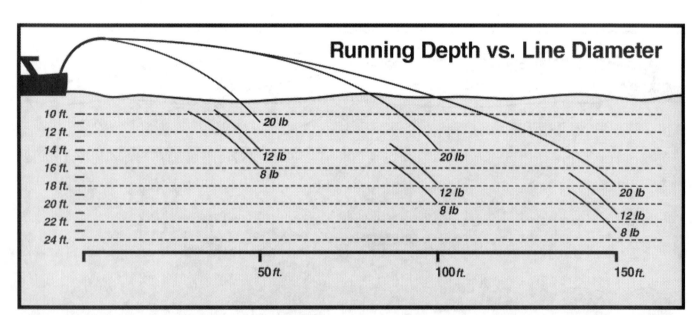

The only way to insure maximum running depth on any deep diver is to pitch out a long cast. Short casts simply don't allow the lure to reach maximum level. Always consider, however, that a short cast might be beneficial if you desire to keep the lure from running too deep in a particular spot.

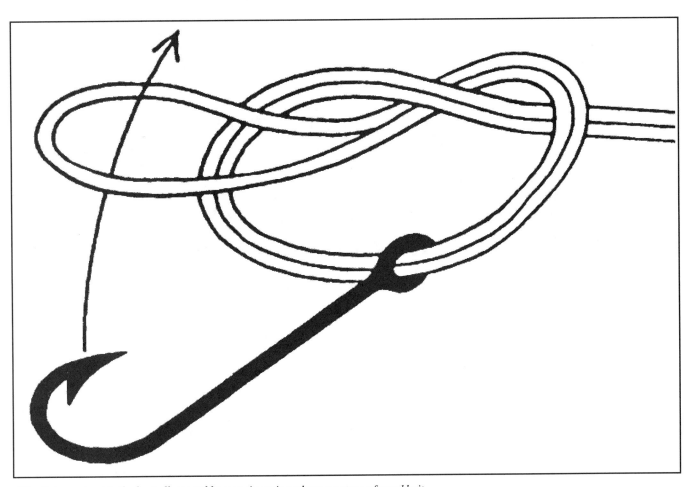

The Palomar knot is the best all-around knot to tie on just about any type of crankbait.

crankbait to run, choose a lure that gets you in the ball park, and then tweak it with various line sizes.

A less known aspect of line test selection is the variance in line diameters between equal test lines. In other words, not all 10-pound test lines are the same diameter. That's why you need to check the precise numerical line diameter on the package to compare. One manufacturer's 10-pound test might be the same diameter as another's 8-pound. A lot of this has to do with where the line is manufactured and the line composition. New line technologies and a variety of new fibers have created a line war of sorts making the issue of comparing lines difficult. The only way to precisely get the desired performance you need and any kind of comparative analysis is to check the actual line diameter on the line package.

A classic example of this is involves my favorite line for muskies and big pike — 50-pound Magnathin. Inquiring parties are nearly always astounded when they hear that I fish with 50-pound test since 30-pound is a more acceptable consumer size. However, a close examination of a package of 50-pound test Magnathin alongside a package of 30-pound test Berkley XT reveals that they're nearly the same diameter, .026. The pound rating is actually immaterial. The real issue, line diameter, is basically the same. My argument has always been – why fish with 30-pound test when 50-pound test is the same diameter? When the chips are down, I'm sure you'd agree that the 50-pound is a better choice. Especially if both cast equally well, and in this case, the 50 actually casts better.

Cast length is another factor that greatly affects

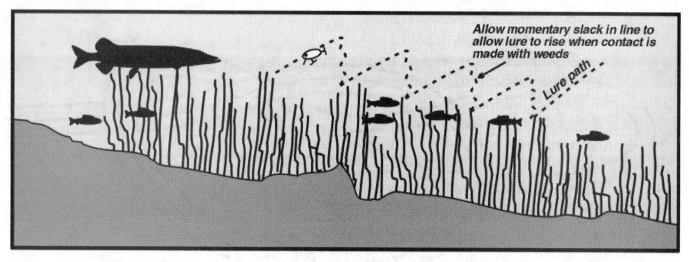

Allow momentary slack in line to allow lure to rise when contact is made with weeds

Lure path

The best weed crankbaits are floating divers with good buoyancy, a fat body design, and a downward angled lip. The lip collects the majority of weeds upon collisions, while the lure's superior buoyancy enables it to back out of these collisions freely by releasing line tension.

true running depth. Shorter casts reduce the running depth potential. Longer casts maximize it. The underwater path of a deep-diving crankbait on a short cast is somewhat "V" shaped. The underwater path of a deep-diver on a long cast is more "U" shaped. No matter what the length of cast, a good portion of the retrieve is always taken up diving the lure down to a specific maximum level. If the cast is too short, the maximum depth might not be reached before a shortening line length from rod tip to lure actually begins forcing the lure back upwards.

The only way to assure maximum running depth on any deep-diver is to pitch a long cast. A long cast provides enough distance between rod tip and lure for the bait to dig to its deepest potential. The longer cast also enables the lure to stay at the maximum depth range longer before it is pulled upward. That's also why trolling takes a lure much deeper than casting. The length of line remains consistent on the troll giving the lure all the time needed to dig to its level-off point. The lure is never being pulled upward by a decreasing line length on a troll. The line distance is steadily decreasing on any cast/retrieve situation.

A good rule of thumb on casting versus trolling is that trolling doubles the running depth. In other words, if a given crankbait runs 6 feet deep with 20-pound test

on the cast, it will run 12 feet deep on the troll with the same line. This generally holds true for most lures, and is an important thing to know for any crankbait application. If you can't hit bottom on a potential hotspot with a cast, a follow-up trolling pass with the same lure will probably do it. This little-known trick has really paid big dividends for me on big bass, whopper walleyes, and monster muskies. I've taken lots of wall-hangers of all species on follow-up trolling passes after failing to hit bottom on the cast.

The actual type of line used also affects running depth to some degree, and in one instance greatly increases it. For example, braided lines drag slightly more water than monofilament and therefore pull a crankbait slightly shallower. If you used braided lines and monofilament lines of the same diameter on the same lure, the rod containing mono will make the lure dive slightly deeper. This is a fact that few anglers realize.

Wire lines and lead-core lines create an entirely different effect. Both wire and lead-core have added natural weighting which pulls the lure down more. When I want to get lures really deep on short lines, I use wire. Of course, this is strictly a trolling application. No wire or lead-core line that I know of can be used for casting. My favorite deep trolling wire is the solid wire variety; one of the most popular being Monel. Monel wire makes any typical deep-diver dig to double the standard depth attainable with monofilament. In other words, if a given plug runs 12 feet on 20-pound monofilament on a troll, it'll dive to 24 feet with wire. Even greater depths are attainable with Monel wire by simply letting out more line. We'll deal more with this specialized method of big fish crankin' in a future chapter.

Speed of retrieve or troll is the final factor in line depth attention. Generally speaking, faster retrieves make floating divers dive deeper. Slower speeds keep floating divers shallower. Crank a floating diver really slowly and it stays right on the surface. Crank it fast and it digs downward. This basic concept works to a point, but there is a certain speed that each individual crankbait reaches where it destroys the lure's ability to dive and track. I like to call this the "torque-out speed." Few lures reach torque-out speed on a cast and retrieve presentation, but many do on a troll. The outboard motor is certainly capable of pulling a crankbait at far higher speeds than any manual retrieve can. Therefore it's important remain below the torque-out speed when trolling and to remain aware of it when casting.

Too much speed also has a tendency to put so much drag between the lure, line, and rod tip that it can also reduce running depth. This is more common when trolling than when casting, but it can occur with a high-speed reel and a small crankbait. Don't crank or troll too quickly with smaller lures. Each lure has a perfect speed. That perfect speed makes the lure track true, and run its maximum depth. Any speed less than this reduces running depth. Any speed above this level will torque out the lure's track and diving ability.

The line diameter and casting/trolling distance has a great influence on overall running depth of any given crankbait. Understanding this basic concept is the first step in truly mastering the art of crankbait fishing. From that point on, it's a matter of learning the diving depth characteristics of each lure in your tackle box. The more you know about each lure's capabilities and how line diameter, casting distance, and retrieve speed affect these sensitive gems, the more fish you're going to catch.

chapter 6

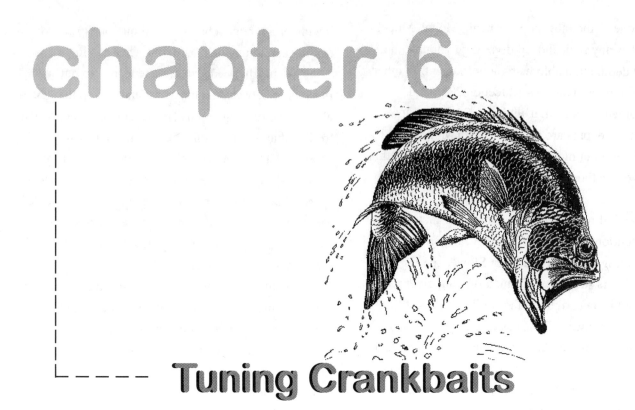

Tuning Crankbaits

I'll never forget my first experience with tuning a crankbait. It was back when I was still a teenager, with no money and few lures. This meant, every lure I owned had to work. And, if I had a good one, I had to not only make sure I didn't lose it, but I also had to keep it running perfectly. But, losing baits and keeping them working is always part of fishing. In addition, the north country where I live has northern pike and musky, that make it a regular habit of engulfing an entire lure and then snipping your line. Sometimes, I think that the fishing tackle industry has employed these fish to generate sales.

Anyway, I remember having this great little balsa crankbait that was really hot on largemouths. Working the weed flats with a bump and rise retrieve, I was taking both numbers and size from late spring throughout the entire summer period. But one late August afternoon, one of the biggest pike I had ever seen, up to that point in my young life, hammered my precious little cranker and tore it to shreds. To make matters even worse, the big fish went absolutely ballistic in the landing net. The violent thrashing, twisting, and rolling

was punishing my fragile little balsa crankbait.

Once I finally got the big pike unraveled, unhooked, and released, I was shocked to see what was left of the plug. The wire frame was completely pulled out of the lure on one side, and partially pulled out on the lower hook hanger. On top of that, the front hook hanger was bent way off to one side. Once I finally got the lure out of the net mesh tangle, it looked doubtful that I'd ever be able to use it again. It was a mess.

Shortly, I made a short cast with it to see how it would run. It didn't! As soon as I began a retrieve, the lure rolled upside down and popped out of the water. I was done, or so I thought. My prize lure was history. Yet, just for kicks, I took a pliers to the bait hoping to reassemble it. This included straightening the hook hangers and forcing the wire frame back into place. I also made an effort to repair the facial cosmetics of the lure, but this appeared to be a lost cause.

Admittedly, I was amazed when the badly battered lure began its tantalizing wobble once again. I was also surprised to see it running perfectly true. My immediate thought was, even though the finish was seriously

Tuning a crankbait is essential to good performance at higher speeds. Adjusting the line tie left or right of center usually solves the problem. This can be done with a pair of pliers, but it is best done with a tool called "The Lure Tuner".

damaged, would this bait still catch fish? It didn't take long to find that out. A few casts later, I had another largemouth, and then another and another. Needless to say, I learned from that point on, that I could re-tune and repair just about any lure in my box. By the way, that same, badly battered Bagley crankbait still adorns my bassin' box today. I keep it as both a fish-catcher and a reminder of what can be done with pliers and persistence.

Recognizing That There Is A Problem

This is a vital chapter in any book on crankbait fishing. Simply put, if you do not know how to tune your crankbaits, it's a sure bet that many of your lures will not work correctly and have virtually no chance of catching a fish. I can assure you that every successful tournament bass fisherman is a master lure tuner. In fact, I'll bet that the majority of these technicians have actually taken the time to individually hand-tune every lure in their tackle box. I'm talking about standing off the end of a dock or even at the corner of a swimming pool and checking the track and wobble of each crankbait. Working with either a pair of pliers or one of the new specialized tuning tools, every effort is made to make sure each lure tracks perfectly. When money is on the line, these top professionals are convinced that a correctly tuned lure does indeed make a difference. You should be, too.

What has always amazed me about the subject of lure tuning is how few anglers actually realize when a lure is out-of-tune. I don't think it's an exaggeration to make the claim that over 90% of today's fishermen have no idea how a lure is suppose to work. They don't know when a lure is out-of-tune, and also have no idea how to correct it. I was reminded of this on nearly a daily basis when I was still guiding full-time. Typically, a customer would snap on a favorite lure and starting bombing away without regard to its performance. I'd often watch in utter amazement as the customer fished with the off-track bait for hour after hour without noticing anything odd. The few who did notice that something wasn't right would simply change lures instead of fixing the problem.

What I'm going to attempt to do in this chapter is help the angler identify when a lure is out-of-tune, and then, what simple steps need to be taken in order to correct the problem. Both of these issues first need some awareness by the angler. Those who blindly cast a lure out and reel it in, with no attention paid to how the lure is tracking, can not hope to ever learn the fine art

of tuning a crankbait. One needs to be concentrating on the lure at all times. This means visually watching the lure work whenever possible, as well as, the more difficult task, studying the lure's vibration patterns.

Once you've identified that a lure is not working properly, the next step is to identify precisely what the lure is doing that you don't like. Is it running to the left? Is its wobble too tight? The first step in tuning a lure is to identify what, exactly, the problem is. Then, and only then, can a lure be correctly tuned. It's also important to identify the exact malfunction with the lure so that you'll know what corrective measured to take.

The next step is in knowing what to do to correct the malfunction. Once you know what to do, solving the problem is actually quite easy. For example, if the lure is running left, simply bending the line tie to the right, to some degree, usually corrects the problem. If the

The action and running depth can be altered on many of the older metal-lipped diving lures by bending the lip up or down. Bending the lip up tightens the action and increases running depth. Bending it downward widens the wobble and decreases running depth.

wobble is too tight, bending the line tie upward usually widens the stroke. In other words, you not only need to be able to diagnose a problem crankbait, but then know what measures will fix it. Like I've said already, this whole process is actually very easy.

Straight As An Arrow

The primary desire of any angler is to have a crankbait track true. This means the lure should run in a straight line during retrieve. Sometimes lures are so out-of-tune that it's blatantly obvious, but other times it's very slight and only reveals itself when under high rates of speed. Speed is the true test of a crankbait's track. A tracking problem rarely shows up when a lure is trolled or retrieved slowly. If it does, of course, the lure is

seriously out-of-tune. Tracking problems jump out when the speed is put on.

My favorite way to "speed tune" a bunch of crankbaits is to actually do it under the power of an outboard. I'll simply adjust my outboard to a fairly quick trolling speed of 3 to 5 miles per hour and then begin tuning my baits. Tuning alongside the boat enables you to closely see the lure's track all the time unlike trying to adjust it with a series of casts where you don't actually see the lure for more than about 20 percent of the time. For this reason, I recommend tuning your crankbaits against the power of an outboard whenever possible. Once you've tuned a crankbait against trolling speeds near five miles per hour, they'll surely stay in tune for any casting presentation.

The first thing I check when a crankbait is running

Bending the line tie up or down will slightly alter the action on minnow baits. An upward bend tightens the wobble, while a downward bend loosens it up.

off-track is the position of all the hook hangers, as well as the line tie. All of these components must be anchored to the lure in-line. If any of these hardware items is bent to any degree, it's probable that the lure will run off-line. Some lures are more sensitive than others, but it's still a basic fundamental of lure tuning – check the hardware first. If any hardware is bent, this is probably the culprit right off the bat. Straighten out the hardware (hook hangers and line tie), and you'll likely correct the problem with no further attention needed.

The next thing to check is the front line-tie. If the line-tie is visibly off-center, this is undoubtedly the problem. The main connection to your line, the line-tie, must be perfectly centered, in-line with axis of your plug. If it is bent left or right of center, it is unlikely that the lure will track true. A bent line-tie is easily straightened with a pair of needle-nose pliers on most lures, although many heavy-duty musky baits contain much stronger hardware which requires a beefier set of pliers.

A few years ago, my good friend Tom Gelb designed a special tool for tuning crankbaits that he simply nicknamed "The Lure Tuner." This is an outstanding device that is shaped somewhat like a pencil with an open slot on one end. The slot fits over the line-tie. One can then bend the tuner left or right to straighten out the line tie. Tom Gelb's Lure Tuner enables the angler to finely tune a lure's line-tie in order to get precision tracking with no fear of damage to the line tie itself. Gripping the line tie with a pair of pliers may actually damage the line tie on some lures as well as pinch gouges in the line tie wire. The Lure Tuner is also a lot easier to apply to a smaller line-tie than a pair of pliers. Finally, the Lure Tuner is far less apt to damage your fishing line than the ridged jaws of a pliers.

If a lure doesn't track true after the line tie and hook hangers have been visibly straightened, the next approach is to actually bend the front line tie to one side or the other in order to straighten it out. The general rule of thumb here is basically to bend that front line-tie in the opposite direction from its tracking problem. For example, if the lure continues to run to the right, bend the front line tie to the left. Continue bending the line-tie to the left until the lure tracks straight. This is the basic fundamental system used to tune a crankbait. Always remember the basic rule of thumb – bend the front line tie in the opposite direction.

Custom Tuning

Beyond tuning the track of a crankbait, there are other things one can do with some crankbaits are that rarely noted. For one, the tightness or looseness of wobble can be adjusted on many crankbaits young and old, as well as the overall running depth. This is done by either bending the diving lip, which can only be done on some of the older metal-lipped models, or bending the line-tie up or down. The latter is the choice with most of today's plastic-lipped versions. In either case, it's important to know that you can alter the action on many of your lures by fooling with the line-tie or diving lip.

I like to play with the diving lip angle on many of my older metal-lipped lures in order to tighten or loosen the action. Many of those older metal-lipped crankbaits such as the Cisco Kid, Pike Minnow, Mudbug, Bomber, and Hellbender can be tuned tighter or looser in order to produce a slightly different action than normal. As we discussed in detail in an earlier chapter, the diving lip angle is critical to both the diving depth attainable and the specific action of the plug. Generally speaking, the more parallel the lip is to the lure's body, the tighter the action, and the deeper the lure will run. Conversely, the more perpendicular a lip is to the lure body, the wider the wobble and the shallower it will travel. Playing with the angle on the diving lip is one way to adjust both the running depth and action.

Decreasing the running depth, a touch, with a favorite crankbait is accomplished by adjusting the diving lip angle downward on most metal-lipped lures. That is, to make the lure run a more toward the surface, bend the lip more toward the tail. Of course, it will also

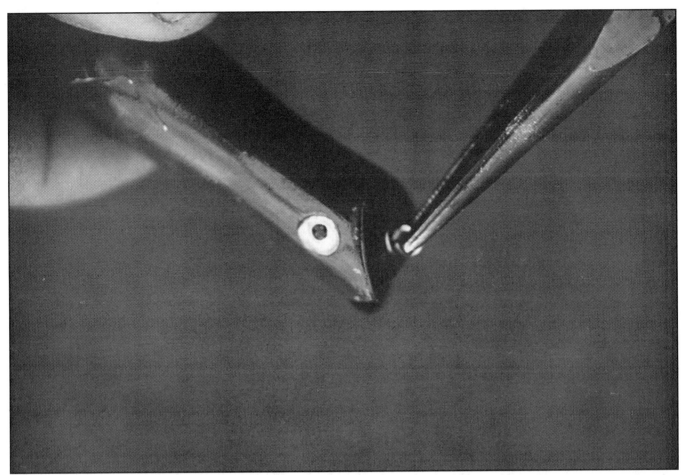

Lures featuring a screw-in line-tie can be altered in action by repositioning the line-tie closer or farther from the lure body. Experiment with various placements until you get the desired action.

wobble wider, too. This small modification can have huge results in some fishing situations where fish are holding at a specific depth, and are reluctant to move up or down to take the bait. This can also help a bunch when fishing around a trashy bottom that levels off at a specific depth that is a bit too shallow for the normal tracking depth of the plug. Bending the lip down might decrease the running depth enough to eliminate bottom plowing, and enable the lure to run inches above the trash.

The running depth can be increased slightly be a reversal of this procedure. Bend that diving lip upwards, toward the point of perfect parallel, and the lure should run a bit deeper, and wobble tighter. If you suspect that your lure is tracking a bit above the fish zone, this slight tune-up, might make a difference. This adjustment has made the day for me on several occa-

sions. Whenever I'm trying to bounce hard bottom and not quite reaching it, bending a metal diving lip upwards has sometimes accomplished the task.

Of course, you can't bend fixed plastic lips. If you try, they'll either break off or simply flex back into their original molded positions. Some gutsy lure modifiers have actually taken a match or lighter to a plastic lip, heating it slightly in order to make it bend. This has worked well with some lures, but is never an exact science. It is also a virtual guarantee that you're going to ruin a few lures when attempting this. In most cases, you're better off switching lures, going to a lighter gauge line, or adding weight in order to gain more running depth. However, there are some situations where, if you get good at this advanced modification, you could create some super-unique fish-catchers. This can be done to either make a lure run deeper or shallower. But be prepared to ruin a few baits until you master this process.

You can alter the action slightly on plastic-lipped lures by bending the line-tie forward/backward, upward or downward. This is best done with a Lure Tuner, but can also be adjusted with a pair of pliers. In fact, if I didn't own a Lure Tuner, I'd suggest attempting this modification with a needlenose locking pliers. Both the Lure Tuner and the locking pliers will fit firmly around the line tie in order to move it without damaging the hardware or the diving lip. Of course, this entire process is much easier done with smaller lures and lighter wire hardware. It's tough to bend the hardware on many of the larger musky style lures to any extent.

However, the action on many smaller bass and walleye crankbaits can be modified slightly by a little-known tuning secret. To widen the wobble, bend the line-tie up. To tighten the wobble, bend it down. On some lures, the improvement is nothing more than subtle. However, it can greatly enhance the wobble on certain baits, and that's why it is worth a try. This rarely used tuning trick is especially effective on minnow baits. I've successfully altered the action on many of my Rogues, Rapalas, and Rebels by bending the line-tie up or down.

There is one more point that may be worth noting on the subject of line-tie alterations. It involves a specific group of lures, older ones for the most part, that have a screw-in line-tie. Whenever you see a screw-in line-tie, the action can be altered by unscrewing the line-tie (screw

Hook sharpening is another essential fundamental of good crankbait fishing. Always hand-sharpen your hooks before each use. Sharp hooks simply catch more fish.

eye), and re-anchoring it either closer to the lure body or farther way in order to alter its action. Just as we learned in one of our earlier chapters, position of the line-tie on any lure body or fixed diving lip greatly affects both action and running depth. Experiment with various placements of the screw-in line-tie to tighten or widen the wobble.

The most important tuning trick you can learn is to simply correct lures that run left or right of center. Keep close tabs on all of your lures to make certain they are tracking in a straight line. Remember that speed is the true test of a lure's tracking ability. Put some speed on your retrieve in order to really check its tune. If the lure tracks straight at high rates of speed, you can confidently use it under any situation. If it doesn't, you now know how to correct it. I own a number of Lure Tuners, both large and small, and keep them in an easily accessible location. When I'm really fishing crankbaits hard, I'll keep a Lure Tuner in my belt pack along with my fish-unhooking pliers.

Once you really know what a crankbait runs like when it's in-tune, and know how to easily tune one, you'll find it hard to tolerate any lure that isn't tuned properly. Whenever possible, it's a good idea to pre-tune as many of your crankbaits as possible. This can be done off a dock or even at the local motel's swimming pool. One of my favorite times to fine-tune a bunch of crankbaits is whenever I'm trolling open water with planer boards. I'll simply let my partner take over the helm, and begin tuning a bunch of my newer lures alongside the boat using the power of the outboard to initiate the action.

No matter how you do it or when, never underestimate the importance of tuning your crankbaits. Properly tuned crankbaits dive deeper, track truer and simply catch more fish. A finely tuned crankbait is simply a thing of beauty. A perfect creation of sorts. A joy to fish. You get the absolute most out of your crankbaits when they're correctly tuned. Personally, I refuse to fish with an un-tuned lure. Once you know better, I'm certain you'll feel exactly the same way.

Crankbait Secrets—69

crankbait
categories

chapter 7

Floating/Diving Crankbaits

Those who've known me for a long time are well aware that my roots are as a bass fisherman. I was extremely fortunate to have had the opportunity to grow up on a small southern Wisconsin lake. Both my grandfather and father were in a resort business together. The water and fishing were at my daily disposal. It also didn't hurt that both my grandfather and father, were ardent anglers. When time permitted, I was out fishing Phantom Lake with either grandpa, dad, or one of the many resort guests.

While big bluegills were the most sought after local species in Phantom at that time, my interest began to shift to those occasional big largemouths we accidentally encountered while bluegill fishing. This interest quickly grew in to an obsession. Anyone in my family would be quick to comment that "obsession" was an understatement. By the time I was a teenager, I was totally focused on Phantom's largemouths. I started learning everything I could about how to catch our local bass; this included reading about bass fishing techniques from other parts of the country and trying to apply those concepts to my own local situation.

When I first took up bass fishing, I could catch spring bass in the shallows, but my success rates really dropped off by late June. I knew that the bass had moved deeper, but had no idea how to get at them effectively. The occasional encounters summer bluegill fishermen had with big bass in deep weed beds told me they were in the same general areas, but other than still-fishing big minnows over these bluegill areas, I had no concept of how to get at them.

During the summer of 1968, I read an obscure article about a southern fellow casting a lure called the Bomber for big, deep-water bass. The angler's name was Floyd Mabry, and he became one of my early fishing heroes. Floyd Mabry was one of greatest bass fishermen of the 1960s, and his pioneering concepts on crankbait fishing pushed me to learn more about this incredibly productive deep-water lure. When I had read that Floyd was crankin' these Bomber lures down along deep timber lines and weed edges, I just had to give this idea a try on Phantom.

Before I ever had a chance to check out the local sports shop in town, which was a major deal back then

A life-long pursuit of largemouth bass has served the author well. Joe Bucher first discovered crankbaits as a young bass angler, and he later applied these same principles to walleyes, pike, trout and muskies.

since we lived out in the country, I had to see if we (my dad's tackle box) had anything that would hold me over until I could get my hands on one of these Bombers. Besides, I didn't know where I was going to get the money to buy a Bomber lures anyway. I never got paid cash for chores from either my dad or grandpa. I did have a birthday coming up, however, and I always asked for fishing tackle. I was hoping that someone would buy me a Bomber.

Dad had a lure in his box called the L & S Bassmaster. While it didn't look like Floyd Mabry's Bomber, it had a fairly large diving bill, a nice finish, and a great jointed body action. I knew the bait was bass-proven since I'd seen my dad catch a few on it. Armed with the L & S Bassmaster and my newly acquired excitement about crankin' deep weeds, I loaded the boat and rowed for the closest deep weed

bed that all the locals were workin' for bluegills. Yes, rowed. I wasn't allowed to use an outboard motor quite yet, and had to stay within sight of our resort. Getting to that deep-water weed bed was quite row, and it also put me on the fringe of my parents accepted boundary lines. No matter how long it took, nor how much trouble I got in, I was going to get there.

I began casting a few hundred yards shy of what I thought was the hotspot, since there were so many boats clumped around the deep weed bed all still-fishing bluegills with canepoles. What happened next sold me on crankbaits forever. I hadn't thrown more than a few casts, when I started catching bass on that old L & S lure. Each bass gave me more confidence in this crankbait. But then, the worse possible thing happened — I hooked a big one, and it broke my line.

I had never hooked a bass quite this big, and the

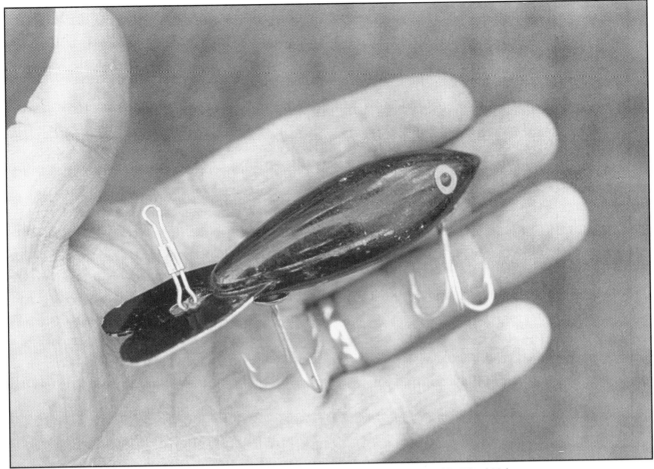

Here's the original Bomber crankbait made famous by great southern crankbait specialists like Floyd Mabry.

crummy, low-grade spincast reel simply failed me. With my bait gone, I rowed back to the resort dejected, but forever sold. My dad was not happy that I'd lost his favorite L & S Bassmaster, but he still took care of me on my upcoming birthday. A few weeks later, my dad bought me a spinning outfit – with a superior drag system – and a few lures, one of which was a Bomber in solid brown. The others included a Creek Chub Pikie Minnow in perch, a Lazy Ike in perch, a Bass Oreno in red & white, a Heddon River Runt in red & white, and a Fred Arbogast Mudbug in the coach dog pattern. This was my initial selection of crankbaits and the beginning of my career as a crankin' specialist.

From this original selection, I quickly learned that there were some noticeable differences in these lures. Some floated, some sank. Some ran shallow, some ran deeper. While I caught fish on all of them, the floating

deep-divers quickly became my favorites for weedbed work. It didn't take me long to see the value of a lure with buoyancy. The natural buoyancy of these floating divers made them go through cover better. What I learned as a boy back in the 1960s still holds true today and forever. Floating divers have a tendency to run tail up/nose down. This tracking action makes them far superior in cover.

Floating divers make cover contact with their diving lip. Most of the weeds, wood, leaves or any other debris that is encountered, collects around the lip area just in front of the line tie. The most buoyant portion of the lure, the tail section, remains pointed upward protecting the hooks and the bulk of the lure body from snagging up. An experienced cranker knows to relax line tension whenever there's a cover collision allowing the lure to literally back itself out of the snag as it floats upward. A sharp rip forward, after allowing the lure to rise, usually clears any remaining "clingers" that hang around the diving bill area.

As we've learned in previous chapters, various diving bills on lures not only create different lure actions, but also determine the lure's ability to run through cover. Lips that protrude off the lure body at some noticeable angle downward run through cover better than diving bills that are anchored directly in-line (parallel) with the lure body. This, however, is not entirely ironclad. Much of a lure's ability to run through certain kinds of cover is unique to the lure's overall design.

For example, my friend Tom Seward designed an incredibly unique floating diver for the Luhr Jensen company called the Brush Baby. Much like the original Bomber, this lure features very strong buoyancy, and a fairly parallel diving lip anchor. But it also has some unique body cams on the lure body that also help to ward off wood from snagging on the hooks. The combination of a severe diving angle to the water in conjunction with excellent buoyancy and some great design features make this the most wood-free crankbait I've ever seen. Yet, surprisingly, just like the Bomber, it is not a great crankbait in the weeds.

A far superior weed crankin' design is a floating diver with a diving lip that protrudes off the body at a downward angle combined with a fat overall body design. The downward angled lip makes the lure run a bit shallower, with a far more exaggerated side-to-side wobble. This is the best possible combination for weed crankin'. The lip collects weeds without plowing into them, while the fat buoyant body backs out of the weeds more responsively. An underrated aspect of these lures is the exaggerated side-to-side wobble, which aids in shaking off clinger weeds. Rip your rod tip forward

Joe Bucher considers the Brush Baby crankbait, designed by Tom Seward, to be one of the best crankbaits ever designed for fishing in woody cover. The combination of its unique body cams, built to ward off brush from snagging on the hooks, a broad based diving lip positioned at a severe angle, and excellent buoyancy make it go through just about any wood cover.

sharply and watch this kind of lure shake clinger weeds right off. Probably the best small crankbait I've ever used in this category is the Bagley Kil'r B series. In a larger crankbait for pike and musky, the straight model DepthRaider would be its equal.

Speaking of "straight model," there are some noteworthy advantages to fishing a straight model over a jointed version in cover. Straight model floaters are far more buoyant and cover-free. In other words, you'll snag up a lot more with a jointed lure than you will with a straight bodied floater. The tail section also has a tendency to fold to one side or the other on the rise, after cover collision, drawing it right into trouble. Whenever I'm fishing in thick weed cover, or heavy brush, I always opt for a straight model floater. It has been the mainstay crankbait for me for over 25 years.

However, a jointed floater has its moments and dark water is one of them. Jointed lures have a natural clicking action that occurs as the body parts collide with each other. This makes them outstanding slow-speed, dark-water crankbaits for walleyes, bass, pike and muskies. Whenever there's a strong algae bloom, muddy water runoff, or any other dark water condition, a jointed floater is going to be a fish-catcher. This also includes nearly all night-fishing applications. The clicking sound of a jointed lure makes it an outstanding choice for night gamefish of all species. As most of you know, there are many excellent jointed crankbaits that run both shallow and deep for all sizes of gamefish.

Never underestimate the importance of line choice when casting floating divers. As we've learned from our earlier chapters, line diameter, length of cast or troll, and the speed of retrieve can all affect the running depth of the floating diving crankbait. Line factors are

The best weed crankbaits are generally buoyant straight model floating divers with a lip that protrudes off the body at nearly a 45-degree angle. The lip collects the majority of the weeds on these lures, and their exaggerated side-to-side wobble aid in shaking off clinger weeds.

more critical in this crankbait category than all others. Sinking cranks still run deep no matter what the line diameter, if you let them sink to the bottom. But buoyant floating divers resist diving. Thicker bodied floaters resist it even more. Add a thicker gauge line and you've reduced the overall running depth even more. Crank it at a slow speed and the floater will run shallower yet. Shorter casts will also keep the floating diver shallower.

The inexperienced angler often gives up on utilizing a floating diver for its true purpose — fishing in and around cover — simply because he or she does not understand the basic fundamentals of cast length, retrieve speed, and line diameter and what effects these have on the running depth of the lure. These factors are absolutely critical to your success. If you want a floating diver to run deeper, use thinner lines, make

longer casts, and crank the lure a bit harder. If you want that same lure to run shallower, do the opposite – use thicker lines, make shorter casts, and crank slower. You need to know how to match your line, cast length, and crank speed in order to achieve the desired results.

It's as important to understand the value of making a floating diver run shallower as it is to make it run deeper. You can easily make a crankbait run too deep on stained waters with shallower weed lines. A crankbait that's constantly plowing the bottom is either the wrong choice or outfitted on the wrong line. The ideal running depth of a crankbait, in and around cover, is to occasionally tick and bump it; not plow through or dig into it. For example, make long casts with a big DepthRaider crankbait on 20-to 25-pound line and it's going to run about 7 ½ to 8 feet down. This is perfect for shallow-

Bouncing the bottom with large-lipped floating divers is one of the best ways to trigger big fish to strike. Spence Petros landed this huge bronzeback bouncing a deep diver over large boulders.

topping rock humps on stained lakes, or a deeper weed edge in a clear lake. But this setup is not ideal for any dark water lake with a shallow weed line in the 4-to 7-foot depth range. Substituting a 40 pound line instead of a 20- to 25- pound test is recommended here in addition to shortening your average casting length.

Quite often I will utilize this reverse psychology when fishing crankbaits. For example, I really like to fish a musky crankbait on a thick, saltwater grade 50-pound test mono, like Stren's High Impact, in stained waters with shallow weed lines. I purposely fish the heavy-weight line along with a short cast in order to keep the lure from traveling too deep. Typically, this setup keeps my big DepthRaiders running no deeper than about 7 feet. I'll adopt the same routine with many of my favorite bass crankbaits in shallow stained lakes. Casting a small diver on 17- to 20-pound line greatly reduces maximum running depth. This is why matching your tackle correctly to the conditions at hand is so important. When done correctly, the combination makes your lure perform a lot better.

Choose the wrong line and you're going to make the lure run too deep or too shallow. This is why it's imperative to learn everything you can. In particular, you need to find out precisely how deep the fish are holding in the cover on your favorite waters. Then match the crankbait performance characteristics to it. You also need to learn

The author prefers buoyant crankbaits with a 45-degree angle diving lip for weed oriented bass, as well as other gamefish, His favorite for bass is Bagley's original Kilr'B (pictured here).

everything you can about a couple of favorite crankbaits so you can match them perfectly to these situations.

Line length or distance from rod tip to lure is one more factor that greatly affects running depth. Generally speaking, longer casts combined with a low rod angle make a floating diver run deeper than a short cast with a higher rod angle. We talked about this in some detail earlier with Paul Elias's kneel & reel system, but it can't be overstated. If you want a lure to attain its maximum depth with the tackle you're using at that time, you must make a long cast. I particularly like to make these "Brett Farve" casts when I'm trying to bump clean hard-bottom spots, like rock humps, for walleyes and smallmouth bass, but it works equally well on muskies. You'd be amazed at how much deeper your lure travels with the long cast versus a short one. It's that significant.

The whole goal with this tactic — casting a floating diver over a deep hard-bottom hump — is to attain that magic depth where it will bump bottom. The entire focus of the technique here is to make the lure run at maximum depth and hit bottom. Once it hits bottom, because it's hard and clean, maintaining a steady retrieve is acceptable and actually preferred. The careening action of the lure's lip skipping across the rocks and gravel is all that is needed to trigger a strike. A long cast, thinner line and a lower rod angle usually accomplishes this very well. It's simply a matter of choosing a floating diver that will attain the correct depth.

On the other hand, the approach is entirely different when attempting to work a deep diver along a weedy flat. I have a tendency to really shorten up my casts with a floating diver when casting around any cover, but particularly around weeds. Here I much prefer the "Bart Starr" cast. Short and precise casts minimize running depth and allow you to vary the running depth of the lure throughout the retrieve. In this instance, you'll often want to run the lure shallow in the beginning, bumping, rising, and ticking it over the high weed cover. This takes a short cast with a rod pumping

action that allows the lure to dive and rise over the shallow weed tops.

By mid-retrieve, your lure will probably have passed by the troublesome shallow weed tops. This is the time to lower the rod tip a bit, increase the retrieve speed a little, and drive the lure down into the lower growing stuff. As soon as any deep weed cover contact is made, the line must be relaxed a tad to allow the bait to momentarily float up out of trouble. This is also a key time to be ready for a strike to occur. Anytime you're bumping and rising, bobbing and weaving a crankbait through variable weed cover, a strike can occur. They usually pound it when they hit, too.

Towards the last 25 percent of a typical weed crankin' retrieve, the goal becomes attaining the maximum depth in order to hit any deep fringe weeds, and trigger a possible boatside strike. This section of the retrieve is of special significance when fishing any gamefish that has a tendency to follow. Muskies will often follow crankbaits to the boat when worked in this manner around weedy cover. Many of these following fish strike on impulse as the lure either hits that maximum depth area, or as it starts to rise at the end of the retrieve cycle. If they don't hit it here, they'll sometimes take a crack at it right at boatside as the lure is drawn in a figure-8 pattern. Never take a crankbait out of the water before pulling it in a figure-8 at the gunwale when you're after muskies.

Finally, trolling floating divers is an outstanding way to take just about every species of gamefish. Floating divers are superior trolling lures over nearly all other crankbaits for any cover situation or bottom-bouncing opportunity. Just as the added buoyancy makes the floating diver the tool of the trade for cover crankin', it's also the bait of choice for cover trolling. The trick with trolling floating divers in cover is to work it much the same as you would in a casting situation. For one, speed control is critical. Fast trolling over cover is asking for trouble. Too much speed drives the lure too quickly through the cover, jamming it in wood or rocks, and plowing it through weeds. There is simply no time to react to a cover collision with high-speed trolling.

Slow down your trolling speed when crankin' through thick cover with a floating diver, and you'll give the bait a chance to rise up after a collision. The right trolling speed is usually one that is fast enough to initiate a good wobble on the plug as well as drive it down to its maximum running depth, yet allow enough reaction room for you to drop the rod when the lure jams up, allowing it to float up and free itself. Some might argue that this doesn't generate enough speed to trigger strikes, but I beg to differ. The whole concept of generating speed in order to trigger a strike is misunderstood. It's not so much that you need to generate tremendous speed in a constant forward motion as it is to generate it at that perfect moment – just after it collides with cover. When you rip a bait forward after it rises up out of weeds, for example, tremendous speed is generated at that perfect moment, but only for a few feet or so. This is all that is needed. In a nutshell, this is the concept that all crankbait anglers need to grasp in order to effectively fish them in cover.

The biggest advantage of trolling a diver rather than casting it is not so much the tremendous amount of water that can be covered, even though that is a significant factor, but it is the depth that can be obtained.

King-sized largemouths can be taken regularly on all forms of crankbaits. This big-time bucketmouth hit a rip and rise retrieve with a floating diver over shallow submerged wood.

Basically, trolling nearly doubles the potential running depth of any given floating/diving crankbait. In other words, if your favorite crankbait generally runs a maximum depth of 7 feet on a cast with 10-pound test, it will run 14 feet deep when trolled. This is a good rule of thumb to follow with almost any floating/diving crankbait. Even greater depths can be reached with excessive amounts of line out and a thinner gauge line, but comparatively speaking, you double the running depth of a floating/diver when it is trolled.

Where this becomes notably significant is when the fish prefer a certain size of floating diver that can not reach the depths where the fish are holding with conventional casting tactics, no matter how long the cast is, nor how thin the line is. For example, if walleyes are holding on a hump at 12 feet and seem to readily strike and prefer the smaller crankbaits like a #5 Shad Rap, you'll have to troll it to get it down to the fish effectively. With an ample amount of 4-pound test line out, you'll probably bump that gravel hump with that small Shad Rap on a trolling pass, but there's no way you'll even come close on a cast.

There are some other noteworthy applications for trolling floating/divers and we'll be discussing many of them throughout the pages of this book in some species-specific chapters. Some of my most preferred trolling applications for floating divers would included: 1) open water planer board trolling for walleyes, 2) bottom-bouncing deep clean bottom for bass, walleyes, and muskies, and 3) short-lining over shallow flats with low weeds for pike and muskies. There are more, and we'll talk about them eventually.

So now you know my relationship with floating divers goes way back. These are the crankbaits that really got me started, and I rely on them more than any other. They are among the most versatile lures for casting or trolling, and they catch just about any gamefish that swims. They come in an almost endless array of shapes, sizes, colors, and actions to suit just about any possible fishing situation. Lord knows I've got boxes on top of boxes of these lures to attest to that. As we examine a number of species-specific and season-specific tactics, you'll notice that I lean heavily on this category of crankbaits. They're fish-catchin' critters for sure.

chapter 8

Lipless Crankbaits

My son, Joe Jr., and I had just idled into our first evening walleye spot about an hour before sunset. The series of rock piles had already given us plenty of walleye action over the past three evenings, so we were anxious to get started. The bait choice was an easy one, or at least we thought. We grabbed our jiggin' outfits and got to work. However, 20 minutes later, neither of us had a fish and we sat wondering what had happened to all the fish.

As the sun crested the horizon, the wind died down and the lake's surface simultaneously erupted with mayfly hatches and feeding fish. This was the first time my son had ever seen a mayfly hatch of this magnitude, and this got him excited. "Dad, we're not catching fish on the bottom with these jigs. Do you think they're all up near the surface, feeding on those mayflies?" Obviously, this was a great observation, and I commended him for it. We both snapped on a couple of crankbaits, and got to work.

Past successful experiences made me lean towards a RatLtrap for this situation. For some odd reason, active suspended fish that are snappin' at mayflies,

really get turned on to this kind of bait. Why? I don't know? But I've really caught fish on this lure, in this situation, on many occasions. Active, shallow, suspended fish seem to love lipless crankbaits. Would they this time? Our first casts would answer that question. Seconds after our lures hit the water we both had strikes. Joe landed a nice walleye, and I bagged a 33-inch northern pike. Moments later, we had another double. This time we both had walleyes. This intense action kept up for at least another 30 minutes before darkness set in. When it was all over, our tally was 23 walleyes up to 25 inches and seven pike with the largest at 33 inches. Not bad for an evening that started out dead.

That, my friends, is one example of what can happen with lipless crankbaits under the right conditions. These lures have the potential to really hammer a lot of fish in a short time. I wouldn't hesitate to say that, when fish are really cranked up, nothing catches fish quite like these uniquely designed plugs. Perhaps it's the tight wiggle or the extra-fast retrieve speeds; and maybe it's the combination of the two. Something really

Lipless crankbaits are awesome fish-catchers. Lots of water can be covered almost effortlessly with this bait. In addition, these lures are highly attractive to nearly all gamefish species.

gets fish turned on to these lures under conditions like I just described. The important thing to remember is, when fish are on a lipless crankbait bite, you're going to have a ton of fun. Let's take a look at this wonderful crankbait design in more detail, in an effort to understand more about why these lures are so effective and the many ways they can be fished.

The RatLTrap, Hotspot, Sugar Shad, Rattlin' Rap, Bayou Boogie, and Pico Perch are all examples of what the crankbait industry calls a lipless crankbait. These unique plugs feature no diving lip, and a teardrop-shaped, baitfish-like body configuration. Nearly all lipless crankbaits sink and have the line tie positioned somewhere on the top of the lure. This line tie positioning provides the lipless crankbait with its tight vibrating action.

Unlike the floating/diver, that features a relatively buoyant body and a diving bill that imparts some built-in natural action, the lipless crankbait has a slim overhead profile, no buoyancy and no diving bill. The action on the lipless crankbait is much, much tighter. These lures barely have any side-to-side wobble, but they have this superbly tight vibrating action that accentuates with speed. The additional flash that's created by the large flat sides vibrating back and forth at high speeds is also worth noting. Few lures match the flash of lipless crank.

While all crankbaits generally vibrate harder with speed, lipless cranks don't generate the additional pull or drag that a diving bill style crankbait does when retrieved faster. Therefore lipless crankbaits can be retrieved or trolled at very high speeds. That, my friends, is one of their biggest assets. The tremendous vibration and flash generated with these lures on fast retrieve speeds, triggers reflex strikes from gamefish that might otherwise totally ignore floating divers.

On top of that, because lipless crankbaits can be retrieved almost effortlessly at high speeds, angler fatigue is minimized. This means more water coverage, and potentially more fish caught over the long haul. The beauty of the lipless crankbait is effortless efficiency. While a number of specialized tactics can be employed with this bait, a simple cast and retrieve gets the job done more often than not, and lots of water will be covered effectively in the process.

While no lure is an all-season, all-situation killer, lipless crankbaits come pretty close to it at times. These are versatile lures that work spring, summer and fall, both deep and shallow, and in either dark or clear water. For example, there was a period in the early to mid-1980s when I'd make a weekly trip to Wisconsin's Lake Wausau shortly after ice-out in early April to chase northern pike with RatLTraps. Water temperatures were

typically in the low- to mid-40s at this time, yet pike by the hundreds would hammer these lures viciously. This pattern is still as good today. Casting for cold water pike in shallow marshy bays with lipless rattling crankbaits is simply deadly on early spring pike. Few anglers are aware of this pattern.

The lipless crankbait, however, could never just be considered a cold water killer. I've caught washtubs of walleyes during the heat of summer on the same plug. In fact, that opening incident with my son Joe Jr. is one such example. These fish were taken during the heat of July with water temps in the upper 70s. On another note, my biggest October smallmouth bass consistently fall to lipless crankbaits when the water temps creep down into the low 50s. These lures are simply all-season killers. It's a rare day when you can't catch at least some fish on these lures.

Lipless crankbaits are, of course, most famous as bass lures. I'll be the first to admit that boatloads of

Here's a selection of some of the more common lipless crankbaits sold today. Note all these lures have a signature teardrop shape, and they generally sink.

bass have also fallen to various lipless crankbaits during all seasons – not just in the spring. One of the most memorable big bass days I've ever had in the fall, came during an Indian summer afternoon in mid-October casting for smallies over large sand flats with scattered fish cribs. These were not suspended fish. They were up on a large sandy flat, competitively cruising for anything that moved. This was very clear water, and the fish seemed to be in an extra high-speed aggressive mood. All I had to do was get a bait close to one of them, and I had a strike. Conservatively, I must have taken close to 100 bass on that beautiful afternoon, and many of these fish were in excess of 3 pounds. Several were over 5 pounds.

I could recite hundreds of success stories with big bass and the lipless crankbait, not only from my perspective, but more so from many of the top tournament bass pros. Lipless crankbaits are speed lures, which makes them a perfect tournament bait for scouring water at a rapid-fire pace. At the same time, the lipless crankbait is highly attractive to all sizes of bass. If any class of bass is present, a few are bound to blast one of these "hi-vibe" gems as they scoot by.

A double on big smallmouth bass! These two brutes were taken on back-to-back casts with a lipless crankbait over shallow bottom grass. Sometimes a speed triggering approach to grass beds produces a higher number of strikes.

But most surprisingly, really big bass seem to like these baits, too, even though they're a high-speed lure. Big bass are generally thought to prefer slower presentations, yet the high speed approach with a lipless crankbait defies this theory completely. The daily big bass awards on any given tournament fall with amazing regularity to pros speed fishing lipless crankbaits. This includes monster bass of 10 pounds or more. One of the largest bass ever taken in a national bass tournament, a 12-pounder, fell for a big RatLTrap. I guess, when it's all said and done, the bottom line is that bass of all sizes are equally attracted to this lure. The lipless crankbait is simply a bass-catchin' machine.

Muskies are no strangers to lipless crankbaits either. In fact, one of my most

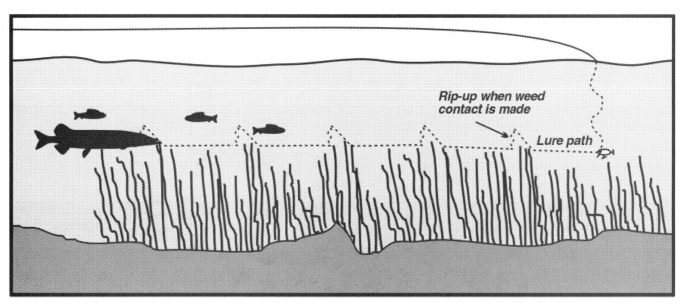

Sometimes the best way to trigger fish hugging tight to a level grass bed is to use an opposite approach. Instead of working slower methodical "bump and rise" retrieve with a floating diver over such an area, simply hold your rod high and crank extra fast with a lipless sinking model such as RatLtrap. When contact is made with grass, a violent rip of the rod tip will usually free the fouling grass and trigger strikes as the lure momentarily drops.

Metal blade baits are also technically "lipless crankbaits", too. They're basically a metal version of the same more popular plastic lipless cranks. Here's a selection of some of the more common metal blade baits available. The top two are original Heddon Sonars. The bottom two are Luhr Jensen Rippletails. The large blade bait is called a "Gay Blade".

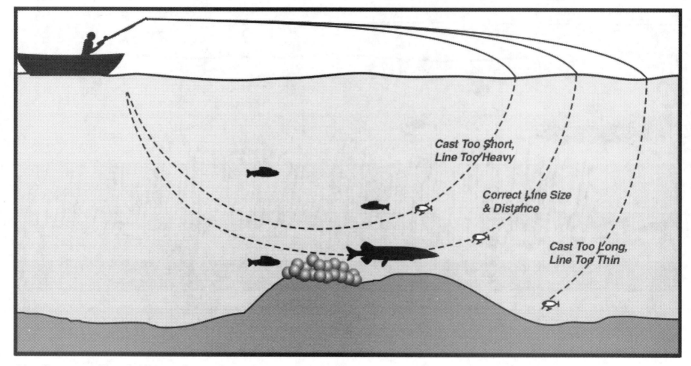

Line diameter and length (distance from rod tip to lure) can greatly effect the overall running depth of any crankbait. Sometimes you want a thin line and longer casts for greater depths, while there are as many applications for thicker lines and shorter casts depending upon the depth of the target you're trying to reach.

productive early-season lures for muskies is a lipless crankbait. I stumbled onto the secret quite by accident fishing for walleyes and bass. I was casting a newly emerging weed bed late one May afternoon a few years back when I ran into five different muskies on one spot. I caught them all on a ½-ounce blue/chrome RatLTrap fishing it the same way I would for walleyes and bass. It has since become one of my mainstay musky lures for the early season.

Surprisingly, I didn't experience a single bite-off that day. I have had a lot of problems with bite-offs on pike and muskies with this style of crankbait over the years. I wouldn't recommend fishing for pike or muskies without some sort of wire leader when using any lipless crankbait, large or small. A small profile snap, a thin gauge wire in the 12- to 27-pound range, and a length of at least 6 inches is a good idea. My favorite wire leader combination for this lure is an 8-inch "Pike Leader" featuring a 27-pound class, 7-strand or an equal diameter single-strand form, with the snap removed. I simply cut the snap off the leader and

discard it. Then I attach the lipless crank directly to the loop in the leader with the split ring on the bait. This keeps the hardware profile to a minimum.

Whenever I'm taking a trip to a big pike lake in the remote wilderness of Canada, I always load up on some big lipless crankbaits in the ½-ounce to ¾-ounce range. Big pike that get pounded with traditional spoons become a bit gun-shy, yet they'll pounce on a big lipless crankbait on these waters simply because so few people use them. Chrome and loud colors such as firetiger are great patterns for big pike on the lipless crank. I've taken several master angler pike on them in Manitoba and Saskatchewan. A master angler pike, by the way, must exceed 41 inches. Try a 3/4 ounce chrome/blue RatLTrap on your next Canadian pike outing and you'll see what I mean.

The lipless crankbait might be the most underrated big lake trout bait of them all. I've had some phenomenal outings on lakers, big and small, with these lures. Few seasoned trout anglers would ever consider trying a lipless crankbait for lakers, but they do work with solid consistently. They're especially effective for early, ice-out lakers that cruise the tops of rock bars in about 8 to 12 feet of water, but I've also had some great, late fall outings with lipless cranks on lakers. Most recently, I caught a bunch of lakers only days before ice up on a blue/chrome RatLtrap in one of my local area lakes. Again, this is a pattern few anglers know about.

"Oil cans" as lake trout are often nicknamed, can be spooky when in the shallow water early or late in the season. These times require a long bomb cast. Lipless cranks cast extremely well on any kind of tackle, but particularly on big baitcasting gear. A big baitcasting outfit featuring a long 7-to 7 ½-foot rod and a high-speed reel combined with a flashy chrome pattern lipless crankbait is a great combination for spooky fish in clear-water lakes. Flash and high vibration are huge attractants to oil cans. Lipless cranks in chrome fit the ticket perfectly. Anytime you find spooky lakers cruising up shallow, whether it's spring or fall, give the lipless crankbait a try. However, hold on to the rod a bit tighter than normal. Big lakers can really smack a plug. I mean, they hit much harder than most of us are used to. Rarely is setting the hook even necessary.

The best tackle for

working a lipless crankbait is baitcasting gear. This is one case where a high-speed gear ratio is a real asset. Lipless crankbaits create almost no drag on a reel no matter how quickly they're retrieved. Lipless crankbaits

also work better and trigger far more fish when cranked ultra-quick. These assets make them perfect for high-speed baitcasters featuring a gear ratio of at least 5 to 1. In fact, some of those super-fast reels at 6 to 1 are great choices for lipless crankbaits.

An extra-long, soft-action rod is also preferred for lipless cranks. One of the biggest drawbacks to this lure is that it has a tendency to shake loose when fish jump to throw it. Perhaps the shape of this lure combined with its heavier than average weight makes it more susceptible to flying out of a fish's mouth during a jump. The extra-long 7 ½-foot medium to medium/light action rod simply has more overall bend, and it exerts a more even pressure on the fish. This diminishes lure shake in the fish's mouth, and thus reduces overall losses.

As far as line goes, lipless crankbaits seem to perform best with heavier gauge lines in the 12- to 20-pound range. I'd even go heavier than this with some of the larger magnum versions; especially when fishing in woody cover for big fish. Casting and crankin' lipless cranks is an aggressive "smash mouth" kind of presentation. There is absolutely no finesse at all in this kind of fishing. You need a line that will stand up to hours of casting and crankin'. Lines less than 12-pound test simply won't give you this option, and they offer no advantages. Stick with heavier lines whenever fishing this kind of bait.

The best way to retrieve a lipless cranker depends upon the situation. More often than not, it's open to experimentation and variation. Most anglers do extremely well with a simple cast and crank retrieve.

Lipless crankbaits are the most effective lures for speed fishing over shallows, but they work equally well in deep water with a slow "rip and drop" method.

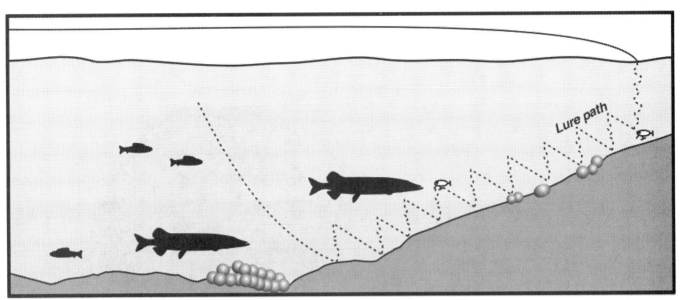

One of the deadliest ways to fish a lipless crankbait is to rip & drop it along a dropoff or any other lake structure. To accomplish this, simply cast the lure out, let it sink all the way to the bottom (until the line goes slack), and then rip upward sharply on the rod. Using a long rod really helps. After the rip, let the bait descent all the way back to the bottom before executing the next "rip".

There's no science or secret here. Just cast it out as far as you can, by the way, these lures do cast really far, and then just wind as fast as you can. This simple system has made the lipless crankbait famous as a fish-catcher with all anglers.

However, there is more you can do with a lipless cranker. I frequently work a lipless crankbait with a rip and drop retrieve. This really seems to turn on fish that are holding a bit deeper and apparently don't want to run down the standard steady fast retrieve. All I do is cast the lure out and just sweep the rod tip to the side or upwards. The sweep should be hard, in order to really initiate a super-fast, super-tight vibration. Follow this up by allowing the lure to fall while you pick up slack line. You'll find that fish hammer the bait when it's worked in this manner. Quite often the entire lure is engulfed during the drop portion of the retrieve.

Another little-used technique with this lure is to cast it out and let it sink all the way to the bottom. Then rip it up, and let it fall all the way back to the bottom again. This enables you to work a lipless crankbait at virtually any depth. Lipless crankbaits can be worked in very deep water effectively with this tactic. The intense vibration generated on the rip triggers fish holding tight

to the bottom to race up and strike hard.

Lipless cranks also work very well over the tops of grassbeds and weeds. Bass, walleyes, and pike are commonly caught on these lures over such terrain. The key here is to retrieve the lure just fast enough to keep it mere inches above the grass or weed tops. Anytime the crankbait catches grass or weeds, it should be sharply ripped in an effort to clean it. This collision with weed tops and the subsequent ripping action, makes fish literally explode on the bait. I'd venture to guess that experienced anglers fish a lipless crankbait this way more than any other method.

All in all, the lipless crankbait is one fish-catchin' son-of-a-gun. As you can see by the examples in this chapter, I rely heavily on this fantastic lure. You really can't fish this bait incorrectly. Simply casting it out and just reeling it in is going to catch plenty of fish no matter what the species. Add a pump and drop to this bait and it becomes even more effective at times. Cast it out, let it sink to the bottom, then lift and drop it, and you've got one heck of a deep-water cranker. Like I said, you really can't fish this bait incorrectly. Cast it out, crank it in, and hold on!

chapter 9

Minnow Baits

Before I even begin to get into specifics on how good a minnow bait is, just think of the fish you've taken on lures such as the original Rapala and Smithwick's Rogue. I don't have to tell you that these baits are simply awesome fish-catchers. Minnow baits catch every conceivable fish species, both fresh and saltwater, on any sector of this planet that has a predatory gamefish. I'd bet that minnow baits, as a lure category, account for more total gamefish than all other lures combined. The reasons for this incredible scorecard are quite simple: 1) minnow baits can be fished on all kinds of tackle from ultra-light to very heavy 2) they can be straight-cranked, twitched, topwater fished or trolled with equal efficiency, 3) they have one of the most natural looks of all lures. They are one of the all-time deadliest artificial lures.

My first exposure to the minnow bait was back in the early 1960s. I remember staring at my first minnow bait, a Rapala, for weeks in my grandfather's local tackle store. I wanted that lure so bad, but I had no money to buy it. I finally convinced my grandpa to

trade it for a day of work. I still can't believe how many chores he found for me. I ended up putting in an entire eight-hour workday for that one single lure. Rapalas were rare and expensive in those days, but was it worth a whole day of work? Grandpa thought so.

Anyway, looking back, I think the fact that I wanted the lure so bad, and had worked so hard to get it, that I was bound and determined to catch fish on it no matter what. However, catching fish on the lure turned out to be easy. I first caught fish on the Rapala by row-trolling it across the tops of weed flats. I discovered this tactic by rowing out to my fishing spots. Back when I first started fishing on my own, I wasn't allowed to use an outboard motor. So I rowed out to my fishing spots. On the way to them, I'd troll that one Rapala. In the process, I discovered a hot tactic and the locations of some bass that I was not aware of.

Later on, I began to discover the many successful ways to cast and work this bait. I not only caught 'em rowing, I also caught fish on this lure by crankin' it, twitchin' it, ripping it, and doing nothing with it.

Fishing it as a surface bait – doing nothing with it – turned out to be one of the deadliest tactics of all. While I had already had lots of success with some of the older, more traditional top-water baits, I found the Rapala, and similar minnow baits, could catch 'em when traditional surface lures wouldn't. The soft landing and subtle natural action of the minnow bait fooled finicky clear-water bass like no other top-water plug I'd ever seen before. Of course, this is no secret any longer, but it sure was back then.

Minnow baits can be fished in a variety of ways. Actually, it's almost impossible to fish a minnow bait incorrectly. Almost any kind of retrieve, including no retrieve at all, catches fish on minnow baits. Let's take a look at some of the more effective ways to fish this lure and cite where specific tactics might be applied most productively. Keep in mind, as we dig into the nitty-gritty of this bait, that versatility is its trademark. If you utilize some easy-to-manipulate tricks, this bait can become even more deadly in certain situations.

Cast & Crank

One of the first retrieves I learned when I started fishing this wonderful bait was to simply cast it out and crank it in. I caught hundreds of bass this way, even though there was absolutely nothing fancy about this technique. Of course, this was always

most productive for shallow water bass in the spring when the fish were scattered over weed flats during the prespawn period. Not so surprisingly, this tactic is still as deadly today, but is not used as often for bass. It is,

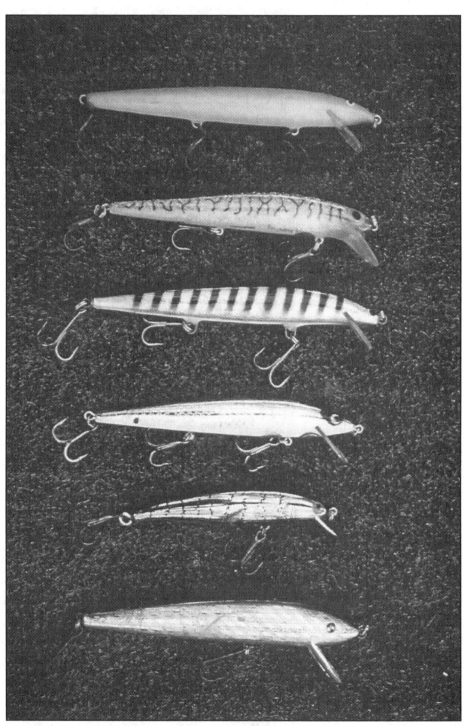

Minnow baits are among the most productive of all crankbaits for all species of freshwater gamefish. Their natural baitfish, true-minnow look makes them one of the deadliest artificial lures ever devised. Minnow baits depicted in this photo include the: Rapala, Storm Thunderstick, Bangolure, Rogue, Bomber Model A, and Garcia Minni.

however, still a mainstay walleye technique.

My original bait of choice, a 13S floating Rapala, is still my preferred weapon for this specific technique, although I've had equal success since then on Bagley's Bangolure, Storm's 4-inch Thunderstick, Bomber's Model A, and Smithwick's larger Rogue. Smithwick's Rogue, by the way, is really an outstanding lure and every bit as good as the Rapala. Not surprisingly, the Rogue is the #1 minnow bait of the touring bass pros. The Rapala is made of balsa and therefore a very lightweight lure. It's best fished on spinning gear. The Rogue is a plastic version and works much better off baitcasting gear. Either bait is outstanding.

Matched with a spinning outfit or a light baitcaster and 6-to 10-pound line, long casts over shallow weed flats are possible. To successfully implement this basic straight retrieve tactic, point the rod tip low and a tad off to the side, and simply begin a slow, steady crank with an occasional twitch. Any-time the minnow bait encounters any kind of cover such as weeds, wood or whatever, follow up with a sharp jerking

action. The jerking action cleans any debris from the lure and helps to trigger strikes.

Today's bass angler is apt to jerk the lure more throughout the retrieve, but the straight retrieve still

The author has been fishing minnow baits since he was a youngster. His first minnow bait was a Rapala, and it's still one of his favorites today.

does work extremely well in many instances. Sometimes anglers have the mistaken impression that fish want more action in a lure, but this is not always the case. A relatively straight retrieve still catches plenty of fish in the early pre-spawn period. Walleyes are especially vulnerable to the straight retrieve when the water is a bit cooler. The larger minnow bait, in that 4-inch range, is preferred for such applications since it casts farther with relative ease. A 4-inch bait throws far better than 2- or 3-inch model.

This same simple retrieve technique works extremely well on early spring walleyes. The productive habitat might also be very similar to bass cover in most cases. Casting a 4-inch floating minnow bait over shallow weeds, over shallow rock/gravel flats, along rock shores, and inside shallow stump fields can really produce walleyes. My wife and I began using this technique on some of our first trips to northern Wisconsin in the early 1970s. In those days, I knew little of how to jig walleyes during daylight hours, and had little knowledge of daytime walleye tactics as a whole. Yet we always caught plenty of walleyes utilizing a simple formula – we'd fish the first and last few hours of daylight over shallow food shelves with # 13 Rapalas. That was all there was to our technique, and all that was needed to be successful.

Best of all, the average size of the walleyes we caught was always impressive using this simply minnow bait casting technique. If the body of water you're fishing has a good batch of walleyes in the 18- to 24-inch range, and they work shallow food shelves in low light, casting the 4-inch minnow bait is bound to catch them. Our daily catches would feature fish in this range, with an occasional lunker pushing the 25-to 30-inch

Smithwick's Rogue is an outstanding small minnow bait, and is the #1 choice of the bass touring pros. It is also equally productive on walleyes. Plastic minnow baits, such as the Rogue, work better than the lighter balsa models on baitcasting gear.

range. I can say, with all confidence, that this tactic will still take that same class of fish in nearly equal numbers today. Nothing has changed – the original floating minnow bait, cranked with a simple, straight retrieve, just plain hammers shallow-water walleyes.

Jerkin' minnow baits has become one of the hottest bass tactics in the country. The best models for this method of fishing have a lower buoyancy which enables them to work slightly deeper and at much slower speeds. You can easily modify a minnow bait's action and buoyancy by adding stick-on weights or changing the hook size.

Jerkin' & Twitchin'

Somewhere along the way a number of anglers, myself included, found out that a high number of strikes occurred on these original minnow baits when they were jerked to clean weeds off them. The eventual result is what musky fishermen call "twitchin'" and what bassers refer to as "jerkbait" fishing. No matter what you call it, working these lures with a constant jerk, twitch, yank and pause action simply drives fish wild. This tactic is especially deadly on cover-tight gamefish that aren't in the mood to chase things down.

Fish in this state, bass, pike, walleyes, or muskies, are generally hugging tight to some kind of cover and are extremely reluctant to leave their sanctuary. Some might classify this kind of gamefish as more "neutral" in mood. They definitely would not be termed "active." Most often this occurs during typical midday conditions during any average summer day. It also occurs quite regularly after the passage of a cold front in the spring and fall.

Whenever gamefish are in this state, they'll often ignore a straight-retrieved lure that scurries on by. The only way to draw a response from a fish positioned in this manner is to get the lure as close as possible to it, and then aggravate it into responding. In some instances, the best scenario is to actually run the lure into the fish. The fish has two choices in this situation: 1) get out of the way – a spooked response, or 2) take a snap at the intruder – a dominant predator-like, territorial response. The bigger the fish, the more apt you are to draw the latter response.

I've used this tricky technique successfully on so many different species of gamefish that I could write a book on these experiences alone. Jerkin' and twitchin' minnow baits for cover-tight gamefish has been one of my favorite tactics for nearly two decades. While this method has gotten a lot of press lately as a bass tactic, it has been a mainstay pike/musky method for much longer. Many noted musky guides across Wisconsin,

Minnesota, and Ontario have utilized this tactic for years as their main gun for any reluctant fish. Musky anglers are as much a part of popularizing and refining this technique as are the bass fishermen.

Most recently, my son (Joe Jr.) and I made an August trip to Rainy Lake for pike and muskies hoping for a big top-water bite, but due to easterly wind and some cold front activity, it just didn't happen. The only top-water action we did get happened for a brief period between sunset and darkness. But the rest of the day, 15 hours or more, we could barely get a raise from a pike, let alone a musky, on a top-water bait. These muskies were cover-tight for sure.

Magnum minnow baits are sure to catch magnum fish. The author has had great success with big walleyes using musky-sized minnow baits.

Musky anglers are as much responsible for popularizing the "jerkbait" technique with minnow baits as the bass fishermen. Many noted musky guides across the U.S. have utilized the tactic for years as one of their main methods on reluctant fish. Musky specialist Jake Novak caught this world record class 51-1/2 inch hybrid "tiger" on a 5-inch minnow bait.

After the second day of disappointing top-water performance, I began following up my son's top-water efforts by jerkin' a minnow bait – one of my hand-made prototype 7-inch straight model ShallowRaiders – around the deeper milfoil, grass, and other cover. In addition, I was fishing those deep outside weed clumps that were not visible from the surface. It only took about 25 casts to draw the first response – a 38-incher, but in the next six days I caught nine muskies up to 46-½ inches, a few hundred pike up to 41-inches, and a couple of big bonus walleyes. Our total tally of top-water fish on this trip was two, and they both came during the classic dusk period. If it wasn't for adopting the method of jerkin' a minnow bait on this trip, we probably would have gone home with only two to three muskies total. Choosing the right tactic made all the difference in the world.

I should also point out that I lost the biggest musky I'd hooked in nearly 10 years on the final afternoon of that August trip. My son had already thoroughly fan-casted the entire weed saddle with his top-water bait, when I began twitchin' my firetiger ShallowRaider around some deep milfoil. About a dozen casts into this pass, I pitched the brightly colored minnow bait over an isolated deep clump of milfoil and gave it two teasing jerks with a long slack line pause in order to make it dance and dart in place with a lot of side rolling action. This is one of the real secrets to this technique, a slack line on the pause and a sharp, short jerk over thick cover.

Anyway, up roars this huge set of

jaws putting the clamps on the tail section of my already beat-up ShallowRaider. After a short battle, I could see that the fish was barely hooked with one hook of the rear treble in the roof of its mouth. This is nearly always a losing deal since the fish can get so much side-to-side leverage on the hook. Well, it only took the big fish a couple of surface head shakes to free the minnow bait and my quest for a spotted, leopard musky of over 54 inches remained unfulfilled. Why this fish didn't get all three treble hooks imbedded like the other nine muskies I'd taken that week is still a mystery, but I guess that's why the big ones get so big. At least I now know where one of these really big leopards lives anyway.

Jerkin' minnow baits has recently become one of the hottest trends in tournament bass fishing. In many instances, the tournament bass angler has gone completely away from a floating minnow bait in order to obtain additional depth, and get more "hang time" near cover. Innovative pros have added stick-on lead tape to the bottom of their minnow baits in order to create a slow rising, or even a neutrally buoyant model. Manufacturers have taken the bait, so to speak, marketing internally weighted models that feature a neutrally buoyant behavior. These newer "suspender" model minnow baits are now mainstays in most

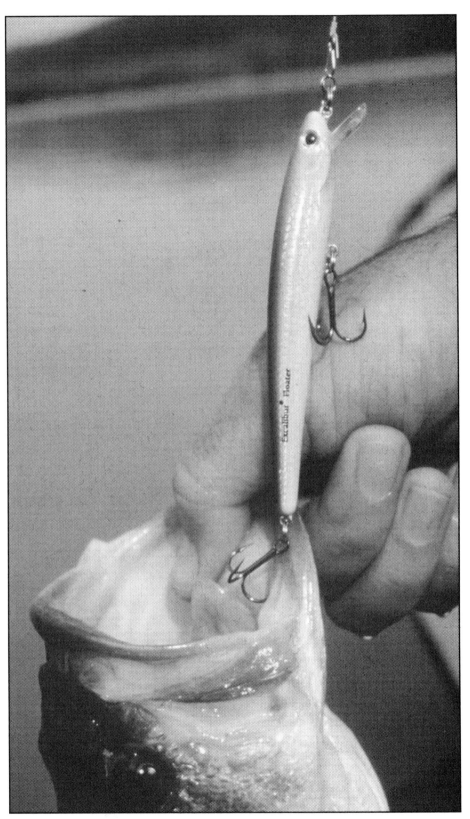

Minnow baits are particularly deadly on bass. Bass fall for them as top-water lures, jerkbaits and even straight-retrieve plugs.

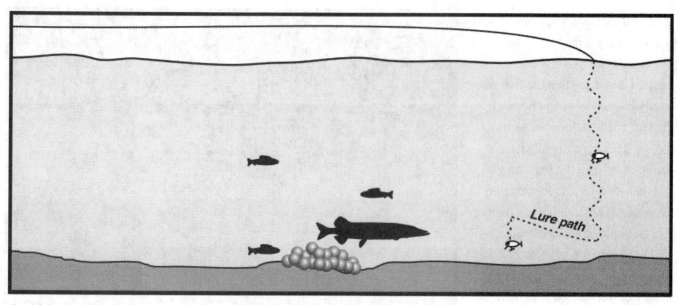

One of the most underused tactics in all of crankbaiting is to cast a sinking model out, let it sink all the way to the bottom and then begin a methodical "crank & drop" retrieve back towards the boat. Counting the lure down also helps to determine the depths you're fishing at as well as give you a reference point. This is an exceptional tactic for deep water gamefish hugging tight to the bottom.

bass tournament angler's tackle boxes.

Suspender jerkbaits have no real advantage in thick, shallow weed cover, but they're definitely superior over deep cover of any kind. In this instance, the original floaters ride too high over the top of cover, and rise up out of the strike zone too quickly. Suspenders can be driven down close to the cover and then nervously twitched in place. The lack of buoyancy helps to keep the lure right there, inches from the strike zone. Sometimes letting it sink a bit further after each jerk, closer and closer to the cover holding the fish, works even better. This is best accomplished with a suspender minnow bait and that slack line pause along with sharp, short jerks that I spoke of earlier.

Keeping a tight line on this lure at all times is not always desired since it reduces the side flash and pulls the bait forward too much. The tight line method works well for hot fish on shallow flats, but not well at all for cover-tight critters. Remember, the longer you can keep this bait in the strike zone on tough days, the more apt you are to trigger a strike. Sometimes repeated casts to the same spot are necessary in order to draw a reluctant fish out of the confines of cover. Persistence and good technique will make a major difference here. The longer

the bait hangs in place near cover, the better your chances of triggering a strike.

Incidentally, never underestimate this suspender jerkbait tactic for walleyes either. While a straight-retrieved minnow bait will no doubt take plenty of fish when they are active in low light, jerkin' a suspender is the way to trigger cover-tight walleyes during midday conditions. I've had great success on walleyes with suspenders and the jerkin' tactic in deep weed clumps, over the top of man-made fish cribs, and along shore-lines that have a lot of downed wood. I really get a kick out of twitchin' minnow baits next to shoreline wood for walleyes in both the spring and fall. The whole key is fishing wood that has a good shadeline, and jerking the bait close to cover as long as you can. Sometimes you have to jerk that lure a half a dozen times in one spot in order to aggravate a walleye enough for it to roar out and nab it. But that's half the fun!

Rock guitarist Frankie Sullivan and I had some great walleye outings this past spring utilizing this exact tactic. A thick jungle of fallen trees along the south shore of one of my favorite U.P. (Upper Peninsula of Michigan) waters had a bunch of walleyes buried during bright midday hours, but they'd venture close to the edge about a half an hour before sunset. Frankie and I cleaned up on these fish on numerous occasions pitching suspending Rogues as tight to the trees as we could. Then we'd simply slack-line jerk these baits in place for as long as we could stand it. Honestly, we'd get a strike on almost every cast.

Larger walleyes are particularly prone to musky-sized minnow baits, jerked over deep grass and milfoil, in the mid- to late summer. While you can consistently take these same fish on a jig, they'll also take a musky-sized minnow bait with surprising regularity. This is a nice way to bag bonus big walleyes while you're searching for big pike and muskies in the same area. They all seem to like the same habitat in late August. Find some deep milfoil or grass on a large flat that gets wind, fish every clump with a minnow bait jerked nervously in place, and you're going to be setting the hook on some kind of big fish.

I've caught countless big walleyes in Wisconsin, Minnesota and Michigan waters with this big minnow bait/milfoil system, but it's also worked extremely well in Canadian musky waters. Twice in one summer I stumbled onto a 25-inch walleye, or larger, while twitching a big 7- inch

straight model ShallowRaider over deep clumps of milfoil. Big walleyes really seem to like milfoil in August, and they're nearly always looking for a sizable meal like larger perch. The musky version minnow bait is the perfect choice for these wallhangin' waldos.

Skimming a minnow bait over the top of thick grass can be deadly on nearly all warm-water gamefish, it's particularly productive on pike and musky.

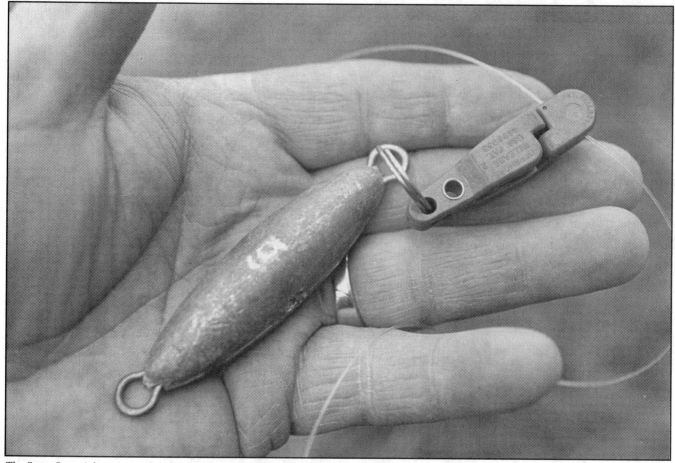

The Snap-On weight system, made by the folks at Off Shore Tackle, provides a simple way to take a minnow bait down to great depths. This is, by far, the most versatile way to weight down a floating minnow bait for trolling.

Top-water Finesse

It's certainly no secret that a floating minnow bait makes one of the best top-water lures for finicky clear-water bass. This method has scored big on bass for over three decades and will always be a top-10 top-water tactic. Lots of bass and big bass are continually fooled by the life-like look of the floating minnow bait. The reason is obvious once you try one. These baits simply look like the real deal to both the angler and the fish.

First off, a small minnow bait lands softly on the cast creating a more natural presentation right off the bat. This natural soft splash entry usually attracts a bass to the lure right away. Quite often no other action is needed in order to trigger a strike. As the lure lies motionless on the surface, its soft ripples waver towards surrounding cover to alert any interested predator. Watch closely and you'll often see a wake approaching

the lure. The key here is to remain still. Resist any temptation to move the lure at all. Just hold on and be ready to set the hook. Most bass will prefer the still lure over any movement.

If, however, the strike does not occur, the next move is also critical. Instead of any aggressive jerk at this point, the best move is usually nothing more than a slight nudge on the lure. I'm talkin' about barely pulling the line taut; just enough to make the lure nod a small ripple. If there's any self-respecting bass lying in wait below, that slight nod is all that'll be needed to draw the strike. These fish are tricked best by the slightest movement. Any more than this may actually be detrimental.

This technique is particularly good when the lure is cast into small pockets inside emergent weed slop. The entire productive part of the retrieve is centered around the lure remaining relatively stationary inside the open-water pocket. As soon as the lure moves toward the edge of the weed mass, its effectiveness dwindles. If a bass is in that pocket area, your best chance to trigger it is with a stationary retrieve. Leave it there as long as you can stand it.

Anytime you're fishing this style of top-water bait on a surface with some wave action or a lack of emergent cover, a pull-down-and-rise-to-the-surface retrieve generally works better. I'll usually finish off any initial work with a top-water minnow bait by pulling it under and pausing for it to return to the surface. Fish that wouldn't take it off the top, may trigger as soon as the lure draws under. Wave action usually encourages this kind of response. It's important to experiment with a variety of retrieves on these fish in order to feel them out and see what they prefer.

I first discovered this technique back in the early 1960s while still in high school. I'm not sure how, when, or why I began leaving the minnow bait rest on the surface before initiating a retrieve, but I do know that this tactic alone accounted for many of my biggest bass catches early in my angling career. There was a period of time when I was winning just about every weekly big bass contest at the local tackle shop with this one single system. It became so deadly for me that I refused to talk about it with anyone. I'd hide the lure I was using whenever my boat was at a dock, and I never discussed this tactic with anyone. Nowadays, it's not such a big deal.

My best bait for top-water fishing in those days was a modified No. 9 gold Rapala. This size seemed to trick top-water fish better than anything, mainly because it landed more softly and had a slightly smaller profile. However the hooks were a bit small for big fish. I tried the larger, No. 11, but found that the three hook design fouled too much, and the hooks, again were too small for big bass. So I began modifying those No. 9s by replacing the size 6 hooks with a larger size 4. This simple revision made a world of difference in hooking larger fish. Especially in terms of keeping them hooked

during the battle. The larger hooks also made the lure cast better on spinning tackle.

Later on I fell in love with Smithwick's Rogue and started to use light baitcasting gear for this same technique. I became much more accurate with the baitcasting gear, and could step up in line strength a bit more with this kind of tackle. Bagley made a 3-inch Bangolure with two larger trebles that also became a favorite. I still use this top-water minnow bait tactic as much today as I did back then. I don't think this method will ever loose its effectiveness as a bass-catcher simply because it looks so much like the real thing. If you're ever faced with finicky bass in clear water that spook off larger, noisier top-water plugs, give this subtle top-water minnow bait trick a try.

Pull & Rise

I can still remember it as if it happened yesterday, yet it was over 25 years ago – just after ice-out. I was fishing a marshy backwater area just off the mouth of a small incoming river on my boyhood lake, Phantom. The water temperature was a full ten degrees warmer in the backwater than in the rest of the lake, and it seemed like every big northern pike in this system was up in this marshy backwater slough. It was late afternoon, and I'd just gotten home from high school.

One spinning rod, 8-pound test Stren, and a 4-inch 13S floating Rapala were all I needed to have a ball.

The water was so shallow around some of these backwater sloughs that few lures would travel freely without scraping bottom or getting hung on various marsh weeds and bogs. I tried some spinner baits, but they appeared to be too noisy on the splash and simply to much lure for these early season pike. Weedless spoons were also tried, but I had absolutely no action on them. Then I reverted to my old favorite Rapala, even though I thought it was way too early to try a top-water approach. But I tried it anyway.

I pitched the long floater towards a slough that I'd spooked a big pike from earlier and let it sit a few seconds. Nothing happened, so I pulled the rod forward driving the lure down. Then I stopped, allowing the bait to float toward the surface again, but it never made it back up. A huge swirl encircled the area around my lure and I instinctively set the hook into a 37-inch pike. Inside the next few hours I took a bunch of big pike with this tactic and two of the biggest largemouth bass I'd ever seen in Phantom up to that point; both exceeded 6 pounds.

All of these fish fell for the pull-and-rise technique. That day still remains so etched in my mind because it was another one of those pivotal learning experiences in my fishing career. I not only found out where some really big fish hung out early in the season, but also how to take 'em when they're spooky in clear shallow water. Since that day, I've honed this early location pattern for pike and big bass, as well as experimented with a wide range of techniques to catch 'em. The pull & rise tactic with a floating balsa minnow bait remains one of the top three ways to do it. But most importantly, success with the pull & rise is not restricted to this situation alone. It works throughout the summer and into the early fall.

One of the key reasons the pull & rise technique is so deadly revolves around the subtle nature of the minnow bait itself. The thin body profile of any typical minnow bait makes it land softly on the cast. This eliminates a large amount of the spooking factor right out of the blocks. Then the lure itself has a subtle underwater wobble and flash. The bait does not boldly advertise its presence. It's subtle all the way. This tactic also requires light line which further promotes the subtle approach. While you can perform the same function with larger minnow baits and heavier lines for muskies, big bass and many saltwater species, it's most effective with spinning gear, light line, and balsa minnows.

Finally, the pull & rise technique takes full advantage of a variety of triggering mechanisms. You've got top-water, a pull down for reflex strikes, an underwater pause for any deeper reluctant fish, and a dying rise as a convincing finale. Add these all together and you're bound to trick a bunch of big fish consistently, especially when they seem reluctant to take a bait off the top, or chase it down on a straight retrieve. The pull & rise trick compliments both of these systems, modifying it to fit the situation at hand.

Trolling Tricks With Minnow Baits

The minnow bait! What a trolling lure! Troll it shallow. Troll it deep. Troll it on a flat line. Troll it off a downrigger. Attach it to a Dipsey Diver. Attach it to a planer board. All of these things work. Simply put, the minnow bait is one of the most versatile trolling lures there is. Minnow baits will catch nearly all gamefish, shallow or deep, by simply modifying your tackle. Yet little needs to be done to the lure itself.

One of the great assets of the floating minnow bait for trolling is its lack of drag. This enables it to be attached to weighting systems, planer boards, and any other form of trolling aid. This lack of drag makes it easy to attach them to a wide variety of trolling systems without problems of any kind.

Like I said in the beginning of this chapter, my first experience with the effectiveness of minnow bait trolling was way back in the beginnings of my fishing career. My dad first started to let me take a boat out on my own when I was about 13 years old. However, I wasn't allowed to use an outboard motor at that time. I had to row. The other rule was I had to stay within sight of our house on Phantom Lake. So, what I'd do was pitch a No. 13 Rapala out and row towards my favorite spot. In the process, I'd take a lot of bonus bass on my way out and way back. Yes, this was one of my earliest exposures to row-trolling, a now-renown tactic for northern Wisconsin's muskies, but I began doing it for bass way back in the 1960s.

This tactic was amazingly simple, yet it produced time and time again, and it still produces well. When bass, walleyes, pike muskies or even trout are scattered across shallow water areas, trolling minnow baits on flat lines is deadly. It catches all sorts of gamefish in shallow water during all seasons. All you need to do to present this technique is to cast the lure out, and hold on.

If you want to run multiple lines with this lure over shallow water, it's easily done by adding rod holders to your boat and attaching some of the lures to in-line planer boards to increase the spread so lines don't tangle. The in-line planer boards also keep the lures away from the boat which usually helps to trigger boat-shy fish. If there's anything that's improved my shallow-water trolling productivity with minnow baits, it is the addition of planer boards. Being able to force the lure out, off to the side, for improved water coverage and boat-shy fish, has increased my productivity with minnow baits over shallow water tenfold.

Some of the best applications for this simple system of shallow minnow bait trolling would include: 1) spring walleyes along shallow rock/gravel shores, 2) walleyes over grass beds in the summer, 3) pike along shorelines and over weeds, 4) muskies over weeds and along any rock shoreline, and 5) trout or salmon riding high. You can adjust the true running depth of the minnow bait by using longer or shorter lines behind the planer board. Using a heavier or thinner gauge line will also affect the running depth.

Deep minnow bait trolling is also highly effective, particularly for walleyes and trout. A number of depth-attaining systems will work with minnow baits depending upon the situation and application. If you're limited to one rod, such as in a Canadian situation, you can get

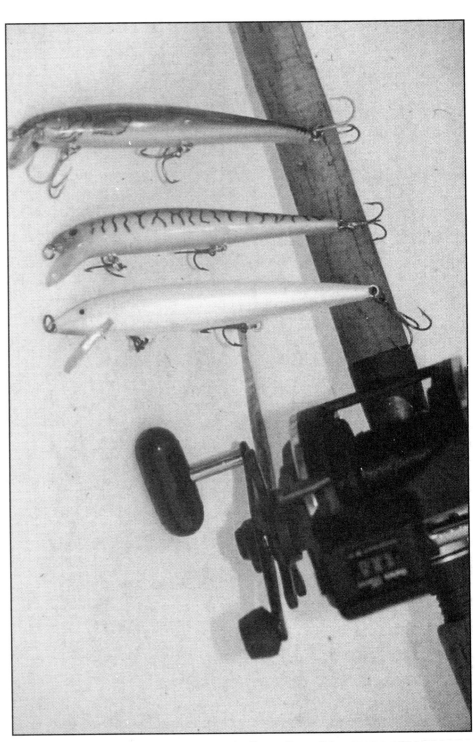

Trolling minnow baits shallow or deep can be deadly on all gamefish.

great depth easily by simply attaching a heavy snap-on weight in front of it. The folks at the Off-Shore Company make a fantastic little snap-on weight device precisely for this purpose. You can attach this weight like a clothespin anywhere in front of the minnow bait in order to make the lure run deeper. This is the system I recommend the most since it is the most versatile.

Get a supply of these Off-Shore Snap-On weights along with a variety of attachable lead weight sizes from 1 to 5 ounces in order to outfit yourself for a variety of situations. One of the neat things about the snap-on weight system is that you aren't limited as to where you must attach the weight. In the past, we've always attached sinkers near the lure, from 2 to 5 feet in front of it. While this works good in most applications near the bottom, there are times when a weight attached farther away from the lure is better. Lake Erie trollers are finding that when walleyes are spooky and suspended over clear water, attaching a snap-on weight 10, 20, and even 30 feet or more in front of the lure is the key to success. This is easily done with a snap-on weight, but not possible with a sinker. The snap-on weight acts like a downrigger, in a sense, but it does not detach on the strike like a downrigger ball does. In this case, the snap-on weight is detached when you're bringing the fish in. By marking the line spot with a permanent magic marker, you can reattach the weight when resetting after a fish is caught.

Attaching minnow baits to downrigger balls is a superb way to take this lure down to great depths where trout and salmon lurk. Of course, your boat must

My first exposure to the effectiveness of minnow baits on gamefish came on largemouths. This trophy took a small balsa minnow right off the top as I worked it like a surface bait.

be set up for this kind of fishing, but if it is, attaching the lure to a downrigger is a sure way to take this highly productive bait down to fish-catching zones never before imagined. Be advised that downriggers are the way to fish this kind of lure for suspended fish of all kinds that work deep open waters, but they are poor choices for bottom-related fish. Do not use them around reefs since the downrigger ball can get hung up on the reef. A snap-on weight is still the way to go if you're around reefs, since the weight will break free.

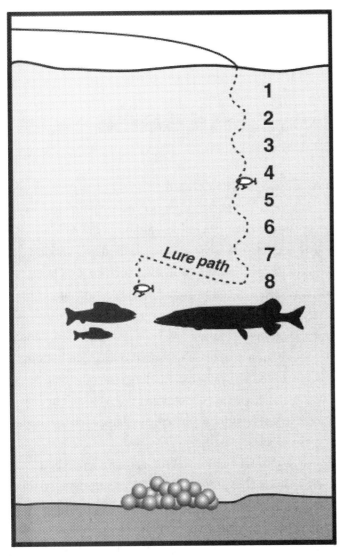

Catching suspended fish is easily accomplished by using a count-down crankbait. The key is in determining the "sink rate" of the lure. Once that is done, simply cast the lure out on a long cast, count it down to the approximate level of the suspended fish, and start crankin'.

What downriggers do offer that snap-on weights do not is precision depth control. Metered downriggers offer precise measurements so you can spot fish on a sonar unit and get a lure to them. Whenever you're seeing deep water fish that hover at depths way below easily attained ranges, over 40 feet or more, the downrigger system is the way to go. However, stay away from reefs. Getting a downrigger ball hung up on a reef is a bad deal.

Another unique depth tool for really deep water applications is the Dipsey Diver. The Dipsey Diver is basically a big diving bill that you can attach to your line. These are great devices for small rental boats and remote fishing trips for lake trout and other deep-water species. I've had some great catches of lake trout on a minnow bait attached to a Dipsey Diver device. The normal rig here consists of attaching the Dipsey Diver to your line and then running a 3- to 10-foot leader off the Dipsey Diver to your minnow bait. The Dipsey Diver has a diving lock on it that enables the device to dig, but it releases when a fish hits so you don't have as much drag when reeling in a fish. For rental boats and remote fishing, this system is tough to beat for really deep applications.

All in all, the minnow bait is one heck of a versatile lure. As we have seen, this bait can be fished on top as a motionless surface bait as well as attached to a downrigger and trolled to depths of 100 feet or more. When you think of it, there probably isn't another lure that is this versatile. That's why minnow baits have been such great fish-catchers for so many years. They catch fish shallow and deep, no matter what the season. Minnow baits should be an integral part of every good angler's arsenal. You now know this to be true.

chapter 10

Count-Down Crankbaits

As much print as crankbaits have commanded in articles, books, and other publications, very little material has been devoted to the sinking "count-down" style crankbait. In fact, few anglers own or even know how to effectively use these highly efficient deep-water tools. Without the proper working knowledge of sinking count-down lures, and what their true functions are, any typical sinking crankbait does nothing more than collect weeds or occupy space in your tackle box. While floating divers and suspender crankbaits continue to get all the press and playing time, sinking "count-down" cranks wait in the wings for a chance to prove themselves. They are the true dark horses of the crankbait world.

Sinking count-down crankbaits are very specialized tools very comparable to a metric ratchet set. While they do have multiple uses, they're primarily designed for clean bottom and open water use. Whenever fish are hugging the bottom in deeper waters, or when they are suspended over deep open water, this style of crankbait is likely to catch more fish than any other. In other words, they get deep, and catch fish that

other lures simply can't reach.

Generally, sinking count-downs are poor choices for any cover-laden conditions, although the sinking lipless crankbait, which can be classified as a sinking count-down, works quite well over such cover. On average however, sinking crankbaits are more apt to get hung up in cover. When that cover is woody, you're probably going to loose a few baits now and then. More often, a sinking cranker is best used over clean bottoms and suspended big gamefish holding at depths below levels reachable with conventional crankbaits. The key is to have a few of these sinkers available, and try them in these specific situations.

The perfect depth level for a sinking crankbait begins somewhere around 12 feet. Not surprisingly, this is the basic cut-off depth where traditional floating/diving crankbaits and their suspending cousins level off in productivity. On a conventional cast few floating divers or suspending crankers attain depths greater than 12 feet with any regularity. However, the sinking crankbait reaches this depth level and greater with no problem at all.

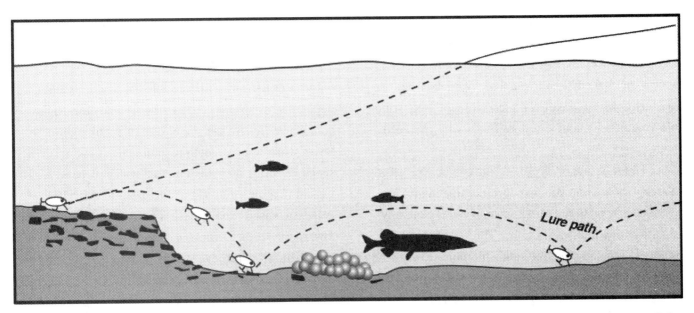

The "rip & drop" technique is one of the most productive ways to fish a sinking, count-down style crankbait. After letting the lure sink all the way to the bottom, rip the lure forward utilizing a sharp sideways or upward pull on the rod tip. Follow this up with a recovery pause allowing the lure to sink back to the bottom while repositioning the rod for the next rip.

The simple secret lies in its ability to sink. Instead of trying to grind a floating diver down 12 feet with a long cast, fast retrieve and lighter line, all one has to do with a sinking count-down is cast it out and let it sink to that level. Basically, it will get there on its own. Because this lure sinks, it can reach virtually any level desired. It can be fished tightly to the bottom in really deep waters or worked at various levels over open areas in search of suspended fish. Because the lure has no buoyancy, it will not rise upward when retrieved. In fact, slower retrieve speeds may actually make the lure run a bit deeper.

Document The "Sink Rate"

One of the basic fundamentals with any sinking crankbait is to document how fast the lure sinks. This is essential if you hope to get the lure down to any precise level for suspended fish. Without knowing the sink rate, precise depth control is not possible and you'll rarely score big on suspended fish. You must take the time and steps to record how fast your lure sinks. This is why I

like to call these lures "count-downs." Because you need to count as the lure goes down.

This whole process is actually quite easy to determine. You can do it on just one cast over the right spot. Simply position your boat over a known depth on a flat, cast the lure out and watch your line as you count during the lure's descent at a rate of "one — one thousand, two — one thousand, three —one thousand", and so on. If the depth you're at is 18 feet and the lure hits bottom at around a count of 18, you've got an easy formula for countdown crankin'. The bait has a "sink rate" of approximately one foot per second. This is the ideal sink rate, of course, since it makes it easy to calculate how deep your lure is going without any math.

Yet, ideal sink rates of one-foot-per-second aren't always possible. Some lures sink faster, while others descend more slowly. Having both fast-sinkers and slow-sinkers is a good idea. You'll find uses for both. I particularly like a slow-sinker for many shallower situations in cold water. The key is to have a lure that sinks, but is easy to keep control of over shallower cover without the sinking nature of the lure overtaking its ability to perform. I prefer fast-sinkers for all deep water situations. The deeper the water, the faster I want a count-down cranker to sink. Imagine how ineffective a slow-sinking crankbait would be over lake trout holding down off a reef at 45 feet. If there's any wind blowing, it'll be double-tough. That's why you need both.

The sink rate of any crankbait will also be greatly affected by the line you use. Just like floating/divers work deeper on thinner lines, count-downs generally sink faster on thinner lines, too. Thicker lines create more drag making the lure sink a bit more slowly. The only way to know the sink rate of a particular lure on any given line is to test and record it. Usually, you'll find an ideal line size that seems to perform best with your count-downs. For bass, I particularly like 10-pound test. For muskies, I'm partial to 30-pound. However, if you prefer a heavier weight line that's fine,

too. Just remember to record that sink rate so you know what it is. Then, you're off and running.

Sinking count-down crankbaits are exceptional on cold water fish since they enable the angler to retain depth at slow speeds. That's why so many top-flight cold water anglers use some form of a sinking lure in lower water temps. Depth retention at a slow retrieve speed is a critical element to cold water success. A typical floating crankbait needs speed to drive it down. A lack of speed usually pulls a buoyant cranker back up toward the surface. This is not so with a sinking crankbait. Slow retrieve speeds with a count-down keep the lure deep, and sometimes make it dive even deeper. This combination is often deadly on big fish resting along deep break lines in the late fall.

One of my favorite places to cast count-downs is over deep-cresting humps that top out way below the tracking range of any typical floating or suspending

Most lipless crankbaits work exceptionally well for countdown crankin' since they sink horizontally. Pumping and ripping them off the bottom, followed by a pause allowing them to sink again, is a tremendous triggering mechanism for bass and other game fish.

crankbait. Those humps that crest in that 14- to 22-foot range are typical of what I'm talking about here. Food shelves in this range get very little angling pressure. Even when they do, anglers are usually casting lures that run way above the tops of these humps. There's no way you're going to get a floating diver to reach this kind of depth level with any consistency, yet all you need to do to get a count-down to this depth is to simply cast it out, and let it sink all the way to the bottom. Then, by simply crankin' at a slow to medium speed, you'll have that count-down cranker bouncing at those depths easily.

I've also had great success utilizing a "rip and drop" technique with this bait on deep water areas. I begin the same way — casting the sinking cranker out and letting it sink all the way to the bottom. Then, instead of beginning a straight, steady retrieve, I rip forward on the lure with a sharp sideways or upward pull on the rod tip, followed by a "recovery pause" that allows the lure to sink back to the bottom while I reposition my rod for the next rip. This has been one of my deadliest deep water secrets for years on big muskies. It also works extremely well on deep water smallies.

For some reason, this retrieval method really ticks fish off, if they're at all active. I'm talking about a retrieve that produces one of those much-talked-about "bone-jarring strikes." The "rip and drop" tactic triggers a violent response from monster muskies and belly-bustin' bronzebacks. More often than not, the strike is so hard that the fish inhales the entire lure! I wouldn't hesitate to predict that you will likely get more super strikes with this kind of crankin' technique than with any other. You also nearly always get a great hook set since you're basically initiating one every time you rip the lure.

My biggest musky in the fall of 1993 hit in just this manner. I was diligently working on one of the first prototype designs of the Count-Down DepthRaider series and one clear October day I picked the right spot to test it. It was a deep rock/gravel point that extended out beyond a large weedy bar that was also part of the same point. My friends and I had seen a big musky on this spot several times throughout the season, but could never get it to hit. Whenever we saw it, it was always on the deep weed edge at the very tip of the point; right where the weeds met the rock and gravel. We hadn't seen the fish in over a month, so we thought it had vacated the spot.

I just finished thoroughly casting the weed tops with various lures, and scouring the weed edge with a floating/diving crankbait, but did not see the big one, or any other fish for that matter. However, deeper hard bottom adjacent to a good weed shelf should never be overlooked in the fall, and I already knew that this rock/gravel extension was a good one. I'd taken many muskies from this deeper finger in the past, as well as some nice strings of walleyes. It was the perfect place to test the new Count-Down DepthRaider prototype.

Three casts into my count-down test told me I was onto something. I fired out a long bomb cast, somewhat perpendicular to the main body of the deep hard bottom projection, and let the big diver sink all the way down. As soon as I hit a count of 18 the line went slack indicating the lure had hit bottom. I immediately ripped forward on the rod tip hard, and let it sink back. Then I did it once more, but the lure didn't sink back, so I ripped it forward again, only this time my rod tip buckled. What followed was kind of amazing. At first I thought I was hung up, but the snag kept moving. Eventually, I got that tell-tale head shake at my rod tip, and I knew I was hooked into something big. The ensuing battle lasted over 10 minutes. This is astonishingly long for a musky fight on heavy tackle. The big fish stayed deep and fought extremely hard literally towing me around. When it finally surfaced, I was amazed to see both the size of the fish, a trophy of at least 52 inches, and no visible lure in its mouth. That's right, the big musky had actually engulfed the entire 9-inch crankbait and about three inches of the wire leader. Like I said, they really get ticked off when you "rip and drop" a count-down.

One of my biggest smallmouths this past spring was also taken with this "rip and drop" technique while filming one of my television episodes. I was fishing with guest, Mark Hesslemen representing Miller Friends Of The Field program, and we were casting lipless crankbaits for spring smallies off rock points and mid-lake humps. It was a very windy day, which made it ideal for smallies to be active, riding high, and eager to chase down crankbaits.

Anyway, Mark and I were both casting various versions of a lipless crankbait including RatLTraps, Cordell Hotspots, and Luhr Jensen Sugar Shads. All of these baits were taking a few fish, but the Sugar Shad was particularly productive. As we crossed a large gravel point, Mark began casting the top of the bar for shallow cruisers, while I turned and fired a long bomb out off the very tip of the point and let the lipless cranker, a red craw Sugar Shad, sink all the way to the bottom. I then ripped up on my 7 ½ foot crankin' stick driving the Sugar Shad upward, followed by a pause allowing it to drop all the way back to the bottom. My intention was to check the deeper hard bottom hoping to find a bigger fish or two. It didn't take long to find one!

The second rip was met with an incredible strike, and an almost immediate missile as the big bronze back rocketed straight up from the depths breaking the surface with a big boil. As the camera rolled, I battled the 21-inch fish all the way to boat and again was amazed to see the entire crankbait buried deep inside the fish's mouth. It took quite an effort to get the lure out, and release this superb trophy unharmed. Like I said, big gamefish seem to get ticked off when you "rip and drop" a count-down sinking crankbait.

One of the very best weed flat walleye tactics I've ever come across

Big smallmouths are particularly vulnerable to the "rip & drop" tactic with lipless crankbaits. The trick here is to let the lipless crank sink all the way to the bottom after the cast. Then, utilizing a long rod, sweep the lure upward, followed by a pause that allows the bait to drop back to the bottom again.

lately involves utilizing one of the old classic Countdown Rapala lures. Actually I was tipped off to this technique by my friend Bruce Nimz, a northern Wisconsin game warden. Before that time I'd used this lure on occasion, and had caught some fish with it, but never to the extent that it became a choice bait. Then Bruce told me that he'd been really catching walleyes with a # 7 Countdown Rapala ripping it over cabbage weeds. Soon after Bruce told me about this tactic, I began really experimenting with the Countdown Rapala and the "rip & drop". Successful outings since then have convinced me that the Countdown Rapala works a lot better with this retrieve than with any of the more conventional methods I'd been using.

What I realized from then on was that the relatively weak action of the Countdown Rapala at slow to medium retrieve speeds does little to trigger less active fish. That's why you never really hear much about this lure as a fish-catcher. Few anglers know how to utilize it properly. Heck, even the folks at Normark don't promote the use of this technique with their lure. I'm now convinced that the rip & drop is the key technique with this bait. Start using the Countdown Rapala with a fast rip & drop technique and you'll see it turn into a fish catchin' dynamo.

There are still a number of other crankbaits that sink, and all of them can be utilized with the various techniques I've presented.

Some of my favorite sinking crankbaits include the: RatLTrap, Sugar Shad, Cisco Kid, Count-Down Rapala, Heddon Sonar, Luhr Jensen Rippletail, and of course my big Count-Down DepthRaider. All of these lures will catch deep-water fish from muskies to bass to lake

Metal blade baits are actually crankbaits in a sense. They are simply a heavier metal version of the lipless plastic crankbait. Blade baits are great deep-water lures, and superb on the "rip & drop" technique. The author particularly likes a blade bait for walleyes and lake trout.

Sinking count-down crankbaits allow you to fish at depth ranges unreachable with conventional casting lures. This big musky came from such a spot, a deep rock/gravel finger extending way out beyond a large weedy bar.

trout, utilizing the right tactics. The "rip and drop" tactic is especially effective with all of these lures. However, never discount a simple slow, straight retrieve either.

Metal blade baits, while not considered true crankbaits, really are a crankbait. I'm speaking of lures such as the Rippletail, Heddon Sonar, Silver Buddy, and Gay Blade. They work superbly with the lift and drop technique. Some of the larger versions of this lure sink even faster than the desired one-foot-per-second making them outstanding choices for really deep applications. They work particularly well on lake trout holding at depths greater than 50 feet. You can vertically jig these lures with equal efficiency, and that's what most anglers use them for. But they can also be great casting baits for a host of deep-water conditions. In particular, I've had outstanding success with the "rip and drop" technique on blade baits for lakers, walleyes, smallies, and northern pike. Southern bassers have done equally well on winter largemouths using the exact same method.

Count-down, sinking crankbaits continue to be the overlooked player on the team. Even today's most astute crankbait anglers often neglect using this outstanding deep-water tool. That, in itself, is the main focus of the lure — deep water. If you want to effectively fish depth ranges never before reachable with conventional crankbaits, start utilizing the count-down. Discipline yourself to fish these deeper areas slowly and thoroughly, taking full advantage of the lure's capabilities. It won't take long for you to build an unbreakable confidence in an entirely new bait category. Just remember what I said about those strikes on the "rip and drop" technique. They are truly bone-jarring.

chapter 11

Jointed Vs. Straight Models

I can't say that I've been more successful with either jointed or straight crankbaits over the years, but there are those times, conditions, and situations when one is definitely better than the other. While the straight model crankbait gets far more water time from anglers, is sold by more sport shops, and is made by more manufacturers, the jointed crankbait still holds its own in terms of raw fish-catching power. Plus, no matter what the species, there are times when the jointed plug proves superior to the straight model. That's why it's important to have both and know the differences between the two.

The biggest assets of jointed crankbaits are slow speed action, what I like to call the illusion of speed, and noise. While many straight model crankbaits work well at slow speeds, most jointed crankbaits excel at slower retrieves. Very little forward movement is needed with a good jointed crankbait in order to initiate a wobble. As soon as a jointed lure begins to wobble back and forth, the jointed body parts react with opposite movements. As the front section moves one way, the rear section moves the other. Usually this results in

a violent collision of the body parts at the joint section. As the body parts collide, they create a strong clicking sound. This makes the jointed lure exceptional in dark waters, where fish have limited visibility and rely much more on sensing vibrations.

Research has shown that clear-water gamefish are basically sight feeders, while dark-water predators are sound seekers. A clear-water environment offers any gamefish far more sight range, enabling it to spot prey. While clear-water gamefish might have senses of hearing and vibration that are just as acute, these senses are not required for predatory success. Sight takes on the primary role in most strike decisions. That's why lures with superior flash catch lots of clear-water fish. In most clear-water cases, straight model crankbaits provide all the flash necessary. While jointed crankbaits definitely work well in clear waters, most often they are not necessary. Straight models essentially work just as well.

What jointed lures do offer the angler in clear water is the illusion of speed. Because many good jointed crankbaits wobble and wiggle so violently at slow to medium speeds, they look like they're moving quickly through the water when they're really not. In other words, you can make a fish think the lure is getting away and moving out of strike range quickly by utilizing a good jointed crankbait. I have found this illusion of speed trick with a jointed crankbait works well on clear-water gamefish in colder temperatures; particularly in the fall.

Jointed crankbaits have also worked well for me on clear-water fish when the bite seems tough overall. For some odd reason, bass, walleyes, and muskies all appear to prefer a jointed crankbait in clear water when they're less willing. Generally, whether I'm casting or trolling, I'll nearly always load up on jointed lures if the fish stop taking a straight model crankbait. Slowing down the retrieve or troll speed is nearly always the other factor that goes hand-in-hand with this scenario. Whenever fishing gets tough in clear water, switching to jointed cranks and slowing down has worked for me more often than it has failed. The illusion of speed is part of the secret trigger here, but you're legitimately providing that fish a bit more of an opportunity to snatch the bait. Usually this little trick works.

Another benefit the jointed lures and slower speeds is more

solid hookups and a higher overall hooking percentage. The result of the speed illusion combined with an actual slower forward movement seems to help fish get a

While jointed crankbaits are very popular with musky anglers, they are often overlooked by bass and walleye fishermen. Jointed crankbaits catch all species of fish with equal efficiency, and are particularly good in any dark water situation.

direct hit on the bait more often. By and large, when gamefish hit jointed lures, they're hooked well. In fact, I also believe that – on average – jointed lures hook big fish far better than straight models. This may have something to do with the overall loose-leverage design of a jointed lure versus a straight model. Big fish seem to be able to get more hook-bending leverage on rigid straight model lures. The larger the straight model crankbait, the more of a problem this seems to create.

In retrospect, if you're going to fish larger lures for big fish, it's a good bet that jointed lures are going to hook 'em better. In many cases, this means having several trebles buried solidly in the fish's mouth instead of one hook or two from a single treble. When the fish hooked is a 50-inch musky or a 30-inch walleye, this might make all the difference in whether you ultimately catch the fish since the battle is likely to last longer with these larger brutes. Admittedly, I have far more confidence in the overall hooking ability of a jointed cranker over a straight model when it comes to big lures and big fish.

This subject of larger lures versus smaller ones will be covered in more detail in another chapter, but its definitely worth discussing. Large, over-sized lures do have their time and place for all big gamefish species. Crankbait selection basically follows the same set of rules. I've done exceptionally well on big bass with larger lures in dark water. This includes up-sizing in just about all lure categories from plastic worms to top-water baits. Larger crankbaits are particularly good here. The bigger bait casts a larger silhouette making it an easier target to find. Larger lures

Fishing magnum lures is one of the best ways to catch the biggest fish in any system. This giant walleye simply couldn't resist a musky sized jointed crankbait.

also push more water, providing a bigger signal to the fish's lateral line much like a Boeing 747 on a radar screen in comparison to a small plane. All of this makes it easier for a fish to find the lure.

Huge crankbaits of 10 inches or more have proven to be highly attractive to the biggest fish in the system. Monster bass of California are regularly taken on plugs of this size. So are really big muskies of 30 pounds or more. Many musky hounds are really shifting to huge crankbaits for big fall muskies in an effort to distract smaller fish of other species, and attract the biggest muskies in the lake, river, or reservoir. Tournament

walleye anglers are finding out the same thing. The rule is: Fish an oversized crankbait when you're into a big fish bite. It filters through the small to medium fish, and attracts the larger fish.

I have to admit that whenever I see darker, stained water conditions, I immediately think "jointed" in a crankbait. I want a lure with lots of action, sound, and vibration whenever the water is dark. I also want a bait that really wiggles and wobbles at slower speeds so the fish has plenty of time to find it and hit it. A big, straight crankbait with a rattle might produce equally well on some occasions, but it's tough to beat a jointed

The jointed crankbait has been the author's key night fishing lure for big muskies and other lunker gamefish. Jointed crankbaits emit tremendous noise and vibration, making them easy targets for night feeders to home-in on. This 51-1/2-incher hit a jointed "Night Shiner" pattern at 1:30 a.m.

version for dark waters. Add a rattle to the jointed plug and you've really got a dark-water dynamo.

Night fishing is another specific situation where I'm certain jointed lures are superior. As many of you already know, I've spent a great deal of time fishing after dark for all kinds of gamefish. As a teenager, I chased largemouths after dark on a regular basis, establishing my reputation for big fish as a big bass specialist. Most of these bigger bass came after dark. In fact, most of the locals that marveled at my big stringer catches in those days were amazed how early in the morning I'd come in. I'd be back at the dock by 8 a.m. These locals always thought I was simply getting up early and fishing the dawn/sunrise bite. Little did they know that I'd been out all night. Jointed L & S lures and Pikie Minnows were my weapons.

Early in my guiding career, night walleye excursions were part of my business and many of my clients caught wall-hanger walleyes under the cover of darkness. The vast majority of these big walleyes were caught on crankbaits. We'd begin a typical guided walleye outing at about 8 p.m. Most of our action would be from 9:30 p.m. through about midnight. Our approach to catching walleyes night after night was very simple. We'd cast crankbaits around weed flats, over the top of shallow rock reefs, and along the edges of stump fields. It was a rare night when we didn't catch lots of fish. It was also a rare night when we didn't catch a few big ones. While we caught plenty of walleyes on straight model crankbaits, I found jointed ones to be better.

Of course, anyone who's been keeping up with the musky game for any number of years knows I made a living for over a decade guiding clients for trophy muskies in the dark. I don't need to tell you that the jointed DepthRaider was the key bait. When I first started chasing muskies after dark, I thought it was a top-water game. However, we rarely got enough good top-water conditions for night muskies so the success rate was never big on top-water baits. A lot of nights had wind and waves. I started experimenting with subsurface lures and had a lot more success. Now, there are plenty of musky guides taking clients out after dark. Back in the early 1980s, there was only one.

While I've had success with all species after dark utilizing a variety of artificial lures and live baits, nothing takes big gamefish after dark like crankbaits. Both straight and jointed crankbaits take plenty of bass, walleyes, and muskies after dark, but I still think the jointed lure is superior. Much for the same reasons that jointed lures work better in dark waters during daylight, the body clicking action along with strong wobble at slow speeds makes them fantastic night baits. If you're seriously considering exploring night fishing, I'd highly recommend that you load up on some good quality jointed crankbaits.

Rattles can greatly improve a straight model for night fishing, just as it does for dark-water applications. Hours and hours of casting, night after night, on all three species (bass, walleyes, and muskies) has proven this to be true more often than not. While there are times when I'm a fan of a crankbait with no rattle, night fishing is not one of them. You'll catch more bass, walleyes, and muskies after dark with crankbaits containing rattles. Night-feeding predators seem to key-in on the sound of the rattle.

From all this talk about jointed crankbaits you'd think that I rarely use a straight model, but this is far from the truth. I'm a huge fan of the straight model and give it equal water time. My tackle boxes are loaded with straight model crankbaits of all kinds; from tiny 2-inchers to giants of 12 inches or more. I use them for bass, walleyes, pike, muskies, and trout in all kinds of situations. More straight model crankbaits are made and marketed than jointed versions. Maybe that's why I have so many more straight ones. Anyway, here are a few of my favorite applications for the straight model.

Whenever there's snaggy bottom cover such as weeds, wood, or brush, I prefer a straight model floating diver over a jointed one. The straight model crankbait simply runs through cover a lot better. My research with underwater cameras reveals that the tail section of any typical jointed lure tends to snag-up a lot more often since it swings farther to the side. Jointed lures also tend to snag on debris when you're trying to let them float back up out of a cover. The tail section of a jointed lure folds to one side on the rise exposing the hooks to snags. Straight model floaters back out of cover perfectly backwards protecting the hooks from fouling on any kind of debris.

Comparatively speaking, straight models are more buoyant than jointed versions, too. This gives the straight model floater a distinct advantage over the jointed lures when trying to work the lure in a "bump & rise" fashion through any kind of cover, particularly weeds. Buoyancy is a big factor in cover. Without it, you're going to have lots of wasted casts. A crankbait that's fouled in weeds, or locked up in a brush pile really kills your chances hooking a fish. Plucking weeds off the lure is bad enough, but having to move your boat over the brush pile, log or crib holding the fish in order to free the lure is sure spook any remaining fish.

I also prefer the straight model for most clean-bottom bouncing situations. Straight models "bump & rise" over the bottom, no matter what the substrate, much better than a jointed version. When the hard bottom area contains big jagged rocks with lots of crevices, the straight model is sure to be a better choice. Jointed baits are much more prone to jam in rock crevices than a buoyant straight model. If any scattered brush or logs exist along the bottom, it's a sure bet that the jointed bait will hang up more often than the straight version. Jointed baits simply don't have the buoyant rise and the precise back-out nature that a straight model does.

Casting crankbaits over clean bottoms is one thing, but trolling them over such terrain in a bottom-bouncing manner is yet another. The additional speed and momentum of the boat has a tendency to hang up crankbaits more regularly. You're sure to get a lot more frustrating hang-ups when bottom-bounce trolling with jointed crankbaits. That's why I choose to avoid them for this tactic. Give me a straight model floating diver with a large triangular diving lip and I'll troll it over just about any kind of bottom with minimal problems, and in the process, catch a lot more fish. I'll rarely troll a jointed lure when trying to bounce the bait across the bottom.

Speed and straight models are also synonymous. Whenever the fish seem to prefer speed, straight model crankbaits are superior. Jointed lures simply are not built for speed. Put too much speed on a jointed crank and it begins to torque against itself in all kinds of ways. Too much speed negates all body clicking. It also makes the jointed lure unpredictable in action. Most, but not all, straight models excel at high speeds once tuned properly. There's nothing working against the lure's built-in action to destroy the vibration and rhythm of the lure. Speed enhances the wiggle and wobble of the straight model.

This speed issue is particularly important when trolling at speeds of three miles per hour or more. Some clear-water fish in warm temperatures need excessive speeds to trigger a strike. Certain straight model crankbaits that can withstand high-speed trolling, are going to be the only lures one can use here. Jointed lures have no possible chance in this situation. They were not designed for this purpose. Thin profile straight-bodied crankbaits with thinner diving lips are built for high-speed trolling. Straight model crankbaits are the lures to use for nearly all high-speed trolling.

Finally, I like a straight model crankbait whenever I'm using it in a jerkbait fashion. Twitchin', jerkin', and rippin' a crankbait over the top of weeds and other debris is a job for the straight model, hands down. The straight model isn't necessarily better on the twitch or jerk part of the retrieve, but it's far superior during the pause or rise. Whether it's a buoyant model that begins to rise or a suspender that continues to hang, the straight model has a more natural look to it at this point. Jointed baits tend to fold during a pause. This causes them to hang up on cover more often, as I mentioned earlier, and it detracts from its realism.

I'm not saying that you can't catch fish on jointed

Jointed lures work well for all big gamefish in dark waters. This summer musky fell to a 7-inch minnow bait.

crankbaits worked with a stop 'n go retrieve, or any sort of jerkbait style, but they're rarely as good as a straight model in this situation. I've put many hours on the water testing both lures under these conditions and the straight model consistently out-performs the jointed one in this instance. Nowadays, I wouldn't even think of trying a jointed lure for this technique. I've come to learn that twitchin', jerkin', and rippin' are best left to the straight model.

As you can see, both lures have their time and place. In order to be a totally outfitted crankbait angler, it's a good idea to have both styles. Generally, I've found that walleye and bass anglers tend to lean on straight model crankbaits too much. They never even consider a jointed version. Old classics like the jointed Pikie and L & S (Mirrolure) plugs were sure productive for me in the past. Newer, smaller jointed baits such as the jointed Rapala and broken back Rebel Fast Trak are really hammerin' fish in tournaments. I'm convinced that walleye and bass anglers would catch more fish in

both dark water and at night if they tried a jointed crankbait once in awhile.

Musky hunters are just the opposite. They're more apt to choose the jointed bait, and fail to recognize how deadly a straight model can be. They also don't know the distinct differences between the two. Both jointed and straight models should have specific placement in the musky-hunting job. Yet, few musky hunters look at it this way. If you're a musky hunter, next time switch to a buoyant straight model when trying to fish thick weeds. You'll catch a lot less weed with this bait, and probably more fish.

All in all, be more versatile. Try both jointed and straight models. In particular, make the effort to match the right lure for the right situations. No doubt there will be plenty of times when it won't make any difference, but then who cares. However, there will be some outings when one clearly outperforms the other. You'll have to fish both in order to discover this preference.

tactics

chapter 12

Weed Flats & Weed Lines

Weeds, whether in a bay, flat, bar, or mid-lake hump, are one of the most productive forms of cover for nearly every big gamefish that swims in freshwater. Admittedly, much of my success with magnum muskies, big bass, and wallhangin' walleyes has come from some form of weeds. This includes every conceivable species of weeds growing at a variety of depths. I've caught big muskies in 2-foot deep tobacco cabbage as well as 18-foot deep sand grass. Some of my biggest bass have come from emergent weedy slop in no more than 2 feet of water. A few of these bucketmouths have even topped the 10-pound mark! Yet deep broadleaf cabbage along a clear lake weed lines at 12 to 14 feet have also produced plenty of big ones, including some of my best overall stringers of fish exceeding five pounds. Hundreds of walleyes have bent my rod from shallow cabbage and milfoil flats through the years when I was a full-time walleye guide. Heck, I even used to make a living catching summer walleyes from deep grass beds. To say weeds have been good to me would be an understatement.

What's most amazing about all of this history is

that the majority of these weed whoppers have come on crankbaits. This would definitely seem surprising to many anglers, since weeds are rarely associated with crankbaits. When most anglers think of weeds, they think of lures that are "weedless." Crankbaits are generally a lure that the novice would AVOID when fishing any kind of weed cover. As you will learn throughout the pages of this book, weeds and crankbaits should be synonymous. Avoid fishing weeds with a crankbait and you're likely to avoid catching fish. Whenever weeds are beneath the surface with some clean water above them, crankbaits become a viable lure choice. However, the specific choice of crankbait here is usually critical. Pick the wrong crankbait and you'll probably spend more time plucking weeds off the lure than unhooking fish.

What I'm getting at here is this; in order to be a truly good weed cranker, you need to be able to analyze the weed situation on any given spot and choose the right lure accordingly. This obviously takes some practice and some experience, but it's really not that difficult. First and foremost is having a solid knowledge of the running depth on each crankbait in your tackle box, and which ones run through weeds the best. Taking this a step further, you also need to know what kind of crankbait action the fish are likely to prefer in and around these weeds. In other words, do they want a fast-moving, flashy lipless chrome RatLTrap, a slow-twitchin'/suspendin' minnow bait, or the bump & rise action of a floating diver. Many times, the only way to know what the fish prefer is to try a variety of crankin' tactics over the same spot.

I've titled this chapter "Crankin' Weed Flats & Weed Lines" for a very specific reason because the lures and tactics for casting **over** weed flats vary a great deal from those needed to cast **alongside** weed lines. Essentially, casting crankbaits **over** weed flats is a **perpendicular** presentation, while working crankbaits

alongside weed lines is a **parallel** presentation. They are two entirely different techniques that require specific kinds of crankbaits and a completely opposite casting approach. You must first understand this basic concept before going any further.

For example, weed flats, no matter what the lure choice, involve fan-casting. The goal here is to pepper the entire weed flat with as many casts as possible in order to search for big fish cruising over the top of the weed jungle or possibly hiding inside isolated thicker clumps. Maximum water coverage is always a main objective whenever probing weed flats. Unlike fish working weed lines, that are much more predictably pinpointed since they're hugging an edge, you have no idea for sure where fish are going to be in the weed flat.

Weed flat gamefish often cruise over the weed

Much of the author's success with big fish has come from crankin' the weeds. However, specific crankbait choice for weed fishing is critical, along with proper technique. Pick the wrong crankbait or fish the right one incorrectly, and you'll probably spend more time plucking weeds off the lure rather than unhooking fish.

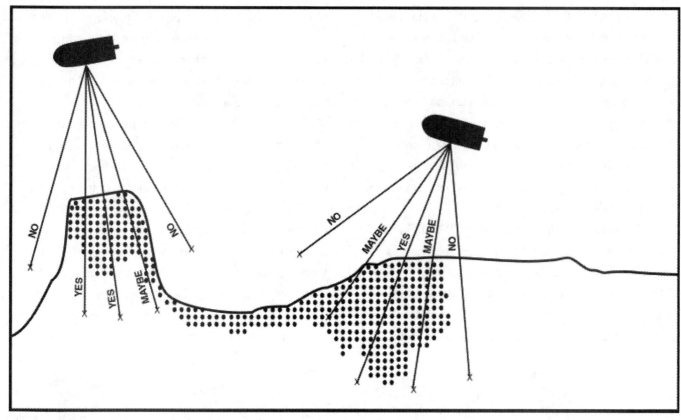

Casting weed flats is generally a perpendicular fan-casting presentation. The goal here is to pepper the entire weed flat with as many casts as possible in order to find the weed clump holding the fish. Maximum water coverage is always a main objective whenever probing the tops of a weed flat.

tops when really active. These fish are swimming, searching, feeding fish. It matters little what the species is, by the way. Every conceivable freshwater predator gamefish that likes weed flats, from northern pike, to walleyes, to largemouth bass, to muskies, cruises weed flats in the same general manner, and reacts to lures thrown over them in the same manner. In fact, it's not uncommon to catch all four gamefish over the same weed flat with the same crankbait when conditions are just right.

A high-speed, run-and-gun casting approach with a relatively trouble-free crankbait is nearly always the best bet here. This might involve a number of potential lures, and the selection along with the size of the crankbait might vary depending upon the species. My favorite choice for bass, walleyes and pike when speed-casting a weed flat is usually a lipless crankbait like the RatLtrap, My favorite size is normally the ½-ounce

version since it casts well, is easiest to fish overall, and attracts the widest size ranges of fish. I'll fish this bait on baitcasting gear, a long rod of at least 7 feet, with lines of no less than 12-pound test and rarely more than 20-pound. I'd lean toward the lighter line for deeper weed flats and clearer water. I'd definitely go on the heavier side, 20-pound test, for higher weeds and darker water.

Cast length should vary with the height of the weeds, the water clarity, and the wind speed. If the weeds are really strong, you might have to shorten up casts in order to maintain lure control and basically keep the lure weed-free. If the water is really clear, longer casts might be necessary to get at fish that would otherwise spook by your boat presence. Calm water surfaces would also promote a longer cast to avoid fish spooking. Strong winds would encourage fish to hit at closer ranges, and force you to shorten casts to maintain

One of the fastest ways to speed check a shallow weed flat is by casting a lipless crankbait. Lots of water can be covered efficiently in very little time. Almost any game fish in the weeds will jump on these highly attractive plugs.

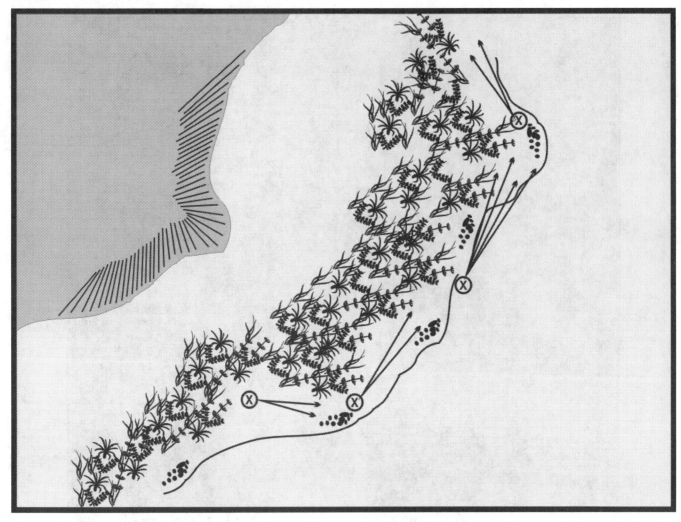

Working deep divers alongside a weed line is generally a parallel presentation. The goal here is to constantly probe the deep weed edge with a disciplined parallel "test cast". Discovering and defining that weed edge is a fringe benefit of weed line crankin' as well as catching fish.

more lure control. As I mentioned earlier and will reiterate throughout, you need to develop a talent to analyze the situation and choose your lure and tactics accordingly.

For muskies, I might try a larger version of the same lure in the ¾-to 1-ounce range, but I've had great success in this situation with a large jointed minnow bait such as a 7-inch ShallowRaider. A straight model floating minnow bait in the 7- to 9-inch range, might be equally good. It has a good flash and vibration, and runs very shallow. If I choose the minnow bait, jointed or straight, I wouldn't necessarily be doing any jerkin' or twitchin' with it. I'd simply cast it out and reel it in at a

fairly fast clip. The only time I'd jerk on it would be to clear any weed encounters.

I've taken many big muskies with this method throughout the years, and so have my friends. When Tom Gelb and I were testing the original prototypes of the ShallowRaider, we caught a bunch of nice muskies on these baits by simply fan-casting them over weed flats and retrieving them. No jerkin', no twitchin', and no rippin'. Just straight crankin'. Some of these first ShallowRaider muskies were featured on my original music action musky video, MTV – Musky Thrashin' Video. The following year I took back-to-back 30-pounders on a prototype color of the ShallowRaider while we were out on another field testing mission. All of these fish were taken with a simple fan-casting, straight retrieve method over weed flats.

Working weed lines with crankbaits is an entirely different ball game. The focus shifts from a wide open, speed-fishing, fan-casting approach in a perpendicular fashion to a much more disciplined parallel casting tactic. Discipline is a good word here. The goal with weed line crankin' is to constantly seek out that deep weed edge, the weed line, with a test cast that is just about parallel to the weeds. Instead of running a shallow diver over higher weed tops, you're essentially trying to dig a deep runner along the side of weed walls, and deeper fringe weeds. This takes discipline as well as concentration.

Once again the four species (pike, walleyes, bass, muskies) will often hug a weed line in much the same manner and react to this parallel presentation much the same way. I first honed this tactic as a teenage bass fisherman back in the late 1960s, and little if anything has changed in the way I now use this same technique for muskies, pike or walleyes. About the only flare I've added to this classic crankin' system since my early bassin' days is to finish the retrieve with a figure eight when in musky waters. That's it. Since muskies follow a lure so much, this addition is paramount and a vital part of the crankin' system when muskies are the target.

Crankin' weed lines basically involves casting a

Sometimes big fish are up on the weed flat itself cruising or holding around thicker clumps or higher weed tops. Skimming a shallow-running minnow bait over a weed flat in this situation can be very productive.

floating deep diver parallel to the weed line. Basically, that's it, but of course, like everything else, there's a lot more to being really successful with this tactic. For one, you must outfit yourself with the right tackle, most notably the right line diameter in connection with the lure being used. Use a line that's too heavy and your lure will not attain the depth necessary to tick those lower fringe weeds. Fish a line that's too thin and you'll spend the majority of your time picking weeds off the bait, since the lure will dive too deep-plowing into the deep weeds.

The perfect line diameter will vary with the depth of the weed line, and the lure you choose. The only way to know for sure what's the perfect combination, is to experiment. Initially, I first like to feel out what lure the fish prefer. This includes experimenting with various colors, too. Once I start to get action on a lure (catch fish), I then hone the tackle combination, more closely tweaking the rod, reel, and most importantly the line diameter. With some fine tuning, you'll develop the system into an art form for your favorite lake.

For example, back in the early 1980s my friend Ron Weber from the Normark Company arranged for Yarmo Rapala from

Finland, maker of the famous Rapala, to fish with me and test some of the first Shad Raps to be marketed in this country. He not only wanted to know if I could find them a few walleyes to catch, but also if they would be shallow enough to tag on a Shad Rap. Worse yet, it was

The Rapala folks from Finland fished with the author back in the early 1980s. One of their head designers, "Matty", poses with a big walleye taken on a small #5 Shad Rap crankin' a grass bed in mid-August.

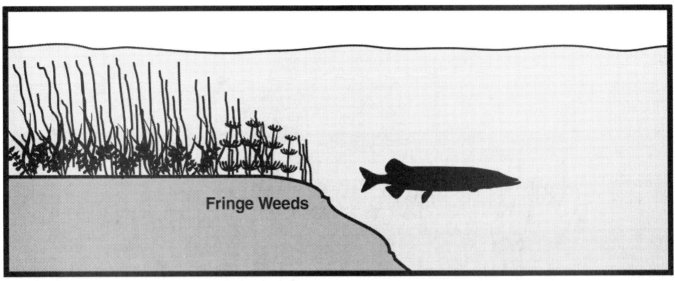

Deep "fringe weeds" often hold the bigger fish along deep weedlines. The only way to get at these fish consistently is by parallel casting a deep diver.

the middle of August! Luckily, I really had a great pattern going on some stained-water weed walleyes that were holding in elodea grass at 7-to 9-feet. This grass bed was huge, and there were plenty of fish in it, but the question was: Could we catch them on Shad Raps during the day? Up to this point, I had only fished them with jigs.

We began the day with four guys crankin' various patterns and sizes of the Shad Rap. Before long one fellow, one of Yarmo's head engineers, Matty, was clearly outfishing all of us. He was also getting fouled in the grass a lot less. Matty was catching about five fish to our one. After netting a 25-incher for him I began to figure out why. We were all fishing # 7 Shad Raps on 6-pound test with spinning gear. Matty, on the other hand, was casting an all-new # 5 on 8-pound test. We were so convinced that we had to use the larger lure with a lighter line to get it down as deep as possible, yet Matty was "cleaning up", with a thicker line and shallower running model.

Matty's bait was running as much as two feet shallower, making it skim barely across the tops of the deeper grass beds. His bait was rarely fouled with grass, and it was obviously running at the perfect depth range

for the active fish. While the # 7 was catching fish, it actually ran a bit too deep for this situation, and fouled in the grass a far higher percentage of the time. I quickly wondered if the smaller # 5 was more preferred by the fish, or was it simply running the right depth? After unhooking Matty's big walleye, I rigged my # 7 Shad Rap on a light baitcast outfit with 10-pound line, and bingo! I started catching a lot more fish, and less grass. Bait size wasn't so much the issue as was running depth. Getting the right depth meant perfecting the tackle combination. By the way, we finished the day catching 67 walleyes up to 25 inches and a bunch of pike. This all happened during daylight hours in the middle of August – on crankbaits I might add, not on jigs.

Matching the tackle is always important in any kind of deep water crankin' application, but particularly so whenever parallel crankin' weed lines. Remember that the right line diameter coupled with the right crankbait can be deadly, and a joy to fish. However, the wrong combination will not only be nonproductive, but also frustrating since your lure is likely to be constantly foul in weeds. And once your crankbait is fouled, it'll no longer catch a fish on that cast.

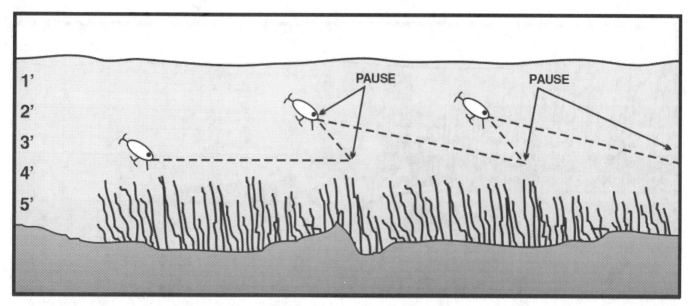

The classic "bump & rise" presentation is the key to fishing weeds effectively with crankbaits. A floating diver is certainly a necessity here. So is developing a knack to release line tension when the lure collides with weeds in order to allow it to back (rise) up.

Fat-bodied crankbaits with a diving lip angled downward, are great for bass over submerged weed cover.

The length of your cast is a factor to consider when crankin' weed lines. As we learned from earlier chapters, not only does line diameter affect running depth, but so does cast length. Longer casts make a lure run deeper. Conversely, short casts make a deep diver run much shallower. When I'm fishing a portion of a weed line with taller weeds, I'll usually shorten up on my casts to reduce running depth and improve lure control. As soon as I get a clean bait (a bait that does not contact weeds)on one of those short casts, I immedi-ately increase cast length on subsequent casts, and change the angle in the cast. I'm hoping to drive the lure a bit deeper to hit some of those "fringe weeds", and make contact with the weed line, just so I know where the edge is located.

A slight change in the casting angle is part of the overall technique here. Always keeping a somewhat parallel angle in mind, probe the weed line with various casts slightly left or right of the one you just made. The job is to maintain contact with the weed line. Short,

precise, probing casts will provide you with this information. What's neat about this style of fishing is you get to really learn the lake you're fishing so much better. As you fish, the deep-diving crankbait acts like a second sonar unit, providing you with constant information on each cast. The bait is telling you where the weed line is and how it is configured. It helps you anticipate any abrupt changes in the weed line before your boat reaches that spot so you can adjust accordingly.

This is really a neat "double whammy" to fishing deep-diving crankbaits. Not only are they great fish-catchers, but also great teachers and boat-control tools. You're fishing a high-percentage big fish lure (the crankbait), along a high-percentage spot (the weed line), but in the process, you're also learning that spot better each time you fish it. Eventually, you'll get to know the contour of that weed line so well that anticipating any points and turns in it becomes easy. This makes for better boat control which further increases your chances of catching more fish.

Like I said before, a great deal of my success with big fish has come from casting crankbaits over weeds. I've caught wallhangin' trophies of nearly every freshwater fish species from some type of weeds on some form of a crankbait. This combination has been absolutely deadly. Anyone who thinks that crankbaits aren't lures for weeds is obviously missing the boat big time. From fan-casting weedy flats to probing the edges of deep weed lines, crankbaits can do it all. Master the art of crankin' weeds and you're simply going to have a lot more success no matter where you fish, no matter what the species.

chapter 13

Wood Walkin' Crankbaits

Timbered flowages and reservoirs exist all across the North American continent, and I have fished many of them. From the stump filled bays of Rodman Reservoir in central Florida to the flooded forests of Ontario's Lac Suel, North America has plenty of wood for the "would be" angler. However, it's important to note that it doesn't necessarily take a lot of wood to attract gamefish. Some of the best wood fishing I've ever encountered involved situations where wood was more an isolated, secondary cover than a dominating one such as in a classic timbered reservoir. Inside this chapter, we'll deal with all kinds of woody cover, both dense and isolated, and how crankbaits fit into the realm of wood fishing.

Of course, wood has always had a great reputation as a fish producer no matter what the geographic location. Plainly put, wood creates cover, and that attracts both baitfish and gamefish. This includes everything from a single fallen tree, to a jungle of brush, stumps, and standing timber. Wood is highly valued as a cover source to nearly every one of our favorite gamefish species at some point during the season. Some gamefish, such as largemouth bass and walleyes, seem to like wood even more than other fish, but pike and muskies spend plenty of time in woody havens, too.

The value of any specific piece of wood in the water, whether submerged or emergent, whether a single log or a thick brush pile, is usually determined by a number of factors. One of the easiest ways to decipher any particular wood as a potential fish attractant is to compare it to what else is available inside that given ecosystem. When very little natural cover, such as weeds, exists, any hunk of wood is likely to have fish holding potential. If there's a lot of wood in the body of water, it's almost a sure bet that the fish will use various kinds of wood at different depths depending upon the season. Each body of water is slightly different, yet one thing does remain the same – if the body of water has some wood, it'll probably hold some fish at some time.

Inexperienced anglers rarely consider crankbaits good lures in wood, yet, just like weeds, nothing could be farther from the truth. Even though crankbaits contain wood-hangin' treble hooks, they can be among the deadliest of all lures in wood for nearly every conceivable gamefish. The trick is knowing what style of crankbait to use in wood. Some crankbaits are designed specifically for use in wood, while others catch more wood than fish. On the same note, there are several things an angler can do, when fishing crankbaits in wood, to minimize snag-ups and maximize their fish-catching potential.

Let's first look into what makes a crankbait good for use in wooded cover. Disregarding the fish attracting qualities of any specific crankbait, the first thing to consider, when choosing a crankbait for fishing in and around wood, is the lure's ability to travel through a woody jungle without getting hung up. That is a very tall order. Few crankbaits can actually travel through woody brush without their hooks fouling. It takes a very special design, by some good lure engineers, for a crankbait with its dangling trebles to travel through wood.

The first prerequisite of a good wood crankbait is **buoyancy**. Sinking and suspender crankbaits are generally poor choices in woody environments. They travel in a straight, parallel-to-the-bottom, kind of way that exposes the trebles to hang-ups. Worse yet, once they do hang-up there's no buoyancy in the lure to back it out of the snag. Buoyancy serves a double purpose in a wood crankbait. It, first off, makes the lure travel in a nose-down/tail-up posture. This posture positions the lure's diving lip as a hook guard. The diving lip collides with most wood obstructions before the hooks do.

Joe Bucher has been crankin' wood for bass, walleyes, pike and muskies for nearly three decades. This old stringer shot features some big bass cranked off of a timbered flat from Toledo Bend Reservoir in east Texas.

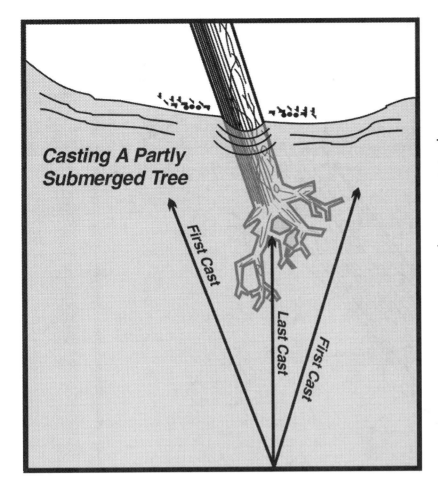

Casting A Partly Submerged Tree

First Cast

Last Cast

First Cast

It's best to test the outside edges of any brush or a fallen tree first, looking for the most active fish. Once you've thoroughly tested the outside edges, then make your final casts directly over the brush. It really doesn't make any difference which side you start from.

That's when the secondary advantage of buoyancy kicks in – its ability to back out of the cover that has collected at the diving lip. Without this feature, the lure would be hopelessly hung-up. The lure must have the built-in ability to back out of trouble. Buoyancy makes this possible. The more that buoyancy is accented in the tail portion of the lure, the better it will be at backing out of trouble spots.

Another positive feature of a good wood crankbait is a fat body shape. A fat body shape further protects the treble hooks, hanging underneath, from snags. In other words, the fat body shape acts like an additional built-in hook guard. This is especially important on the rise, as the lure backs out of a snag. When a lure is backing out, quite often it's going to encounter some additional branch work from a sunken tree. This is where the fat-bodied bait wards off a potential hang-up

allowing the lure to rise up freely without the hooks fouling. A thin-bodied crankbait provides no protection here, and usually gets hung up on the back out.

The best wood crankbait I've ever seen is a lure called "The Brush Baby" marketed by the Luhr Jensen Company primarily as a bass lure. The Brush Baby was designed by a friend of mine, Tom Seward. Tom took this fat body, hook-guarding concept a step farther by adding some additional built-in cams on the lure. These cams are uniquely positioned on the lure's body to protect the hooks even more during forward travel as well as when the lure is backing out of a woody snag. I can tell you from personal experience that these cams definitely work. The Brush Baby will travel through the thickest woody jungles imaginable without snagging. It also catches bass like crazy.

Once you've chosen a fat-bodied, buoyant

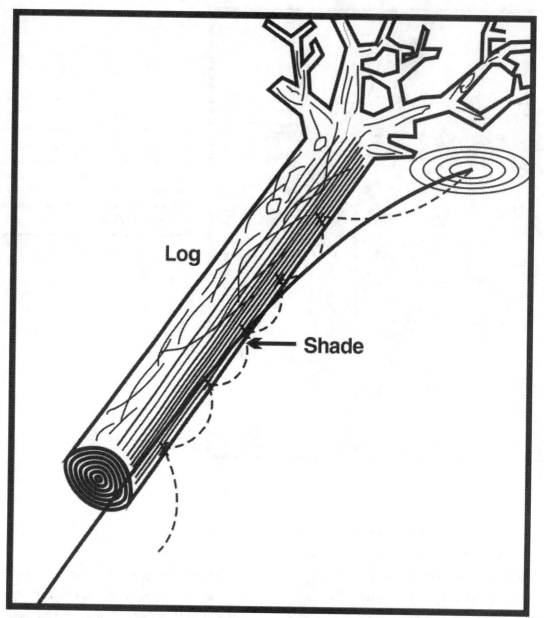

Whenever possible, it's best to fish a sunken horizontal log with a parallel cast. Take the time to line your boat up correctly, and then make two perfectly placed casts that run the crankbait down both sides.

crankbait for wood crankin', the next step is to match it up with the right tackle. Rarely is it wise to fish in wood with lightweight lines. A lightweight line will not hold up to the constant abrasion caused by the line rubbing along wood for hours. Lightweight lines, more often than not, also make a lure run too deep. But most of all, the lightweight line does not give you enough insurance when you need to horse a big fish away from the snag. This is an essential part of the whole wood crankin' process. Once a fish is hooked, it is imperative to muscle it out of the trouble spot as quickly as possible. This is not possible with light lines and, if things go well, large fish. What's the best overall line for wood? That really depends, but if the wood is thick, I wouldn't consider anything less than 20-pound if bass is your target. If it's muskies you're after, you'd be taking a big chance with anything less than 50-pound test.

I also like longer rods and baitcasting reels for wood crankin'. I like the additional accuracy and control of a baitcasting outfit for this situation, plus

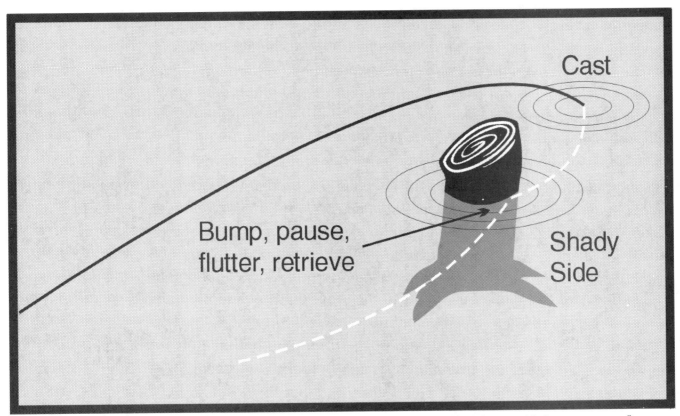

Cast

Bump, pause,
flutter, retrieve

Shady
Side

When looking for fish near a stump, cast beyond the target and try to bump it with your crankbait. Once you hit the stump, pause, flutter your crankbait and continue the retrieve.

baitcasting gear simply handles heavier line better. While I'm a big fan of spinning for a variety of situations, this is not one of them. In my opinion, spinning is the way to go with lines up to 10-pound test. After that, baitcasting is first-string.

Cast placement in wood is very much like a weed line situation in that a short, precise, probing cast is usually the best approach. Long casts in wood are rarely a good idea here, since you loose control over many factors. For one, a crankbait is likely to get hung up more on a long cast because of overall lack of feel and control. Secondly, your chances of landing a big fish in thick timber on a long cast are severely reduced. Therefore, short casts are the rule. In general, I like to search out submerged brush piles, and thicker clumps of wood with a series of short casts. Once I hit an underwater woody obstruction, I'll take a visual bearing of where that cast was placed, and then pepper the spot on both sides to thoroughly cover all sides of the woody tangle.

Of course, woody cover varies a great deal. Some wood such as sunken logs and standing timber are somewhat easier to fish than sunken brush. Single large trunk-like trees are easier to target and thoroughly fish without snag-ups than invisible, inconsistent brush. Whenever possible, I like to fish horizontal logs with a parallel cast. This involves nothing more than two perfectly placed casts made once you line your boat up correctly.

I approach standing timber and visible stumps much in the same way. The only difference here will probably be in the depth, and therefore the lure choice might vary a bit. Stumps are usually shallow-water wood cover, while standing timber could be in a variety of depths including really deep water. However, the crankin' goal on both spots is to run the lure on both sides of the trunk so close that it collides. With stumps, the exposed root sections are often the key holding area when the fish aren't as active. Of course, this means running a crankbait right into the root area with a bump

Stump fields can hold walleyes bass, pike and muskies. Crankbaits are one of the best to use in these areas. Make certain you cast both sides of every stump. Pay attention to the lead stump _ the one that first catches incoming waves. That's where the most active fish hang out.

& rise retrieve.

When fish are really active in stump fields, a high-riding crankbait such as a floating Rapala or similar minnow style, will likely take more fish than anything. One of the best walleye patterns my dad and I ever found for late May and early June walleyes was casting stump fields with Rapalas during low light. You didn't need to "bump the stump" with these baits since the fish were usually very active. All you needed to do was fish these spots carefully, making a soft cast with spinning gear. It was always a real experience trying to muscle larger fish of 25 inches or more from the middle of one of these stump fields with 8-pound test and spinning gear, but we won more battles than we lost.

Whenever fish are in standing timber with deeper water, they have a tendency to suspend alongside the trunk at a preferred depth level. The only way to know what that ideal depth level is for sure is to experiment with a variety of crankbaits that run at different depths.

However, running the crankbait into the trunk is still a key triggering mechanism when the fish are less active. The closer you can get to cover, the more chance you have of triggering less active fish no matter what the species. Standing timber is no exception.

Man-made fish cribs are one of the easiest of all woody structures to fish. In the first place, they're usually placed on lakes with a lack of natural cover. This makes them isolated targets, which eliminates a lot of dead water while you search for fish. The whole key with cribs is finding them. In clear water, you can often see them with a good pair of polarized sunglasses. Then it's just a matter of fan-casting the crib. When you can't see the crib, you'll need to make several more exploratory casts in an effort to locate the crib. Once you hit the crib, again take an approximate visual bearing from that cast and pepper both sides of that line until you're sure you've covered it well.

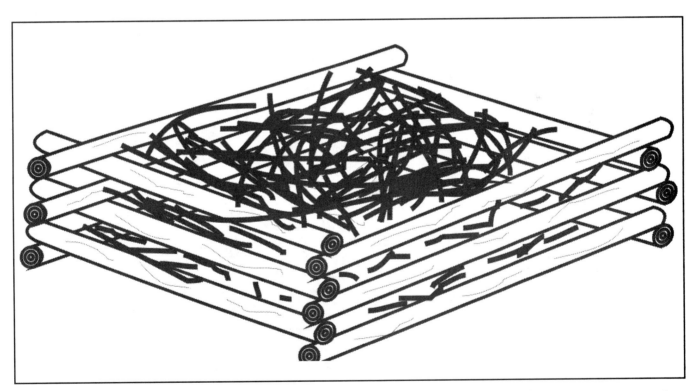

Man-made fish cribs can be outstanding fish magnets on sterile lakes that lack natural cover such as weeds. The best cribs have been sunk along deep breaklines, and are best found using a deep-diving crankbait.

By the way, man-made fish cribs have coughed up some really big fish for me over the years. This includes big smallies, lunker walleyes, and trophy muskies. In fact, rarely does an October go by that I don't catch at least one braggin'-sized musky from a fish crib on one of my favorite local lakes. One recent fall while testing some of the first "classic Pikey" colors of our new DepthRaider, I had a barrage of big crib muskies including a 30-pounder while fishing with my good friend and noted guide Lunker Lou Eich. What's important to note here is that we had already fished these same cribs for days with a variety of conventional shallow-running musky lures to no avail. It was only when I ran that DepthRaider right into the crib, feeling it tick and bounce across various parts of the loggy structure, that any hits would occur.

The most difficult woody cover to fish with a crankbait is dense sunken brush that's inconsistent in depth. My first approach in this situation is to try some shallow cranks in an effort to catch "high riders" which are active fish suspending over the top of the highest portions of the brush. Once this pattern is burned out, or if it doesn't work in the first place, I'll then go to deeper divers that drive the lure much closer to the dense stuff. However, it's important to choose the lure carefully or you'll most surely get hung up a lot and loose a bunch of baits. Keep your casts short, and use a very buoyant, fat-bodied bait. You might also want to employ one of the many good lure-retrieving devices available through catalogs, just in case.

I first perfected this style of fishing back in the late 1970s when I made annual winter treks to the

Horizontal submerged logs like this one are easily fished with two parallel casts using a quality floating diver.

famous southern bass reservoir Toledo Bend, which sits on the Texas/Louisiana border. Anyone who's fished Toledo Bend knows there's no shortage of timber anywhere in this place. My southern bassin' buddy of those days, Burt Cox, and I spent several years deciphering where the big bass staged early in the pre-spawn period before moving into coves. Eventually we discovered a dense brushy flat with scattered standing timber in it. Most of this flat had a depth of 5 to 7 feet; perfect for crankbaits. We lost plenty of lures in the brushy underwater brambles until we perfected our technique. But once we mastered it, man did we catch a bunch of bass from that spot. Most were in the 4- to 6-pound range. Short casts, 14- pound test, and fat-bodied, balsa crankbaits did the job time and time again.

Hopefully, after reading this chapter, you'll feel more inclined to try crankbaits in various woody situations. As you can see now, crankbaits are often the bait of choice for wood fishing, but everything has to be matched up perfectly. The right style of crankbait is the first part of the equation. Don't forget how important buoyancy becomes when the cover gets dense. Without buoyancy, you're going to get hung up a lot more often. But either way, you're going to have to invest in a lure retriever if you're going to spend any amount of time fishing around wood. Otherwise, you'll probably have to buy some stock in a lure company!

Walleyes provide some of the best fishing year-round. Once thought to be strictly a finesse fish, walleyes are often caught on a variety of crankbaits in the spring, summer and fall. One of the best ways to tag walleyes hugging woody cover is with crankbaits. Open-water walleyes are more easily taken on crankbaits than any other presentation.

chapter 14

Bottom Bouncing Crankbaits

Barely 40 feet of line registered on my line counter reel when I felt the straight model DepthRaider begin to tick hard bottom at 12 feet. Immediately, I engaged my reel and began a trolling pass along one of my favorite rock walls. Keeping my boat as tight to the wall as safely possible, I tried to follow the rock wall's contour toward the large prominent point ahead. Adding a bit of a challenge to this whole situation was a strong wind pounding large waves inward.

I was a bit concerned with going too fast, especially since it was late October with water temperatures in the low 40s, but I had to gun my 60-horsepower Mercury in order to avoid crashing the boat into the rock wall. This made the firetiger DepthRaider vibrate my rod tip like a jack hammer as it cleared the high spot in the rocks. Temporarily, I lost interest on the crankbait's performance as I instead turned my focus to revving the outboard and steering the boat clear of the rock wall. All the while gripping tightly to my rod.

It was a good thing that I was indeed "gripping tightly" since the rod was nearly ripped from my grip with an explosive strike that doubled my 8 ½-foot rod,

making the reel's drag scream out line. Feeling excited, but at the same time a bit helpless, I simply held on to the rod and continued steering the boat clear of the dangerous rocks and pounding waves. The big fish bulldogged deep and continued to pull line as it performed a series of heavy head thrashes that shook every inch of the rod. My only option was to keep pulling the fish out away from the rock wall until it was in open water for safe landing.

Eventually I accomplished just that – and had a chance to enjoy the final portion of this battle uninhibited by the torque of the outboard, but still plagued by the strong waves and high winds. This made it difficult to net the wildly aggressive cold-water musky, but nonetheless, I eventually got the job done. After a few quick photos for my scrapbook, I released the fat 46-incher. It was the first of four nice muskies that would fall victim to this incredibly effective tactic on that late October day.

This was yet another page in the very successful book of bottom-bouncing with crankbaits. The technique has its roots with me sometime back in the late

1960s. It was then I began reading about the legendary Buck Perry and his success with bottom-bounce trolling. It didn't take me long to start testing some of Buck's bottom-bouncing principles on the bass in our local lakes. My early successes spawned a new way of fishing, giving me a whole new perspective on the underwater topography of my lake, and a whole new understanding of how to make lures run at the right depths.

I credit Buck Perry for many of my successes since it was initially his knowledge that opened my eyes to how fish relate to the bottom. It was Buck Perry who initially coined most of the structure fishing terminology that we now consider standard. It was also Buck Perry who pioneered many of the bottom-bouncing concepts that are used by hundreds of anglers today. His original book on "Spoon Plugging" described in detail

the steps needed to make crankbaits run to the desired depth, and how to effectively fish them over a variety of bottoms. In fact, Buck Perry even coined the term "bottom bouncing".

In my opinion, it's important to note Buck Perry's contributions to the entire sport. He was the first to describe "structure" and helped anglers understand how fish relate to it. He developed tactics for crankbait trolling and casting. He was the first to decipher how much the depth of crankbaits varied with the amount of line out and the diameter of the line used. He was the first to recognize the importance of controlling depth as well as controlling speed. He was, indeed, the grand master of bottom bouncing, structure fishing, and trolling.

Incidentally, the term "bottom bouncing" does not apply strictly to trolling and should never be intended in

Ron Miller, left, and Joe Bucher have taken some of their biggest fish bouncing hard bottom with deep diving crankbaits. This is particularly true during the cold water months.

this way. Whether an angler casts or trolls a crankbait over a spot strictly depends upon the situation at hand. In general, casting works best over depths of less than 12 feet with bottom topographies that contain a lot of trashy cover such as weeds or wood. Trolling excels in most deeper-water applications including bouncing across clean, hard bottom areas. I suggest you take the time to understand the limitations and applications of both casting and trolling crankbaits over hard bottoms, and then make it your goal to master both techniques. The technique of bottom-bouncing, either in a casting or trolling application, is truly one of the best ways to improve your angling skills and learn the water more intimately. The knowledge you'll obtain from even one day of serious bottom-bouncing is sure to pay big dividends down the road.

I've always placed a high degree of emphasis on making a crankbait collide with something. It matters little whether this "something" is weeds, wood, rocks, gravel, sand or silt, but keep hitting stuff until fish contact is made. Once a fish is caught off a specific type of cover or from over particular type of bottom substrate, more emphasis should then be placed on making your crankbait collide with that cover or bottom type as much as possible. This philosophy of constantly trying to run the crankbait into things has worked very well for me, as well as most of the other well-known crankbait specialists in this country. My braggin' board of big fish taken by bouncing baits across the bottom includes hundreds of big bass, several giant pike, a load

Buck Perry pioneered bottom bouncing as well as coining most of the structure fishing terminology that we now consider standard dialog. Buck was the first angler to describe "structure" and how fish relate to it. He was also the first to decipher how much the depth of crankbaits varied with the amount of line out and the diameter of the line used.

of trophy walleyes, and some of my largest muskies. Needless to say, this has been one fantastic tactic for me.

I know I've been a bit emphatic about knowing the limits of your lures and the tackle you're using, but it truly is essential and it plays right into being effective at bottom-bouncing, as well as any other crankbait tactic. You simply must know what it takes to make a certain lure run a specific depth in order to bounce the bottom. In a basic sense, this first means choosing the right lure and tackle combination for each situation. That's why it's also important to have a variety of crankbaits as well as several outfits for bottom-bouncing. In particular, you should realize that casting tackle varies somewhat from trolling setups for this tactic.

My favorite tackle setup for serious bottom-bounce casting also varies a bit with the species, but for the most part it's an extra-long medium to medium-light action baitcasting rod, a quality baitcasting reel with a semi-slow gear ratio of 4 to 1, and a responsive low-stretch line. The diameter will vary depending on how deep I need the crankbait to run. I like the longer rod for bombing baits a long distance, which is usually a key part of this technique. The long rod also helps me keep big fish hooked on crankbaits that hit from long distances or great depths. But most of all, I like the longer rod for this style of fishing because it substantially lowers the pivot point from which your retrieve begins. In other words, your rod tip will be at a much lower position with a longer rod than with a short one. This adds more running depth to the lure.

Trolling is the most effective way to bounce across the bottom at depths of 12 feet or more. The whole key to successful bottom-bounce trolling involves precision boat control utilizing information provided by your sonar unit as well as the deep diver.

Spence Petros (pictured) landed this big autumn musky by trolling a crankbait quickly along a deep hard bottom.

Ideally, when I approach a hard-bottom area I want to cast, I like to have a floating marker buoy out on the spot as a reference. Then, I'll initiate a fancasting procedure that thoroughly probes the entire surrounding area. The basic system on each cast goes something like this: First, make a long cast in a specific direction noting where the lure lands in reference to the marker so you can adjust your cast placement on the next pitch. Next, point your rod tip low and begin cranking hard in order to drive the lure quickly toward the bottom. Once the lure hits bottom, immediately back off on the retrieve speed. The ideal speed is one that allows the lure to continue to tick bottom, but under a slower, controlled speed.

The slower, controlled speed usually results in far less snags than a faster one. Excessively high-speed bottom-bouncing tends to jam a lure in rock crevices or under logs and brush. It doesn't allow the lure a chance to back itself out of any snag before it's driven hopelessly head-on into it. Too much speed on a bottom-bouncing crankbait has the same effect as an automobile that's driven too fast on a narrow winding road with heavily wooded surroundings. There's simply no room for error and not enough recovery time. Understanding a "controlled speed" is critical.

This doesn't necessarily mean "slow" as much as it means "controlled." The right speed enables the angler to control the bump and rise action of the lure better as it careens off of various obstructions. Far less crevice jamming occurs as a result. This slightly slower bottom-bouncing approach usually triggers more strikes, as well. Perhaps excessive speeds here are simply unnecessary as a triggering mechanism when the lure is bouncing and ticking the bottom. In any case, the fish definitely has more time to check out the bait when it's traveling slowly.

Concentrating on crankbait vibration is always an essential part of this tactic, too. The best crankbait fishermen I know constantly study the "vibe" of their lure as it walks along bottom. That optimum vibe is a feel that experienced anglers develop as they study their rod tip and sense the characteristic vibration of that individual crankbait. If it appears to have lost its vibe it probably has collected a few "clinger" weeds, leaves, sticks, or some other bottom debris around the diving lip area. Simply letting the bait float up a bit with a touch of slack line followed by a sharp rip forward on the rod tip usually cleans the bait and returns that vibe.

Always allow the bait a chance to back out of the debris on its own, and follow it up with a rip. This not only cleans your lure, which prevents any wasted casts, but also often triggers a strike. In fact, you'll find that the majority of your strikes occur either when the lure is ticking bottom or when you're ripping it to clean it. A good number of strikes also seem to occur just as the lure clears bottom, and starts traveling over a deeper section of open water. Very few strikes will occur when the lure is freely traveling over open water.

Preferred length of cast for different styles of crankbait fishing obviously varies a lot. As you know by now through reading previous chapters, I'm generally in favor of a shorter cast whenever there's cover present such as weeds or wood. The heavier the cover, the shorter the cast. On the other hand, I usually prefer a longer cast over clean, hard-bottom areas. This is especially true when the hard-bottom area is situated in deeper water, and the water is ultra-clear. As much as I have emphasized the short cast for many crankin' applications, the long cast is usually the way to go when bottom-bouncing clean, hard substrates.

The same could also be said about the importance of a long cast in establishing contact with the bottom. Short casts with most deep-divers simply do not allow the lure to reach maximum depth. The deeper the hard bottom area that you're attempting to fish, the more important the long cast becomes. In fact, if you want to bounce across the bottom at depths of 8 feet or more with a crankbait, a long cast becomes essential. So does a thin line and a large-billed diver.

Your choice of crankbait for bottom-bouncing is often essential. While both sinking, suspending, and floating crankbaits can be used to bounce the bottom, I still prefer the floating diver for this style of fishing whenever its feasible. The floating diver, traveling with its tail up and its nose down, bounces over various bottoms almost effortlessly with a minimum of hangups. The diving lip on a floating diver receives the majority of the contact and abuse. The diving lip also collects the majority of any bottom trash when a floating diver is used. The buoyant nature of the floating diver then becomes a major asset in releasing the debris, by simply releasing line tension allowing the lure to rise up a bit. This suggested choice of a floating deep-diver for bottom-bouncing is steadfast whether it's casting or trolling.

I'm a particularly big fan of large triangular-shaped lips on crankbaits for bottom bouncing. This fanfare has been developed through more than 20 years of fishing various models and styles of crankbaits. To say "I've tried 'em all" would be an understatement. I still continue to "try 'em all." But, by and large, floating divers with a large triangular lip get my vote time and time again. They're simply superior for this style of fishing. On top of that, I also like straight model floaters over jointed versions for this style of fishing, especially when the bottom contains large, jagged and broken rock. The straight model floater has far less ten-

A floating marker buoy helps you locate hard-to-find deep hard-bottom spots so you can thoroughly scour the area with crankbaits.

dency to wedge in between rocks and crevices, and its superior buoyancy allows it to back out of any such trouble spots.

To me, trolling the bottom is both a science and an art form. It is truly one of the top techniques in all of fishing because it is so effective at covering depths as well as teaching the angler about the lake's topography. On top of that, it accomplishes both of these tasks with speed. Few other methods can rival its efficiency as a total package. Plainly put, if you want to really learn water and fish at depths beneath the norm, then take the time to master bottom-bounce trolling. It's a truly awesome technique.

While your favorite casting outfit will suffice as a trolling setup, The ultimate rod & reel combination for bottom-bounce trolling is an extra-long rod of at least 8 feet, coupled with a metered line-counter reel. The extra-long rod has many trolling advantages. For one, it is far more forgiving on the strike, absorbing the power of a violent short line hit

without fear of breaking a line or bending out hooks.

Longer rods are also superior for manipulating a lure through snags. I always like to point my rod high, near the 12 o'clock position, when trolling. This makes the rod tip transmit every vibration in that crankbait as well as let me know when it is making bottom contact. With the high rod, I can quickly drop the rod tip down

Large triangular shaped diving lips on crankbaits are outstanding for bottom-bouncing. This lip configuration enables the lure to careen left or right of an obstruction, and keep its action intact. The author's good friend Tom Gelb poses with a mega-musky taken bouncing a hard rock bottom lip off an island.

to nine o'clock whenever a snag is encountered. Providing this quick slack line gives the lure a chance to back itself out of the snag.

I also like the way a long rod fights big fish. I can easily steer a big fish clear of dangerous line-cutting edges around the boat. The long rod also keeps such a deep bend during battle, it makes it nearly impossible for a big fish to tear out hooks and shake loose. You'll lose a lot less fish with the longer rod; especially if it has a parabolic action.

The metered line-counter reel is also a superb trolling tool. As we already know, line distance from rod tip to crankbait can greatly influence running depth. With a metered line-counter reel you can easily make adjustments on the length of line you have released to

hit precise depths. As you feed line out in 5 to 10 foot increments, watch your rod tip respond. As soon as the crankbait starts to tick bottom note the depth number on your line-counter. It's even more important to make certain to note that depth number, when a fish hits. This makes it easy to get that lure right back to precisely the right depth again.

Having the metered reel also enables you to quickly adjust the running depth of your crankbait as you troll over various bottom depths. This can really come in handy any time a big fish mark appears on your sonar unit over a deeper piece of structure. I have taken advantage of this on many occasions and it has paid off a lot. For example, just this past fall, my friend Tom Gelb and I were trolling over a newly discovered deep

Straight model floaters are my favorites for bottom-bouncing while trolling. They hang up a lot less than any other style of crankbait and hook bigger fish extremely well.

hard bottom hole that was situated in a shallow narrows. It contained a massive school of baitfish. As we passed over the deepest section of the hole, a big hook suddenly appeared on the sonar over a boulder. Tom yelled "big fish at 28 feet – right over that rock!" I quickly pulled off another 20 feet of line from my metered reel in order to drive that DepthRaider right to that precise depth. A few moments later, I felt the crankbait hit the rock and within seconds I had a tremendous strike and a fantastic battle ensued. A few minutes later our first musky of the day was posing for photographs before being released.

Knowing how much line you have out is, of course, essential in coordinating correct running depth. Without the knowledge of line length, the whole process becomes guesswork. If you don't own a line-counter reel, you can accomplish the same thing by stripping line off your reel in two foot increments or by simply counting level-wind passes. Marking the productive line length with a permanent magic marker somewhere near the reel is also a good idea. This makes it a "no brainer" to set out the precise amount of line again, and get your lure right back into the hot fish zone.

Anyone who's spent anytime trolling like this knows it takes a great deal of concentration. You not only need to worry about precision boat control, but you also need to be in constant study of your lure. While trolling open water admittedly can be monotonous, bottom bouncing is never boring. It simply takes too much concentration and effort. Working the boat correctly is only one part of the equation. Making sure your lure is performing properly at all times is yet another. This is precision trolling in every sense. It is a fish-catching system that began with the legendary Buck Perry, yet is only practiced by a select few today. If you truly want to learn more about the underwater topography in your favorite lakes, plus catch more big fish from deep water, take the time to master deep bottom-bouncing. It's one deadly way to catch big fish.

chapter 15

Open-Water Trolling

I had just finished attaching an in-line planer board to the last of six trolling rigs, when my partner Tom Keenan barked "Joe, fish on!" I quickly jammed the newly rigged rod into a rod holder, and grabbed the steering wheel so Tom could go for the rod containing the sinking planer board. I was just getting the boat pointed in a safe, open-water direction when Tom yelled again "Oh my gosh Joe, we've got three more boards down! Start grabbing rods."

My first inclination was that we had run up on a reef and the crankbaits were all snagged on rocks, but a quick glance at the sonar along with my general knowl-edge of the lake told me that no reefs were in our path. The four bending rods all had fish on. The dilemma we both now faced was which rod to grab?

We finally decided to simply keep the motor in gear and drag the hooked fish along while we attended to each line as quickly as possible. It took nearly 15 minutes for Tom and I to crank in the four hooked fish, but when finished, four fat walleyes from 18 to 25 inches were swimming in the livewell. It took at least 15 to 20 minutes more to reset the rigs, but just as

quickly, they started to go off again. By the day's end, Tom and I had caught over 50 walleyes, seven northern pike, and three smallmouths. All of these fish were taken during the hot, flat, dog days of mid-July with water skiers and jet boats buzzing us from every direction. Needless to say, open-water trolling with crankbaits unlocked the mystery of suspended fish once again.

I was exceptionally pleased to have captured this entire escapade on film for one of my television episodes. Afterwards, I had hundreds of letters, phone calls and e-mail about this amazing system. No doubt, this subject really hit home with a bunch of frustrated dog day anglers. Most of these interested inquirers had no idea that these fish could be taken so easily in the open-water. But the simple truth is just that: It is easy, once you know how to do it.

This story is but one example of how deadly open-water trolling with crankbaits can be on sus-pended gamefish. To put it bluntly, this tactic is nothing short of amazing, and virtually has no equal when fish are cruising off the bottom. The trick is in first finding the fish in open-water, and then have a basic knowledge of how to get lures effectively to them. Some anglers might think such a system is simply too complicated to master, yet quite the opposite is true. Once you've spent a few hours practicing this technique, I'm certain you'll be amazed at how easy and effective it is.

The basic components of open-water trolling include the following: 1) a wide selection of crankbaits in all sizes, shapes, colors, and models, 2) at least four to six small in-line planer boards, 3) at least four to six trolling rod and reel outfits, 4) a boat rigged properly for trolling including such basic necessities as rod holders and a quality sonar unit. I generally carry every crankbait I own in my boat when trolling with planer boards. When state regulations allow you to troll more than one line, you can try a wide variety of plugs in order to establish a pattern. In almost every case, you're going to be surprised at how selective these fish can be

in terms of specific lure actions and certain color preferences.

Of course, the other components needed for successful open-water trolling is a basic knowledge of: 1) the species your after, 2) the water you're fishing, and 3) potentially where the fish are located. It's initially important to understand and accept that nearly every freshwater gamefish spends some time suspended over open-water – off the bottom, not on any type of structure. This includes largemouths, smallmouths, northern pike, walleyes, and even the mighty musky. It also includes all members of the trout and salmon family – lakers, cohos, browns, brookies, kings, etc. All of these gamefish are sure to suspend to some degree. Some will suspend more than others depending upon a number of factors. I've caught all these species in great numbers over open-water at various times of the year. It's also worth noting that any one of the species

Some of the essential components of open-water trolling would include a selection of crankbaits along with a planer board or two.

mentioned may suspend more on certain bodies of water.

What makes gamefish suspend is certainly open to debate, but I speculate that most of this suspending behavior is related to following schools of baitfish and other forages. Recent radio telemetry studies on walleyes, trout and muskies also suggests that all gamefish suspend over specific sections of open-water perhaps for another reason – it might be their summer home. In other words, they know exactly where they are even though they're not relating to any recognizable structure or other underwater signposts. They simply know where their summer home is and instinctively head for these spots at certain times of the year. Almost without fail, these fish end up in these same spots at the same times year after year.

The depth these fish suspend at is another very important factor, and a study all in itself. What I've found is the productive depth varies somewhat with the species. For example, cold-water species such as trout or salmon invariably suspend at much greater depths than do walleyes or largemouths. Individual species of trout will often be separated further by specific depths according to temperature and light preferences. Lake trout will normally suspend far deeper than brown trout. Warm-water species that exist in the same body of water will be far above these trout species under most circumstances, usually just above a lake's thermocline.

Admittedly, I spend most of my time chasing suspended walleyes and muskies, but in the process I "accidentally" catch lots of pike and bass, too. One of my true fishing passions has been to study the open-water walleye and musky in depth in order to understand them more. In the process, I've become quite

Big fish will sometimes suspend over small, isolated deep holes in shallower lakes. This is particularly true in the fall. The author poses with a 36-pound musky taken while row-trolling a crankbait 18 feet down over 38 feet of water.

proficient at catching them under these conditions. What I've found quite often is that walleyes and muskies suspend regularly at the same depths and in the same areas. Again, I speculate that the two must be closely related in the food chain. In some cases, muskies may be following the walleye as a food source, but more often I believe they are both chasing another forage such as perch, shad or ciscoes. Their paths simply intersect.

My general approach at finding open-water suspended fish such as walleyes and muskies depends upon the season. In the summertime, I've found both species, along with bass and pike, to be over large mid-depth flats with deep-topping rock and gravel humps nearby. The depth of these "mid-depth flats" varies quite a bit between different lakes. On one lake, the majority of deep open flats might be only 20 feet or so, while it could be 40 to 50 feet on the lake next door. Both may have equal populations of suspended fish. It's only the depth that varies.

Late fall fish suspend in spots that vary much more. Shallow flats might still be good, but isolated deep holes can sometimes

be super magnets for big fish; in particular monster muskies. I've often found that scattered schools of walleyes, perch, and muskies will suspend across a large mid-depth flat in the summer and then migrate

Several manufacturers are now making excellent in-line planer boards for open-water trolling. Off Shore Tackle's planer board is the author's personal favorite.

The in-line planer board is the key component in open-water trolling a group of crankbaits. The main function of a planer board is increased water coverage. The planer board forces your lures off to the side of the boat providing a large swath during a typical trolling pass.

toward these small, deep, isolated holes just before ice-up. As you can imagine, when they get in these smaller isolated holes, they really school tightly making them rather easy to catch once you find 'em. However, the depth at which fall fish suspend is far less predictable since there is no thermocline at this time. Quite often these fish will remain at the same summer depths relating to what I call an "imaginary thermocline." In this instance, I theorize that the fish in each given lake have gotten so used suspending at a certain depth and so familiar with it because of the lake's consistent thermocline that they use this depth level no matter what. However, there are times when late fall fish will hold below that imaginary thermocline level, so don't hold this rule as gospel.

The general trick here is to troll these suspected spots thoroughly with a bunch of lines set at various depths watching your sonar closely for signs of fish activity. Note the depth of the marks closely. These markings are indicators of how deep you should set

your lines. For example, if I'm seeing a lot of hooks on my sonar at the 18- to 22-foot level, I'll make sure I'm setting the majority of my crankbaits to run at this depth. Usually, this system of depth searching works.

Of course, as we learned from earlier discussions on the running depth of crankbaits, you can control the depth of your lures by: 1) changing the length of line out, 2) changing the diameter of the line you're using, and 3) changing the speed you're traveling. That's why it's important to know how deep your favorite lures travel and keep a detailed log on these facts. Also, it's a good idea to make notes on how much line you had out along with the line diameter and speed when you score on a fish or two. Duplicating this is the ultimate key to bagging numbers of fish on a consistent basis. Obviously, remembering all of these numbers is tough. That's why I keep a little notebook aboard so these things are easy to duplicate on future outings.

Metered line-counter style reels are no doubt a big help for this style of fishing. This makes it very easy

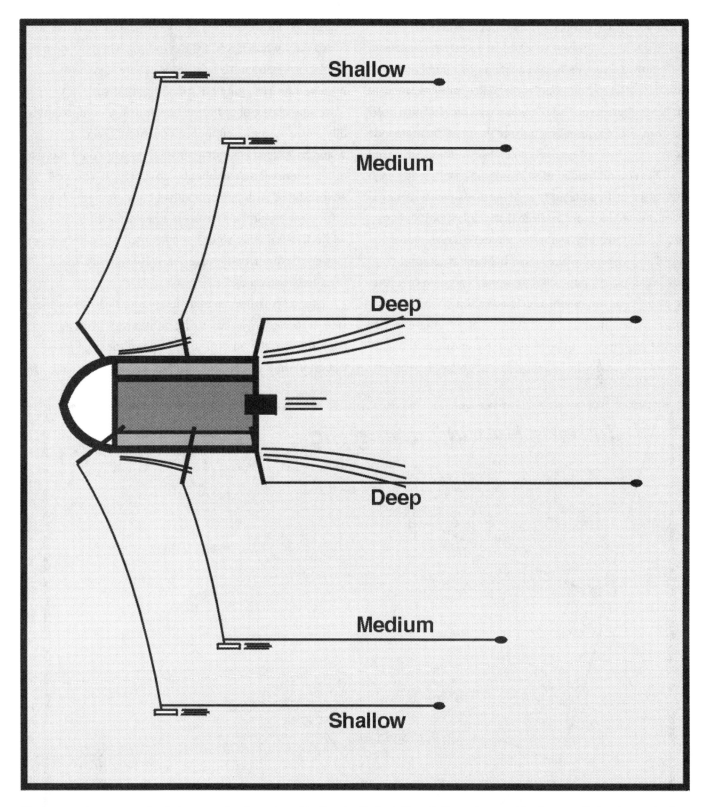

Shallow

Medium

Deep

Deep

Medium

Shallow

Maximum water coverage is what open-water planer-board trolling is all about. Essentially, you're searching for a needle in a haystack when attempting to find open water suspended fish. The increased coverage provided by planer boards makes finding open-water fish easier.

to accurately set and reset lines to precise depths. When you're dealing with four to six rods, and the prospects of rigging and re-rigging after catching a number of fish, the metered line-counter reel takes away many of the headaches. Even though you could successfully troll the open-water without metered reels, I still recommend them.

Several manufacturers are now making great, innovative in-line planer boards for this style of fishing. As of this writing, my favorite is the Off-Shore Planer Board. They feature a snap-on clip design and a large flag. The large flag makes these boards easy to find if they break free in large choppy water. The snap-on clips are also so easy to attach and detach from your line. This is a great improvement over the older wing-nut, screw-tight models. Incidentally, I prefer to attach these planer boards steadfast so they will not break free after

a strike or during battle. Ideally, I like to detach the board only when it reaches the rod tip. Then the board can be dropped on the boat floor, where it is easily retrieved for rerigging after landing the fish.

The planer board is the absolute key component in this entire system. Without it, you simply can't get the water coverage. That, in a nutshell, is what the function of a planer board is all about – coverage. If you've never trolled with planer boards before, imagine how difficult it would be to troll six lines off your boat without them. How would you keep all these lines from tangling? How would you effectively separate these lines to get coverage?

Once you drop an attached planer board over the side, it immediately travels laterally away from the boat, moving the lure off to the side of the boat path. The more line you let out, the farther off to the side, the

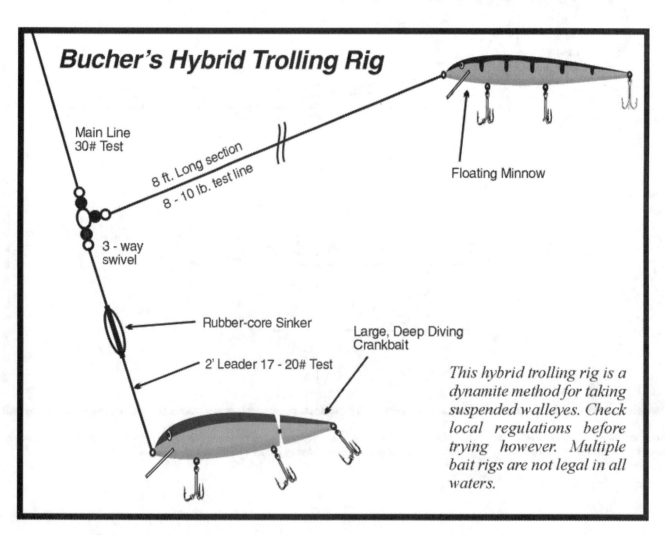

Bucher's Hybrid Trolling Rig

Main Line
30# Test

8 ft. Long section
8 - 10 lb. test line

3 - way
swivel

Floating Minnow

Rubber-core Sinker

2' Leader 17 - 20# Test

Large, Deep Diving
Crankbait

This hybrid trolling rig is a dynamite method for taking suspended walleyes. Check local regulations before trying however. Multiple bait rigs are not legal in all waters.

planer board carries your lure. By adjusting the amount of line from the rod tip to planer board, an experienced planer board troller could easily separate three to four lines on each side of the boat with no tangling problems. The distance between your farthest planer board on the left versus the right side of your setup could be as much as 100 feet. In other words, instead of covering the open-water with a narrow eight to ten foot slice, you'll comb through it with a huge wingspan and multiple lures. The difference in your success rate, because of this increased coverage, will be significant.

A quality sonar unit is the most underrated part of the open-water trolling system. While I'm a big advocate of the traditional flasher style sonar units for many casting applications, I'm convinced that the newer LCR (liquid crystal recorder) sonar units are better for open-water trolling. Having fish markings displayed on a large LCR screen provides the angler with easy-to-comprehend information that can be quickly used and reacted to. These units have the technology and power to read thermoclines and spot various fish holding on and off the bottom no matter what the terrain. This information is exactly what you need in order to set your lines correctly. Without good sonar equipment, a lot more guesswork is involved.

Another feature that I really use on newer computerized sonar equipment is the GPS and "plotter"

features. GPS, of course, is an abbreviation for Global Positioning Satellite Systems. If your sonar has an installed GPS system, you can quickly mark the exact position of a suspended fish with the touch of a button when a strike occurs. Within a split second or two, the sonar's GPS will lock onto a satellite, triangulate your

Professional walleye angler Ted Takasaki has done exceptionally well on the tournament trail using crankbaits. Ted leans heavily on crankbaits when he's after open-water suspended fish.

Big smallmouths are some of the easiest gamefish to catch with crankbaits. This lunker fell to a small crankbait trolled over open water in search of walleyes.

position and record it in your GPS log. Since these GPS systems are usually accurate to within 50 feet or so any place on earth, you have a very accurate marks as to where the suspended fish are hanging out. Returning to this spot for follow-up trolling passes is then possible.

The "plotter" feature on many of today's good sonar systems enables the open-water angler to retrace the productive trolling pass, as well. In other words, the GPS system is also recording the trolling path of your boat constantly. When you graph a fish and mark its position on your GPS, you can then retrace that trolling pass directly over the same spot again. This not only gives you a solid reference point, but also the exact travel path the lure took before the strike. When suspended fish are selective about the directional path of a

lure, the plotter can save the day, and really increase your catches. And believe it or not, there are those times when fish want the lure passing them in a specific direction.

More often than not, I've found that downwind passes are most effective, but there are those times when it's just the opposite. I theorize that strong winds make fish face into the increased current. Lures that cross their path in this manner are more quickly seen and identified, and the fish are positioned to ambush prey better from this angle. Of course, when fish are really turned on, factors such as trolling path direction are not as critical. Then it's only a matter of getting a lure over the fish. This is particularly true on flat calm days with no wind at all. The lack of underwater

Large metal-lipped crankbaits like this old Hellbender produce a maximum dive with the tightest possible wiggle action. They are great choices for clear water, hard bottom and any place where great depths need to be attained.

current means the fish could be facing in any direction during flat, calm conditions.

Whenever you get a strike while trolling with multiple-line planer board sets, the best battle approach is to haul in all fish from directly behind the outboard to avoid tangles. What generally happens after a strike is the angled line containing a planer board and crankbait is pulled backward with the drag of a heavy fish. This pulls the angle out of the line eventually forcing it almost directly in back of the boat. Also, after a fish grabs your lure, it is forced upward towards the water's surface as the boat drags it along. This automatically pulls the fish out of tangle trouble from the other lines. So, no matter what planer board goes off (with a strike), rarely do you get fouled in other lines.

When it's time to reset a planer board/crankbait rig, the same principle applies. First move the other two rods on the side you're going to reset (already in rod holders with planer boards set and running) up to alternate rod holders and let out some more line on each in order to move these boards outward some more. Then simply zero out your line counter reel, drop the crankbait over the side directly in back of the boat (in the prop wash area of the outboard) and feed out line while watching your line-counter meter register. When the reel's line meter hits the magic number stop, reattach the planer board, and then drop it directly over the side in the same prop wash area again. Feed line out freely until the planer board is way out. Then engage the reel and place the rod in the lower inside rod holder.

With this reset system, there is rarely a tangle since the lines never actually cross over each other except during a fish battle. Tangles occur when this system is not followed. Tangles also occur occasionally when a bigger fish has the power to remain deep and cross laterally during the fight. This happens most often with big salmon, larger pike, and lunker muskies. These fish mess with the best-laid trolling plans, but are worth the trouble, for sure.

Planer board trolling works best over open-water for any suspended gamefish, but it should be noted that also has some valid shallow-water applications, as well. I've had great success trolling shorelines for walleyes with floating minnow baits off planer boards. Increased coverage is again the advantage here, along with keeping a lure off to the side of the boat's path. Whenever shallow shoreline fish appear to be spooky, especially in any clear-water situation, trolling a lure off of a planer board is the answer. It keeps the boat away from the shoreline while the lure travels over the target area.

When bottoms are relatively clean and snag free, you can get away with trolling crankbaits off planer boards, but admittedly, the technique takes some guts. I've had great success with smallmouths, walleyes and big muskies trolling over clusters of mid-lake humps with this system on occasions, but I've also had lots of troubles with it. The majority of the time you're actually running the bait over open-water between these humps, but occasionally, you're bumping bottom with any number of the board lines. The big fear is hanging up. Hang up a line off a planer board setup and all you can do is helplessly watch it drag back until the hooks either pull out or the line breaks. Stopping or turning in order to free up the snagged lure usually results in a total disaster with multiple tangled lines or even worse, multiple lines hung up on the reef.

If you're going to use planer boards for any amount of trolling over clusters of reefs that contain some serious snags, it's a good idea to set the lines to run shallow so you just tick the tops of the shallowest cropping humps. Minimizing the amount of time your crankbaits are bouncing across or plowing bottom is sure to reduce snags. It's also a good idea to bring along a large supply of your favorite crankbaits when attempting this kind of trolling tactic. Accept the fact that you're going to

Lake trout can be readily caught on crankbaits over open water. This dandy fell for a deep-diver trolled off a planer board along a deep rocky shoreline in early spring.

loose some lures and you'll be better off. Otherwise, avoid the humps and stick to the open-water.

Like I said, open-water trolling with crankbaits off planer boards is one of the deadliest fish catching systems ever devised. The Great Lakes salmon charters originally developed and perfected, this system. Many of today's top walleye tournament pros continue to hone this technique for inland waters, adapting some unique modifications to suit their needs for a variety of situations. More walleye tournaments are now won with this technique than with any other. Striper guides of the southern states have also discovered the incredible effectiveness of planer board trolling with crankbaits. The technique has produced some awesome catches of giant fish. Some of the stripers being caught with this tactic are near record size. Some of the most innovative musky hunters today are also taking full advantage of this system with incredible results. There simply is no better way to take suspended gamefish than with planer boards and crankbaits.

chapter 16

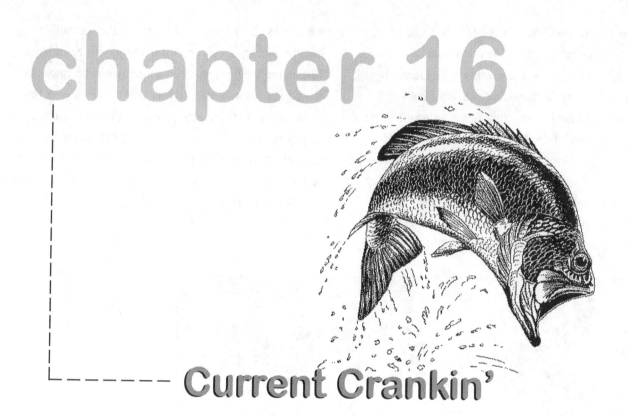

Current Crankin'

It was the last quarter of my freshman year in college, April of 1973, and the class Water 101, a beginning class on limnology. Yet all I could think about was the nearby Wisconsin River and the walleyes that my girlfriend, Beth, and I were going to chase that afternoon. My professor wasn't exactly boring, but the subject matter didn't compare to what was going to happen in the next class – Wisconsin River Walleyes 202. Beth and I had clobbered the walleyes the night before. All I could think about was meeting Beth immediately after this class so we could head back to the river.

It isn't hard to get excited about any kind of fishing after a long winter of ice, snow, and cold winds in northern Wisconsin, but this was extra-special because we were onto an incredible walleye bite. Beth and I had just recently discovered an easy way to catch lots of walleyes from the snag-infested bottoms of the river without losing a single bait. I'll describe our secret in detail in a moment, but first imagine that prior to this discovery, we were going through lead-head jigs and Wolf River Rigs (a bottom-bouncing live bait rig) like

we had stock in a tackle store. On top of that, we simply didn't have much money back then so this high-dollar tackle damage was really tough on our budget.

When the class bell rang, I sprang up from my chair and made a beeline for the door. Several classmates wanted to chat, but I had no time on this day. Beth was waiting, with rods and gear in the car, and I couldn't wait to get after those walleyes. I ran out of the lecture hall and continued to hoof it all the way back to the dorm. I was doubly excited to see Beth parked out front, ready to go. Just as I cleared the front door several dorm mates cut me off wanting desperately to find out more about the walleye rumors they'd heard about last night. They continued to follow me to the car begging for information like a couple of reporters covering a big story, when suddenly we were all stunned as Beth opened the trunk to display a big stringer of walleyes she had already taken that morning.

I was both stunned and proud, but my dorm mates appeared to be in shock. Imagine, these guys were all serious big-time natural resource majors and hadn't caught much of anything yet that spring, and here this

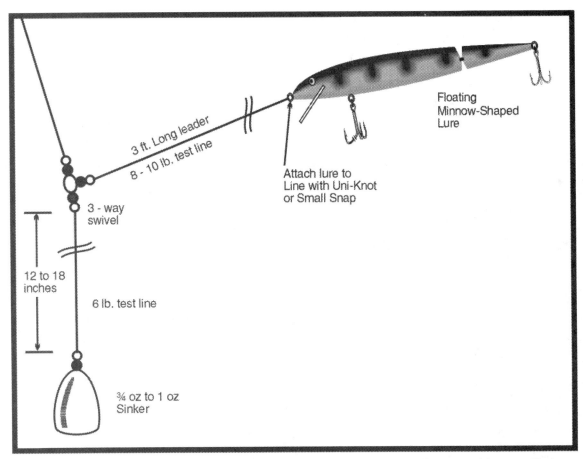

Rigging a floating minnow bait off of a three-way swivel that contains a "dropper weight" is one of the most effective ways to fish snaggy river bottoms. The author has used this technique successfully for years.

little 125-pound redhead had already smoked a bunch of big walleyes that morning. They were also fully aware that she'd done the same thing the night before! Of course, I was along on that prior outing so I knew what this was all about. As my dorm mates stood there stunned, Beth and I headed down the highway back to the river. Now I'm not one to rub it in usually, but I have to admit that 25-plus years later, this incident still makes me chuckle. It still makes my old college buddies chuckle, as well.

Now, about catching these fish and the secrets we discovered. Actually, finding those big river walleyes was easy. When I first went to the University Of Wisconsin-Stevens Point I had heard about big walleyes on the Wisconsin River. I simply checked out all the dam sites and fished every one of them. All of them produced to some extent, but one spot was a lot more productive than the rest. Understand that I didn't even

own a boat back then. I did all of my fishing from shore while attending college. As many of you already know, you don't necessarily need a boat to catch fish from rivers in the spring. Shore fishing can be just as productive. The only thing you have to contend with is competition from other anglers.

When Beth and I first fished below our most productive dam site, we did just what everyone else did. We fished with jigs and various styles of live bait setups like the famous Wolf River Rig. We also had about the same success that every one had. We'd catch an occasional fish, but in the process we'd lose dozens of jigs, sinkers, swivels, hooks and minnows. Each outing was costing us a fortune and we weren't exactly catching a comparable amount of fish.

The problem here was one of the most snag-infested bottoms you can imagine. In fact, it was beyond what you could imagine. River bottoms are typically snag-ridden, but this spot had everything from jagged broken rock to full-grown trees along the most productive stretches. Heck, there was even an old box spring from a bed down there. It was tough on tackle. Yet, inside these snaggy spots were walleyes. At times there were lots of walleyes in them. They could hide out of the current behind the rocks, trees, and all the other stuff down there, and snatch a meal at any moment. Getting a bait to them without snagging up was a challenge.

White-bodied lures are exceptional for deep open-water applications where gamefish are more likely to be feeding on ciscoes, shad or whitefish.

I tried light-weight jigs and heavy jigs. I experimented with live bait rigs of all kinds. I even tried weedless worms. While all of this stuff worked to a degree, none of it really tore 'em up. Most of it ended up hopelessly snagged, and eventually it became part of the underwater collection of trash.

Almost out of frustration one afternoon, I gave up on trying to present things tight to the cover and instead tied on a floating Rapala hoping to catch a high-riding pike. I knew I wouldn't get it hung up. I'll never forget what happened next. I pitched out that Rapala into a swirling eddy, and began a slow retrieve while watching my line get naturally swept around and pulled through the current. All of a sudden I had a strong bend in the rod like a snag. At first I was crushed. I didn't want to loose that expensive Rapala, but my attitude quickly changed when I realized it was a fish.

My first thought was this fish had to be a pike, so I gingerly played the big fish downstream until it was out of the heavy current. Finally, the fish tired enough for me to muscle it into the shallows. The turbid water of

The author's biggest northern pike to date, a 48-incher, was taken on a crankbait in current. This big fish was resting behind a big boulder just out of the strong current pouring out from the falls in the background.

the river didn't allow me to see the fish until it was just a few feet from the shoreline. That's when I saw, for the first time, a walleye pushing 30-inches. Keeping a strong bend in the rod, I began to back up until the fish was washed up on shore from the current. I then got between the fish and the water's edge and nudged it safely up onto dry land with my boot.

"Wow," I thought. "Was this a fluke? Didn't I have to jig the bottom in order to catch early spring river walleyes?" Well, as it turned out, this was definitely not a fluke, and no I didn't have to jig the bottom. A few more hook-ups with big fish in the next hour told me all I needed to know. Beth and I then rigged up with floating Rapalas, and started pounding fish on every outing. We rarely lost a lure from then on, and caught 25 times the amount of fish. This included not only walleyes, but big pike and bass, as well. This was

indeed my first experience with crankin' in the current. A year later, by the way, I married that little redhead.

When casting shallow areas, Beth and I found the simple floating minnow bait, with nothing else added in the way of hardware, was all that was needed to trigger strikes. In deeper stretches, we found that attaching a floating minnow bait to the old standby Wolf River Rig with a much longer dropper line (see illustration) was even more deadly. This rig, in fact, turned out to be our best for years to come.

What we found out was that subtle-action crankbaits like the Rapala and similar minnow lures, were perfectly suited for current. Current actually replaced the need for us to retrieve the lure. We could cast any crankbait into current and watch it wiggle in-place. As the current washed over the lure, the force of the water activated the lure's action. Our best retrieve, in many cases, was no retrieve at all. We'd simply cast the lure out a variety of distances and let the current carry the lure through eddies and over the top of snags at different angles. The only time we'd crank on the reel handle was after the lure had washed through all the eddies and was hanging directly downstream. Then a slow, stop-'n-go, retrieve would clean up on any additional fish.

Since those early successes with crankbaits on river walleyes, I've encountered countless current conditions where crankbaits have been the answer. This includes everything from summer smallmouth bass in smaller streams, to the fast trout waters of Canada. Current crankin' has also tricked many big muskies from all sorts of river situations during every season, spring, summer, and fall. It's a deadly method for all kinds of fish in all kinds of conditions.

The whole trick with crankin' in current is to choose a lure that matches up well with the current speed at hand and the depth you want to attain. Always remember that current speed and its force is going to activate your lure without any mechanical retrieve. There are tremendous advantages to this once you fully understand it. The biggest asset of all is the fact that you can keep your crankbait in front of the fish much longer, in an active, wiggling, strike-triggering state because of the aid of current. Forward retrieve is not as necessary in order to initiate action from the plug.

Once you've fished a variety of currents, you'll quickly realize that lure choice can make a huge difference. For example, in softer, slower current areas larger-lipped deep divers work extremely well. It takes minimal current to activate the action along the large surface area of a big-lipped diver. This minimal current also makes the lure dive more quickly. However, that same lure may be overwhelmed by heavy, fast current. Large-lipped divers will often torque out in heavy, fast current spots. Sometimes they might even roll over and pop out of the water. The overpowering current is simply too much for some big-lipped divers. This is where a narrow-bodied, small-lipped, subtle-action

diver might be more suitable. The only way to know for sure is to try a variety of lures over a productive spot until you find the perfect match of diving depth versus current drag.

Sometimes fish seem to want a big-lipped diver that digs and crawls over large rocks and logs, literally rooting along every inch of the river floor. Other times they prefer a crankbait that skims inches above them. When Beth and I found those first early spring crankbait walleyes back in April 1973, we found the latter to be true. The subtle-action minnow bait, skimming inches above them, was the perfect presentation. Even though the water temperature was only in the low to mid-40s, these walleyes were more than willing to jump out and snatch up this offering. More than two decades later, in September 1997, my friend Jeff Guenther and I found big river walleyes hugging tight behind big shallow boulders in moderately heavy current that would only respond to a bottom-digging, crawling big-lipped diver. That's why you need to be aware of all sorts of crankin' possibilities. The common denominators were still crankbaits and current.

I have several favorite current crankin' tactics that are worth sub-chapters. They have taken many big fish for me over the years, and they relate to specific current situations. Here are a few of my most-used current crankin' systems.

Still Fishing A Minnow Bait In Current Holes

That original method Beth and I discovered back in 1973 is part of a larger system of minnow bait fishing in current. The minnow bait can be successfully fished in so many ways in rivers. Beth and I had great success initially just casting the lure from shore and letting the current carry it around eddies in a natural fashion. Another tactic is to rig the minnow bait with a 3-way swivel, Wolf River-style, and still-fish it in deep heavy current. When you choose the right amount of weight, which is usually much more than you think is necessary, you can actually fish the lure over any heavy current spot at virtually any speed you choose. You can hold the lure in place allowing it to wiggle teasingly just above bottom hugging fish anywhere. One of my favorite tricks here is to anchor the boat above a good spot with heavy current, cast the rig out, and slowly inch it along the bottom pausing often. You won't have to worry about feeling a strike – fish rise up from their hideouts and pound the lure.

The trick to not losing lures with this 3-way swivel system is to rig a lighter line on the dropper going to the weight. Most often, the weight dangling off the dropper rig is what gets snagged up. If you rig up with the lighter line, you'll only loose the weight, not the lure. All you need to do is make certain you have lots of spare weights along. Traditional bell sinkers will do, and that's what I used for years. Today many weight systems are available for snag fishing that are far better. Pencil-shaped weights with a wire protruding below them are particularly good here.

This same rig can be cast from shore with equal efficiency for everything from walleyes to stripers. Even catfish will occasionally take this rig. This is very similar to the original rig that Beth and I used years ago on those Wisconsin River walleyes. If I were to go back to that spot

today, I'd substitute the bell sinker on our dropper lines with one of the newer pencil weights to further minimize snag-ups.

Crankbaits are exceptional producers in moving water. Make certain you crank good-looking eddies from a variety of angles using several different lures.

Casting Cranks In Current

I could cite scores of examples of my catches with crankbaits on current fish of all species which all started with that original Wisconsin River experience, but here I want to talk about a different type of crankbait casting in current. This deals more with bass, muskies, and pike, but it will also take walleyes efficiently at times. In this case, I'm looking for fish hiding behind cover such as big boulders, logs, broken rock and other possible current breakers. In addition, these are fish that aren't responding to lures that skim above them.

When faced with this situation, choose a buoyant big-lipped diver. Cast the bait well beyond the intended target in order to give it time to get down to the right depth before arriving. The ideal retrieve here is one that will make the crankbait crawl along the bottom until it collides with the large obstruction holding the fish. Then it virtually walks up and over the obstruction and back down again towards the

bottom. When big gamefish such as bass, pike and muskies are hugging tight to cover in current, I've seen them annihilate lures worked in this fashion.

My biggest northern pike to date, a 48-incher which, as of this writing, is still a line class world

Neck-down swifts usually contain rocky cliff banks and hard bottom. They're great for bottom-bouncing trolling.

record, hit in just this manner. I was fishing with my good buddy Tom Gelb on Lake Of The Woods in Ontario, right after daybreak one cold October morning in front of a falls area. Current was pouring out of the falls and over several large rocks along a steep breaking shoreline. I pitched my big crankbait well past one particular shallow boulder and began winding it down when POW! I had a strike of such incredible magnitude that it almost pulled the rod right out of my hand. I may have fallen out of the boat if the anti-reverse gear in my big baitcaster hadn't failed.

The mega-strike actually blew the anti-reverse gear right out of that reel, and the big fish peeled line as the reel handles spun backwards. I didn't actually see the fish for the next five minutes or so until it finally roared out of the water in a tarpon-like tail walk. Luckily Tom grabbed my video camera in enough time to capture this jump, as well as the rest of the battle and landing, on film. A monster pike to say the least, that passed up Tom's jerkbait, but couldn't resist the roto-rooting deep-diver.

Heavy Current Bottom-Bounce Trolling

This is a tactic that catches big fish from those impossible-to-reach spots; deep bottom rocks with lots of heavy current overhead. I first figured out how to fish such a situation with my friend Gabor Ujvary on the famous French River in eastern Ontario. The French River is a large system with lots of really deep water. However, it has these neat little narrow swifts that contain rock cliff walls and hard rocky bottoms with water 15 to 35 feet deep. We had heard rumors about big walleyes working these swifts at times, but never actually had any success with these fish.

What we eventually found was that walleyes were nearly always in these fast-water narrows, but they were underneath one heck of a lot of current, resting behind rocks down below the fast water in depths of 15 feet or more. Getting a lure to them was tough. We found two methods that worked on them. One was the same old rig

that Beth and I used years back. We had to add a lot more weight to the dropper line, but it worked. Using a crankbait with minimal current resistance, like the floating Rapala or similar minnow bait and anchoring it to a 3-way swivel with a very heavy sinker of 1 to 3 ounces attached to the dropper line. Today I'd probably use one of the new bottom-bouncers in the same weight range.

The extra weight was needed to cut through the tremendous current. The type of lure we picked was necessary to reduce drag and allow the entire rig to stay down in the fish zone. We then very slowly trolled up stream, against the tremendous current and treacherous rock walls, occasionally holding the boat in place under the power of the outboard. Every once in awhile I'd initiate a slight turn left or right while holding in the current to push the lure laterally around the bottom rocks below all that fast overhead current. To say we caught a few big walleyes this way would have been an understatement. We hammered 'em. This included several topping the 10-pound mark.

I've also had great success with big muskies in the same situation, trolling with wire line and big-lipped divers such as our straight model DepthRaider. Wire line really increases the running depth of any crankbait since it acts as both a long weight and has a water-slicing effect. Trolling against the heavy current at a snail's pace so that the crankbait isn't torqued in the heavy current, I've caught several really big muskies out of seemingly impossible fast-water stretches with this system. One of the secrets here is not only the wire line and a well-tuned crankbait, but also trolling at a snail's paced with a lot of lateral maneuvering.

The immense current puts plenty of action in the lure with no additional boat movement needed. Lateral boat shifting triggers fantastic bottom-bouncing action as the lure careens off various rocks. There is considerable drag on the rod tip when attempting this technique and intense lure vibration at the rod tip. There is also a much stronger chance of fouling the lure in rock crevices using the tactic. But, man, does it trigger strikes from big muskies, pike and walleyes. I've caught a lot of big ones using this tactic.

If I had to pick one, I prefer the wire line trolling tactic over the heavy weight system for fast water because there is so much control and response. The no-stretch wire line in combination with the strong resistance and vibration of the big-lipped deep diver provides an intense trolling situation. You feel every rock the lure crosses over. You know instantly when it is fouled. The strikes are incredible.

Wire line also greatly shortens the line length needed to get deep, while maintaining overall line strength and response. Short-line trolling means control. This will enable you to work the lure closer to the bank, walk it over and around tight spots, and keep it free from snags. I generally use Monel 50-pound test wire line for this system – that's strength. You'll never have to worry about losing a big one to a broken line when utilizing this system. You get control plus power. It's my all-time favorite for tough current spots.

Dragging the crankbait in a figure 8 at boatside is a great way to trigger a hit from a following fish. Followers are most common while musky fishing, but the technique works well with pike and many saltwater fish.

chapter 17

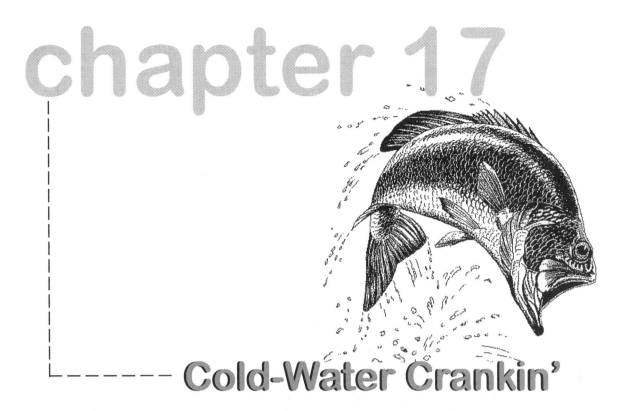

Cold-Water Crankin'

"Look at it snow," my partner "Lunker" Lou Eich hollered. "Joe, I can barely see the shoreline." I shook my head in both agreement and amazement. We were no more than a short cast from the steep rocky bank, yet we could vaguely make out the exposed rocks and downed trees. There we were, in the middle of an early November snow storm with icicles forming on our rod guides and water temperature readings in the low 40s, trying to catch a fish without freezing to death. The heavy, wet snow had us both thinking more about a warm bowl of chili than a big musky. That was until Lou's rod suddenly took a dip.

"Joe, I'm snagged in the rocks," Lou excitedly yelled as he struggled to free the 8 ½-foot trolling rod from the rod holder. "I don't think so, Lou," I barked. "Rocks don't move. You've got a good fish on there." I carefully began edging the boat out away from the bank into open water to make fighting and landing this fish a bit easier. Just when I thought we were home free, my rod also doubled all the way to the reel seat, and began bouncing violently as line begrudgingly peeled from the reel. "Wow!" I exclaimed, "Look at that strike!".

Lou and I were both locked in simultaneous battles with cold-water muskies – oblivious to the snow, the icy cold wind, and even the thought of a bowl of chili. I reached over and threw the outboard in neutral so Lou and I could freely enjoy battling our fish as we drifted across the open water. Both fish fought long, hard and deep before succumbing to my big landing net. Lou's fish hit first, and cried uncle first. As soon as it surfaced, I grabbed the landing net and scooped his 43-inch with my left hand, while still battling my musky with the other. Lou quickly freed his fish from the net, and then secured mine, a slightly smaller 41-incher.

Of course, any day with a pair of muskies longer than 40-inches could be considered a success but neither Lou nor I were finished. Before the day was done, we had boated five muskies from 34 to 43 inches. A good day in anyone's book, but on a cold, snowy November afternoon, it was down right superb. Now, surely this wasn't the first time that a pair of musky anglers had hit on some hot late fall action, but this was not on live bait. All of these fish, including three more that we took on the following evening, fell to crankbaits. Before ice-up that fall 17 more muskies would fall to the same method.

Odd as this may seem to the unknowing, crankbaits are absolute killers on cold-water gamefish. My on-the-water research has shown that crankbaits are more often the superior lure during almost any cold-water conditions. I've taken many late fall, cold-water muskies on crankbaits. This includes fish in excess of 50 inches and 35 pounds. I've also taken some of my biggest lake trout on crankbaits during the coldest water periods. This includes "oil cans" pushing the scales over 25 pounds. Huge bass and big pike are also very susceptible to crankbaits at this time.

Why so many anglers still fail to realize the deadly effectiveness of crankbaits in cold water is beyond me. Somewhere long ago, someone convinced the angling masses that live bait was the only way to catch fish when the water temperature dropped below 50 degrees. This must-fish-live-bait-in-cold-water concept was written about so often that it eventually became gospel of the fishing world. The live bait/cold water mentality is especially prevalent in the walleye, bass, and musky communities. It brings to mind one more quick example involving the so-called finicky walleye.

Sometime in the late 1980s a couple of local deer hunters stumbled onto some big walleyes on Lake Michigan's famous Little Bay De Noc a few days before the annual deer gun season. Now, catching big walleyes from Little Bay De Noc is certainly not earth-shattering news by any means, even this late in the fall. But these fish were taken on crankbaits, not live bait.

Some anglers have the mistaken impression that fish won't hit lures in cold water. Nothing could be farther from the truth. Big fish will actively hit crankbaits in the coldest of waters right down to ice up.

Eventually other anglers caught on to this rumor and the rest, as they say, is history. Today, trolling crankbaits on Little Bay De Noc, from November right up into early December, is considered the "in" thing to do. Throughout the month of November hundreds of anglers venture to Gladstone, Escanaba, and neighboring towns to chase big walleyes with cranks. The result has been massive catches of lunker walleyes, including record-class fish of 15 pounds or more.

Now that's production, and that's the power of crankbaits in cold water. When I first contemplated various chapters for this book, I paged through many of my big fish scrapbooks in order to compile a list of good crankbait tactics. The photos revealed the facts and jogged some of my best memories of lunker catches. The most obvious common denominators were: big fish, cold water, and crankbaits. No matter what the species, if the fish was big, and caught from cold water, crankbaits were likely involved. This has given me an unshakable confidence in crankbaits during the cold water periods, spring or fall.

Of course, this doesn't mean, for a New York minute, that all one has to do to catch cold-water fish is drop a crankbait over the side and start trolling. Just as with any fishing technique, several other key factors must be considered. For one, you definitely need to have some idea of where the fish are. In the very early spring and again in late fall this not only means knowing where in a general sense, but more specifically, **how deep.** Cold-water gamefish generally inhabit deeper waters. This means depth control is a key issue. I firmly believe that depth control is THE issue with cold water crankin'. No other factor even comes close.

This subject of depth control, first coined by the

Big lunker class lake trout are particularly susceptible to big crankbaits in the cold water periods. This 40-inch, 25-pounder hit a deep-diving crankbait trolled over hard bottom. (Angler Scott Miller)

Trolling is the best way to deal with ultra-cold inclement weather conditions. Tom Gelb took this brute musky right before a major snow storm while bottom-bouncing with a blue/white crankbait.

great Buck Perry, should always be the number one goal of the astute cold-water cranker. Cold water fish are less apt to move vertically, to take a lure. This means the lure must travel by the fish at the precise depth of the fish. Otherwise, success to any great extent is doubtful. Therefore, every effort must be made to determine exactly how deep your target species is. Then it's a matter of matching the right tackle with the right crankbait in order to achieve that depth.

One of my favorite ways to take cold-water gamefish on crankbaits is by motor-trolling or row trolling. Trolling is preferred for a number of reasons. For one, we've already discussed how much more

effective trolling is at getting crankbaits down deep. You'll definitely have a lot more success getting crankbaits down below 12 feet by trolling rather than casting. As we've already discussed, cold-water gamefish are more apt to be in deeper waters, below that 12 foot level.

Trolling is also superior in terms of dealing with inclement weather. Whenever air temperatures are below 32 degrees Fahrenheit, rod guides begin to freeze shut and reel pawls struggle to work through ice buildup. The colder it gets, especially if there's some additional wind chill involved, the more of a problem this becomes. Mechanical breakdowns are so common to the cold-water caster, that most of these diehards have also become master reel repair artists. My buddy Tom Gelb is one such cat. He carries a box of reel parts on all his late fall trips. He has pawls, gears, springs, anti-reverse dogs, crankshafts and a host of other no-name parts at his immediate disposal. Tom knows that freezing weather is brutally tough on reel parts. He considers it part of the game when fishing cold water with a casting presentation.

This isn't to say that I discount the effectiveness of casting for cold water gamefish. No way. Heck, I've taken lots of big muskies, walleyes, and lakers by casting. I made a big reputation as a guide throughout the 1970s, '80s, and early '90s catching big fish in the fall with crankbaits. I prefer to catch 'em casting whenever possible. But, it all comes down to how deep the fish are. If I can catch 'em casting, I'll definitely do it that way. But both the depth of the fish and, to a great extent, the air temperature, dictate whether I can catch them on the cast.

Water temperature dictates how deep big fish like muskies, walleyes, and bass will be, and therefore, "the temp" can tip you off on what to expect. Generally speaking, when I see fall or spring surface temperatures in the 50s, I'm confident I can catch fish crankin'. However, when surface temps dip down into the 40s, the majority of the fish start to move deeper, below that magic 12-foot mark. That's when I consider the trolling option.

Line choice is another factor during the cold-water period. Braided cloth lines are nearly always a bad idea in cold weather situations. Braided line freezes quickly to the reel spool. Musky hunters commonly prefer various low-stretch braided lines, but they'll have to give 'em up if they want to seriously attempt frigid crankin'. Line freeze-up is a serious problem with braided lines. Any nylon monofilament style of line is desired when air temps inch below the freezing mark. Personally, I'm a big fan of extra-tough lines designed for saltwater for use in cold-water crankin'. They have additional abrasion-resistance and durability built in.

Superior abrasion resistance is a major plus when jagged ice edges rub on your line all day long.

Speed control, another term coined by Buck Perry, must always be considered no matter what the season, but it has some special significance in cold-water crankin' applications. Speed control is the most misunderstood part of cold-water crankbait fishing. Many anglers have the mistaken impression that the only speed that works when the water is really cold is slow. In fact, most anglers think of cold and slow as synonymous. As obviously simple and clean-cut as this sounds, it's just not true. I won't dispute that ultra-slow retrieve speeds with certain lures can be deadly at certain times, especially with spinnerbaits and jigs, but slow speeds are rarely necessary with crankbaits. I've had surprising success with fast lure speeds in cold water. Admittedly, I stumbled onto the oddity of fast crankin' speeds and cold-water fish quite by accident.

This all started when I was trolling one windy, cold November afternoon a number of years back. I was fishing for muskies. I remember that the wind was blowing like mad and the waves were huge rollers. Big waves were crashing so hard across one of my favorite points that it was almost impossible to troll across it without taking on water. Originally, I made every effort to troll against the wind in order to maintain some boat control and keep the lure speed down. Disappointed with the lack of success on my first trolling pass, I quickly turned 180 degrees, and made another shot across it headed downwind. The big rollers and gusty wind pushed my boat at nearly three times the desired speed. I cussed my lack of speed control, as I struggled to hold the boat off the rocky shore. My rod tip vibrated like it was going to rattle right out of the rod holder. Traveling at this high speed, with water temps in the low 40s, I never considered that a fish would hit. Boy, was I amazed when the rod doubled with a bone-jarring strike.

It took me nearly 10 minutes to land that musky because of both the size of the fish and the howling winds. Nearly 46 inches and at least 25 pounds told me that speed control in cold water doesn't necessarily mean "go slowly." I should also point out that this incident was just the beginning. I caught two more muskies and a couple of lake trout that day, and all of them came on the downwind trolling pass over that same point. The water temperature was 41 degrees.

Since that day, I've never hesitated to "crank it up" when things seem slow. I've also talked to a number of other experienced cold-water crankers about this cold water/speed phenomena. I was surprised to find some similar success stories. Eastern musky hunters, in particular, are big fans of fast trolling in cold water. They purposely troll at high speeds and don't believe in ever trolling slowly. Noted New York musky maniac Mark Magrahn is one of the most successful at this tactic. Rarely does Mark troll slowly no matter

what the water temp. Mark catches a lot of really big fish, too.

Don't get the mistaken impression that I am advocating you should always troll fast in cold water with crankbaits. There are definitely many times when a slow "crawl" speed catches more fish in cold water. So much depends on the species being fished and the style of lure being used. Generally speaking, muskies and lakers seem to like speed in cold water. Walleyes appear to always want it a bit slower. Bass can go either way. However, again it depends upon the bait. High-vibrating, big-lipped crankbaits seem to trigger gamefish with both fast and slow retrieves, but minnow baits appear to work better with a slow speed.

One of the best ways to take big walleyes during the cold-water periods is by slow trolling a suspender-

New York musky pro Mark Magrahn holds one of his many big fish taken on a crankbait during the frigid waters of November.

style minnow bait off planer boards. Some of the biggest tournament catches in history have fallen to this system utilizing a lead-core line and a suspender minnow bait. The lead-core line acts like a weight, taking the bait deep, and keeping it there no matter what the speed. Utilizing a trolling speed meter, serious tournament trollers slowly drag these suspending minnow baits all over deep flats for big 'eyes. This continues to be one of the best ways to take those Bay De Noc walleyes during the late fall period.

Bass fishermen were among the first to popularized cold-water crankin'. Legendary catches of big bass on crankbaits filled the early pages of Bassmaster and many other outdoor magazines. While many southern bassers waited for warm weather to arrive, a handful of bassin' pioneers, such as Floyd Mabry, would crank the creek channel edges and tree lines with deep-divers. Their early catches have now paved the way for today's crankbait anglers to cast crankbaits for big bass no matter what the water temp.

Bass will hit crankbaits in a wide variety of water temperatures, as will muskies and walleyes.

However, on the low end of the spectrum the 50-degree mark stands out. It seems that in the spring, as soon as water temps crack the 50-degree mark, crankbaits catch

This big beast of a lake trout hit a crank bait trolled deep just days before ice-up in the late fall. Some of the biggest fish in any system can be taken by trolling late in the year.

bass. Smallies will hit 'em in lower water temps than largemouths. The ideal cool-water temp seems to be near 55 degrees. My good friend Roland Martin, a tremendous crankbait fishermen, has always maintained that the 55-degree range as an ideal benchmark for cold-water bass on crankbaits. Of course, he's caught a few thousand bass on crankbaits to back up this claim.

I've taken walleyes on crankbaits in the most frigid water temps; right after ice-out in the spring and right before ice-up in the fall. Walleyes will readily hit crankbaits in water temps well below 50 degrees. The key, as mentioned earlier, becomes depth and speed control. It's always important to remember as the water gets colder, depth and speed control become more important. So does lure choice. Cold water walleyes like minnow baits. They'll hit other styles of crankbaits in cold water, but they nearly always like the minnow bait. The trick is to fish the minnow bait on a variety of weighting systems in order to make it travel the right depth and speed.

Muskies love crankbaits in the cold water. They also love 'em in warm water. But cold-water muskies, those in truly frigid water of less than 50 degrees, want a crankbait that travels close to them. They'll chase a lure, all right, sometimes right to the boat. But you'll catch a lot more muskies if you pay attention to depth control closely. Lunker Lou and I took those November muskies at 22 feet. We trolled a number of depths,

Monster-sized minnow baits of 10 inches or more are super producers of big muskies and pike. They are best used in trolling situations because of their size and weight.

both shallower and deeper, but all of those fish came at exactly 22 feet. If you remember anything from this chapter, I hope it's not only that fish like muskies will hit crankbaits in frigid waters, but that depth control is vital to success. Pay attention to how deep the fish are, and get a lure to them. The rest usually takes care of itself.

The topography that holds the most fish in cold water can also vary with the species and the water temperature. I've taken a lot of big bass, walleyes, pike and muskies in weeds during cold water periods, especially when water temps are in the 50s. In the spring, crankbaits help seek out those newly emerging weeds. Without question, the crankbait is the ultimate weed-finder. Crankbaits combine both speed and raw fish-catching ability that's unmatched for finding active gamefish in weeds in early spring. The first fish to enter the weeds in spring are generally pike, but walleyes and bass are always close behind. Crankbaits are the best way to find 'em.

Fall weeds can also be hot for cold-water gamefish, and crankbaits are again the best weapon to locate both the remaining stands of weeds and the fish using them. Fall weeds are usually in a decaying, dying mode. The key in the fall is to find healthy, green standing weeds. Crankbaits will search the best weeds out better than anything else. Water temps in the 50s are again the best benchmark of good fall weed crankin'. As water temps drop below the 50-degree mark, fish use the weeds less often. Really clear lakes may contain healthy green weeds all the way through ice-up. This is the epitome of great cold-water crankin' conditions for the caster. Find clear water with healthy green weeds in the late fall and it's a good bet that you'll have good crankbait fishing no matter what the temperature gauge says.

However, weeds are sure to decay in most lakes, and when this happens, the fish usually vacate them. Stationary cover such as wood and rock then becomes primary fish attractants. Of course, crankbaits are great lures in this kind of cover no matter what the water

temperature, but they excel in cold-water applications. The depth of this stationary cover determines the method of crankin'. If the wood or rock is less than 12 feet, casting is a good idea. Any depths greater than this demand a count-down cranker or a trolling presentation.

This is one of those times when I love to cast or troll rock walls, bluff banks, and steep breaking shorelines. Cold water, crankbaits and rock walls are what late fall crankin' is all about. I've taken hundreds of muskies, pike, walleyes, and lakers from such spots on crankbaits in the fall. Any rock wall, bluff bank or steep bank is likely to hold fish in the cold-water periods, but the best ones seem to be situated in some kind of necked-down, funnel area. Anytime you see a large shallow bay with weeds and a shallow basin that necks down at the mouth like an hour glass, look for a rock wall, bluff bank or some other steep-breaking bank area in the hour glass area. This is sure to hold some big fish at some time during the cold-water period. Crankbaits will be the best way to catch 'em.

Open water can also hold plenty of fish in the cold-water period as can dark silty bottoms. I've had great success trolling crankbaits over small, deep holes near large shallower silty basins in the very late fall, just before ice-up. In fact, my first really big musky on the original DepthRaider was taken during a snow squall in early November trolling around such a spot. The bulk of this particular lake had a basin that was only 19 feet deep, but the far northeast end had a small 40-foot hole. I was row trolling a new prototype of the DepthRaider around this area and saw a bunch of baitfish marks between 18 and 28 feet down suspended over the hole. I knew the DepthRaider ran about 18 feet deep with 120 feet of 30-pound line, so I was confident it was traveling at the top of these baitfish marks. Just as I was turning to go back over the hole on my first pass, the rod buckled and I was in for a 20-minute battle. Eventually I landed one of the area's biggest muskies of the year. It tipped the scales at 36 pounds. It was definitely suspended over the top edge of these big baitfish schools. The smaller fish, by the way, turned out to be crappies.

Cold water and crankbaits are indeed synonymous. Hundreds of gamefish are taken each year during the cold-water periods on crankbaits. My recent correspondence with several noted pike, trout and zander anglers in Europe and the Scandinavian countries confirms that they too catch 'em in cold water on crankbaits. The worldwide web has definitely opened up an entirely new avenue of communication with these anglers. One of Great Britain's most prominent big fish guides is particularly adept at bagging big trout and pike during the cold-water periods. His recent world record Ferex Trout, taken shortly after ice-out, is a testimonial to cold-water crankbait effectiveness worldwide. So you see, no matter where you fish, the crankbait is simply a cold-water killer.

chapter 18

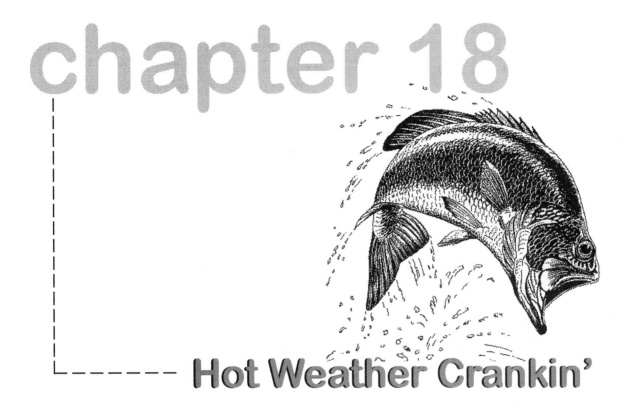

Hot Weather Crankin'

We were fishing in the "dog days of August." It was beyond hot, particularly for Canada. With only an occasional light breeze to soothe our skin from the scorching 90-degree heat, my son Joe Jr. and I set out for our first day on the water. The water temp gauge was reading 81 degrees. I expected dealing with the heat would prove to be more of a challenge than actually catching fish. How true this hunch turned out to be.

Our initial game plan was a simple one. We'd get out on the water as soon as there was daylight and fish our best spots until around 11 a.m. As soon as the heat became unbearable, we'd take a long midday lunch break. As soon as our spirits were recharged, we'd hit the water hard again from late afternoon 'til dark. Although this sounded good on paper, I wondered whether we could actually take a prolonged break each day if the fish were responding right before break time. Heat or no heat, it would be tough to leave if the fish were biting.

My son started out casting a big surface bait, while I backed him up with a variety of other plugs.

Admittedly, we both fully expected early and late day top-water fishing to be the highlight of the trip. This was quickly confirmed when Joe Jr. had a 34-inch musky explode on his TopRaider minutes into our first pass of the morning. It was 6:15 a.m. A few quick photos, the release and a victory handshake got us going for the rest of the morning. Boy, we were really poised to hammer 'em now!

However, two and a half hours later we were still talking about the 34-incher. We did have three more short strikes on top-water, but that's all they were. A lot of noise and some explosive water eruptions, but no hook-ups with muskies. During this time, I'd tried several top-water lures too, along with a variety of bucktail spinners, but I hadn't drawn a single response from any of these offerings. "Is it just too hot, dad?", Joe asked. "Do these fish shut down when the water temp gets that high?" Of course, I didn't have a good answer at the time, but I was sure thinking about it.

Finally, I snapped on a big 7- inch minnow bait, and began a series of short casts over the same weed cover that Joe had just fished with his top-water plug.

Instead of trying to match Joe cast for cast, I opted to tick, bump and bang the weed cover more thoroughly. Even if I only got half the casts in, I was attempting to trigger a fish that wouldn't come up for a top-water plug. At the same time, I figured I had a good "pitch back bait" to any of the fish that blew up at his TopRaider, but wouldn't take it.

As Joe and I began discussing lunch, I launched a cast that sent the big minnow bait right over a thick patch of isolated milfoil weeds. My first pull drove the minnow bait straight into the center of the clump. I immediately stopped retrieving, created a small bit of slack in my line and began a series of rod snapping twitches that made the minnow bait pop back and forth with a very exaggerated side to side action. The slack line also allowed the bait to slowly rise up and over the milfoil. I could feel the bait clear the weed clump, but also see it in the calm shallows.

Just to make certain it was weed-free, I then gave the rod tip a quick rip forward. This made the minnow bait grind forward with an intense vibration. But suddenly, right at the end of the rip, I felt a violent jolt. Instinctively, I set the hook and 46 inches of mad, thrashing musky surfaced with the entire 7-inch minnow bait buried

One of the best ways to trigger big fish in hot dog-day weather is with crankbaits. This particular musky passed up a surface bait, but couldn't resist a minnow bait twitched tighter to cover.

crosswise in its mouth much like a dog with a big bone. Arrogantly, I then answered, "No, Joe I don't think the water's too hot for these fish! We just need to knock on the door!" A few minutes later, I was posing with one of 11 nice muskies that were to fall to this technique on that week.

This is an example of the many successful experiences I've had with hot-weather, dog-day fishing conditions. Most warm-water gamefish can be taken in hot-weather, hot-water conditions. Their locations aren't always the same, nor are the tactics that will trick 'em, but it's definitely worth noting that I've had a high degree of success with hot-weather fish on crankbaits. This includes big catches of bass, walleyes, pike, and even the mighty musky.

Many anglers have been led to believe that crankbaits are better in colder waters. This misnomer has even been written up as gospel in several noted national outdoor publications over the years. Yet, it has been regularly proven wrong. Take for example the successes of the many touring walleye pros. By and large, the best hot-weather technique for mid-summer, dog-day walleyes continues to be planer board trolling in open water with crankbaits. This pattern seems to be equally effective on small shallow lakes and large deep sprawling ones. When the chips are down in the walleye tournament world, the pros go for crankbaits. With such a glowing endorsement by so many top walleye anglers, how could anyone consider using anything else?

The natural perch pattern is one of the best all-around colors for warm-water gamefish. Nearly every big predator, bass, walleye, pike and muskies feed on perch when these striped baitfish are available.

If you remember back in Chapter 11 and the subject of weed crankin', I told the story about fishing with the folks from Rapala from Finland. That event took place right during the dog days of mid-August. It was also hot then, too. Hot air, and hot water temps. We took 67 walleyes on that day – all on crankbaits. I don't know how anyone could call this "unproductive".

Bass anglers have really been led down the wrong path with this "crankbaits are cold-water lures" dogma. I continue to read such rubbish in the pages of many bass magazines on an annual basis. It simply isn't true. It's not even a little bit true. Some of the nation's top tournament bass fishermen have proven beyond a shadow of a doubt that crankbaits will catch both numbers and big fish in the hot weather no matter where they're fished, north or south. The latest exploits of bass pro David Fritts have really solidified the effectiveness of the crankbait in all water temps and seasons.

David Fritts has been perhaps the most successful tournament bass fisherman in the 1990s. He's very adept at finding and catching big bass in a variety of situations. David's specialty is crankbait fishing. David has even designed and endorsed special rods and lines for his crankbait fishing. His name now appears on bass fishing gear all across our country. But David Fritts made his name, fame, and fortune on crankbaits. Many of those wins came during hot weather as he fished in hot water. Tell David that the crankbait isn't good during the dog days, and it's a sure bet that you'll get an argument. Better yet, he'll probably take you out and prove you wrong.

One of the best ways to catch bass from open water is to troll crankbaits. Walleye pro Ted Takasaki occasionally "stumbles" on big smallmouth bass while searching for open water walleyes.

Dusk is a key time for big fish during the dog days of summer. Mike Novak took this monster 55-1/2 inch, 47-pounder on a jointed crankbait right after sunset following a hot muggy afternoon.

My own experiences with crankbaits on dog-day bass have been much the same. Most of my top bass catches, early in my fishing career, came on crankbaits during July and August. My biggest Wisconsin largemouth to date was caught on a crankbait in mid-July. Back when I was still fishing tournaments in the 1970s, my biggest catch, a tournament win no less, came casting a weed line in mid-August with the original Arbogast Mudbug. How anyone could claim that crankbaits lose it on bass during hot weather is baffling.

Then, there's muskies and crankbaits, too. I've made the statement many times that crankbaits are the only true all-season musky lure. I stand by that statement today. Bucktail spinners are definitely more productive during warmer water. Big fish on spinners in the autumn are a rarity. Jerkbaits do take fish during summer and fall, but struggle in the spring. Top-water plugs are obviously most effective from late June through early September. However, crankbaits take muskies regularly from ice-out 'til ice-up. There is no time of the year when a crankbait won't take muskies. The opening story in this chapter is one very good example of just how deadly they can be when the water gets warm.

My favorite summer tactic for hot-weather muskies is still night crankin', and we'll deal with this subject in detail in another chapter. But I will tell you this – crankbaits are clearly the best lure for muskies after dark. Fish the crankbait alongside a top-water lure or a bucktail on any given night and see for yourself. If you want to bag both numbers and big muskies consistently after dark, I'd suggest you fish with one lure – a jointed crankbait. Leave the rest of your lures in your tackle box.

I've also had great daytime summer success with crankbaits on muskies, too. I've caught 'em trolling over the open water with tactics almost identical to that used by the walleye pros. So have a number of other top-notch musky hunters. Summer charter captains on Lake St. Clair have some of their best action during the mid-summer. They're best weapon, bar none, is a crankbait. In fact, most of these charter boats don't have many other lure styles in their tackle boxes.

Many Wisconsin musky anglers prefer not to troll, yet they continue to catch these same suspended summer muskies on crankbaits by casting the small lakes that dot this state. Their main weapon is the crankbait. Instead of trolling across the open water, they simply use the wind to drift them across large expanses of open water while peppering the water with fancasts. Few anglers are adept at this technique, yet those who know how, enjoy a high rate of success. These open water casters prefer midday, sunny conditions. Their reason is simple: the fish do, too.

Crankin' tight to cover such as weed flats, weed lines, rock humps and woody cover can also produce muskies consistently during the dog days. My experience in Canada is one such example. Canadian waters are particularly made-to-order for summer musky crankin'. I'd highly suggest that any Canada-bound musky hound add crankbaits to his or her list of summer

lures. Start bumping rock humps and pounding weeds with crankbaits in those hard-fished spots that get pounded with bucktails and top-water plugs. Once in awhile, you'll find those reluctant followers turn into strikers when you switch to the less-used crankbait.

Speaking of Canadian summer muskies, I can tell you that crankbaits have usually been my top producer. Of course, I'll always catch a few on top-water baits and bucktails, but almost without exception, the crankbait ends up being the best producer on any summer musky trip. As fall approaches, the top-water lure and bucktail eventually lose their punch, while the total amount of fish taken on crankbaits increases. Yet, as productive as the crankbait has been for me and my close friends, the vast majority of Canada-bound musky hunters don't even take crankbaits along on their trip! What a mistake.

The best choice of crankbait along with the best location to fish them for hot-weather gamefish is sure to vary with the species and any given situation. Also, the productive time of the day will certainly differ from lake to lake. For instance, open-water trolling with crankbaits is sure to be productive for walleyes during the mid-summer period simply because so many walleyes suspend during this time period. However, there are also plenty of walleyes up along weed edges in shallow lakes during this same time of the year. The big catch that the Rapala folks made with me in August occurred in a weedbed on crankbaits.

My son and I have had numerous memorable Canadian trips during July and August fishing with crankbaits for walleyes and pike. Our typical fishing pattern was simple; cast deep divers over rocks. We've never had a bad trip utilizing this tactic. Yet, we're always amazed when camp operators are surprised by the techniques we used. The general mentality of a Canadian walleye fisherman is to fish jigs, but most of the time they're simply not necessary. Crankbaits will catch 'em just as well. Bottom-bouncing the tops of rock humps and rock points with crankbaits will catch plenty of summer walleyes throughout most of Canada.

It matters little whether it's July or August. It also doesn't make any difference what the thermometers say.

I guess, if there's been one common denominator in all of my summer successes with crankbaits it's been hitting something. I'm talking about bumping, bouncing, and ticking the lure into some cover or the bottom itself. With the exception of my experiences open-water trolling for suspended fish, almost every warm-water species such as walleyes, bass, pike and muskies hold tight to cover or the bottom in most situations. This is particularly true when the fish are holding in relatively shallow water, and the sun gets high in the sky. Midday shallow fish tuck up tight to cover or the bottom. You must get a lure close to them. Nothing works better in this situation than a crankbait.

Exceptions? You bet there are. Anytime you witness a summer evening mayfly hatch, make certain you check the upper column of water with a shallow-running crankbait. I've had great success in this situation with RatLtraps and other lipless crankbaits. Some of my most exciting summer evening filming excursions for walleyes have occurred while casting lipless crankbaits over surfacing fish that are feeding on mayflies. These fish rise up off the bottom with the hatching mayflies. They're usually cruising only a foot or so below the surface. Usually they have no relation to bottom structure

or any kind of cover. They're simply out cruising the open water. Machine-gun, speed-casting the entire area around the surfacing fish splashes is the surest way to find these cruising fish.

I've also done quite well casting minnow baits for these mayfly munchers. Minnow baits seem to be a better choice for shallower gamefish cruising over the

Some of the author's biggest largemouth bass have been taken on crankbaits.

tops of high weeds or inside stump fields. While these gamefish will also be high, off the bottom, they're not actually cruising over deeper open water. Instead they're simply over the top of the weeds or brush. Thick mature summer grass beds offer up a similar circum-

Solid rock walls are best fished in a more parallel casting pattern. The fish will most likely be positioned tight to the wall, but suspended. The spot should be probed with several types of lures to make sure you are reaching a variety of depths.

stance. In the evening, insects are rising to the surface and so are the gamefish. A straight retrieve with a buoyant minnow bait is all that is needed in order to be successful here.

Of course, these same fish will likely be down inside cover or on the bottom during midday hours, and are sure to be much more catchable on a deep diver then. The key here is to be versatile as well as observant. You might start out the day catching a few "high riders" on a lipless crankbait or minnow plug, and then have to switch to a deep-diver for the bulk of your midday efforts. As evening approaches, watch for surfacing fish to tip you off. Almost without exception, the big mayfly hatch occurs right as the sun hits the horizon. As soon as you start to see a few bustin' the surface, give 'em a shot with a lipless crankbait or minnow plug and see what happens.

Early mornings carry a special magic for all summer fishing, and crankin' is no different. When the amount of daylight peaks during the dog days of July and August, early mornings are sure to be a hot time for crankin' big gamefish of every species. Early morning crankin' is especially good when the night air temperatures remain fairly warm. Any cold front activity, or the cooler high pressure systems that follow, will probably drop the night temps down more. This usually dampens early morning activity. You can then usually bank on better evening fishing in this instance. However, if the night is warm, get ready for an early bite.

The deep weed edge, what many of us refer to as the "weed line," is the pivot point for most good summer bass and musky crankin'. Walleyes and northern pike may utilize this edge with equal interest depending on the lake's overall topography and the mix of other predators available inside the same ecosystem. Back when I first discovered the crankbait as a teenager basser, it was the weed line that got all my attention. I'd pound those weed lines from June through September. I found that, once the weeds matured in June, the entire food chain would center around it. I'd catch bass from the weed edge all summer long.

Many years later as a full-time guide, I practiced the same philosophy. No matter what species I was hired to produce, my first inclination was to head for the weed line during the dog days of midsummer. Inevitably, I was successful in doing so. I'd catch walleyes, pike, bass and muskies all from the same pivot point, the weed line. The same place I learned to rely on back in my boyhood days turned out to be the "bread winner" later on.

Whenever I approach a summer weed line for the first time, I generally fish it with a deep-diving crankbait. I might

also make a pass across the top, hoping to find a few "high riders", but I'll generally end up probing the weed edge methodically, like a surgeon. As I've stated before, working a deep-diving crankbait along a weed line enables me to thoroughly learn the configuration of it while attempting to catch a fish. No other lure

Summer lake trout can also be taken on crakbaits, but you might have to attach the lure to a down rigger in order to reach the depths these cold-water creatures like to hang at in summertime.

provides this kind of information in such a quick and effective manner. In this process, I'll discover precisely where the fish prefer to hold along the weed edge. I can then follow-up working this "spot on the spot" more thoroughly with a variety of other lures.

Once you've cranked as many weed lines as I have, you'll find that each one has its own distinct personality. There might be a small projection of low-growing grass the fish seem to prefer. Or there could be a series of isolated deeper weed clumps growing just outside the main weed bed that are holding most of the bigger fish. Sometimes it's even a change in weed species that's the hot spot. It could just as easily be a small pile of rocks nestled in the middle of the a grassbed the fish are preferring. You'll only learn these nuances by fishing a given spot time after time, and a deep-diving crankbait is the only lure that will provide you with this kind of information quickly and efficiently.

So, the next time you read or hear that crankbaits are just spring and fall lures, and that they loose their punch in the hot-weather months, you'll know better. Let those people preach what they want, while you go out to your favorite weed line and crank up a few walleyes for supper, a bunch of bass for sport, or a trophy musky for the wall. Crankbaits are not just cold-water killers. They're just as productive in the heat of mid-summer. Now you know the truth. I'll bet that once you give the hot-weather crankin' techniques I've described here an honest try, you'll be catching dog day gamefish more consistently than ever before.

chapter 19

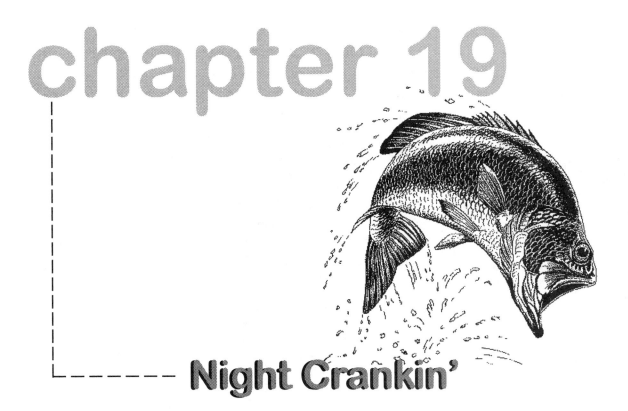

Night Crankin'

A heavy mist made it extra tough to see the high tension tower's silhouette just to the left of the narrows between the two lakes. I then realized just how much I had relied on this landmark to keep my boat on the spot during the night. Using my flasher unit as an additional reference, I launched another probing cast in the general direction of the weed line, knowing that my deep-diver would tell me, in a few cranks, whether I was on target.

A few hard turns of the reel made the big, jointed night shiner DepthRaider race downward at a fast clip, vibrating as it descended. A sudden gust of wind splattered water on the back of my exposed neck making me pause momentarily to flip up my raincoat hood. As soon as my hand resumed its grip on the reel handle, I ripped hard on the rod tip to drive the lure downward once again. This made the big-lipped diver shake violently, and insured that it was working well.

It also made it collide hard with some tall cabbage weeds. Instead of yanking upward on the rod tip in order to clear weeds from the bait, I dropped a small amount of slack in the line and shook the rod vigor-

ously. This somewhat off-beat technique made the buoyant bait jiggle itself upward. Eventually, it cleared the weed stalk and wobbled forward. I again ripped hard on the rod in order to clean any weed clingers from the diving lip. However, this time the lure was abruptly stopped dead, doubling my rod tip over with a solid lockup.

Within seconds the big fish erupted, roaring out of the water with its giant mouth agape. Luckily my hookset was positive, driving the newly sharpened trebles solidly into the big fish's tough bony jaw. Beating it through the initial jump and several more head thrashes, I leaned hard on my 7-foot stick in order to keep good pressure on the fish with hopes of tiring it quickly. Unfortunately, this plan didn't sit well with my adversary on the other end of the line.

I could feel the bow of the boat slowly turning away from the tower and realized that the fish was now towing the boat around. All I could do at this point was simply hold on. Nearly ten minutes went by before the fish began to show signs of tiring. Eventually it rose, revealing an awesome musky of over 50 inches that was well-hooked. So well-hooked, in fact, that I had to cut all three treble hooks out of the fish. It had engulfed the entire 8-inch lure. After some careful hook removal surgery and a brief revival period in my livewell, I released the fish. It was my ninth musky of 50 inches or better taken on a crankbait after dark.

Now, any musky maniac reading this story would agree that nine muskies in the 50-inch class is an incredible scorecard no matter how they're caught. Muskies of 50-inches or more are the true benchmark of a trophy, much like the 10-pound largemouth. While I've certainly caught more than my share of these fantastic fish during daylight hours, I can tell you that nothing matches the thrill of taking one in the dark. Night fishing for any kind of big gamefish is exciting when the fish are biting. Nothing quite compares to the strike of a big musky in total darkness. Simply put, it's awesome. On top of that, night fishing is one of the surest ways to catch a really big musky, and crankbaits are the best lures in this situation, bar none.

When I first started fishing after dark, I relied heavily on surface baits like most other anglers. The common misconception is that at night gamefish must look up in order to effectively zero in on the silhouette of prey in total darkness. Of course, experience has proven this to be totally false. Subsurface lures of many styles will readily take gamefish after dark. Spinners, crankbaits, and even jigs catch night fish of many species with regularity. Top-water baits actually account for only a small percentage of fish caught after dark.

As a guide, I began experimenting with night fishing as a means to beat the crowds and get my customers on top of big fish more

Night-crankin' is one of the most effective ways to take big fish from lakes with heavy boat traffic. The author has caught many big fish like this one utilizing sound night-fishing tactics.

consistently. I tried the "banker's hours" mentality for a number of years, fishing the traditional 8 a.m. to 5 p.m. schedule. While I caught plenty of fish on most occasions, big fish were nearly always tough. As the summer wore on, fishing got steadily tougher, particularly on big muskies and eye poppin' walleyes. You could catch an average musky or two during most daytime trips, and surely a respectable string of walleyes, but lunkers were rare. A few flexible clients encouraged me to try a few night trips, and the rest just kind of fell into place.

I quickly built a reputation in the 1980s as the night guide. Eventually, my night guiding got so popular that I totally eliminated daytime trips from July 4 through Labor Day. This worked out great with many of these trophy-seeking clients since they could avoid missing family time, and work. We'd meet at the boat landing around 9 p.m. and fish until midnight or so. If the fishing was average, we'd quit at the strike of 12 and go home; usually with at least one good musky or two, or several big walleyes. However, if things were really happening, we'd stick it out, staying as late as 3 am. What happened on some of those outings was nothing short of phenomenal.

During my best single night-time musky outing ever we boated 11 muskies with the top fish at 50 ½ inches. How about my best week? We landed 29 muskies in five days. Remember that old lure advertisement that would brag "31 muskies in

31 days! A record still unbroken?" Yeah, right! How does 54 in 14 days sound? All these muskies were taken on one lure, too. I guess the new ad should read "54 muskies in 14 days! A new record!" Maybe the most

Crankbaits are exceptional lures for any gamefish that feeds after dark. The author has found that both jointed lures or straight models with rattles are best in this situation.

amazing night fishing statistic of them all was the fact that, when I was guiding full-time from July 4th through Labor Day, my average catch per summer, over the course of a 10-year period, was about 105 muskies. Not bad for an average three-hour tour, hey?

I realize I'm a bit arrogant about these night fishing stats, but I wanted to slam the point home. Nighttime fishing works. Nighttime fishing with crankbaits is exceptionally deadly on big fish. I know this for a fact since I made a living at it. Again, as with many of the other subjects inside this book, it's important to take in the big picture as it relates to all gamefish species. Nighttime fishing is not just a musky tactic, nor is it just meant for walleyes. Once you learn the solid basics of night crankin', you can catch virtually any gamefish that feeds under the cover of darkness. The techniques are basically the same. That's why it is not uncommon to catch a mixed bag of big bass, walleyes, and muskies on any given night. They are all active after dark under the right conditions.

Just exactly what makes for the "right conditions" for good night fishing is actually very easy to predict. Usually it all begins with a tough daytime bite. Anytime you run into tough going during daylight hours, expect better results after dark. This can be caused by a number of factors. Gin-clear water is one such culprit that promotes a night bite. Whenever you encoun-

Big lunker walleyes are most active under the cover of darkness, and will readily take big crankbaits. If you're looking for a wall-hangin' walleye, your best bet is to fish a trophy lake after dark with a big crankbait.

ter a gin-bottle lake that lacks ample shallow cover for fish to hide in, nighttime fishing becomes a viable option. Most gamefish, in this situation, suspend deep over open water thermoclines during nearly all daytime conditions. A few of these fish venture shallow after dark and fall to crankbaits.

Fishing pressure and increased boat traffic are other factors that create a strong night feed. Anytime a large-scale tournament is held for a number of days on any popular local lake the night fishing is sure to be exceptional in short order. Noted angler Spence Petros and I took advantage of such a situation a few years back when over 800 anglers pounded the lakes around Eagle River, Wisconsin during the annual National Championship Musky Open. Spence was the emcee of that tourney and found that anglers were having a tough go of it for the first two days. In fact, less than 25 muskies had been taken up to that point. Spence and I hit the water around 10 p.m., right before a rain storm. By the time we put the boat back on the trailer, we'd taken eight muskies up to 49 ½ inches, and 15 walleyes up to 25 inches. The heavy daytime boat traffic and increased fishing pressure forced the majority of the gamefish into a nocturnal mode. They acted much the way a whitetail deer will bed in thick swamps and refuse to venture out during the gun season.

Water skiers, jet boats, and all the other pleasure boating tourist traffic really drives fish into a night mode, too. I purposely take full advantage of this situation whenever possible, and head for these kind of lakes to do the majority of my night fishing. All the tourist traffic actually works as an ally here holding the fish down, off any strong, shallow, daytime feed. After only a short time, fish actually develop a sense of waiting until almost all outboard traffic subsides. In some of the really busy waters, this might not occur until well after dark; maybe close to midnight. Accordingly, the best fishing on these waters might not occur until well after midnight.

Best Night Spots

What constitutes a good night fishing spot largely depends on the lake and the time of the year, but some good general guidelines nearly always apply. Inexperienced anglers often make the mistake of throwing good fishing fundamentals to the wind after dark, and simply become "bank-beaters". The misconception here is that night gamefish move up close to the shore (bank). Rarely are these bank beaters successful since most banks are void of fish. Only a few rare shorelines produce after dark. Usually this is related to walleyes, a gravel bank, and the spawning season. A handful of other bank-beating opportunities do exist, but they are not nearly as productive during the summer and fall months as mid-lake spots.

The best night spots are usually also good daytime spots. In other words, the fish are probably on or near this same spot during the daytime, but are inactive. When nightfall arrives, they simply move up on to that shallow food shelf and actively feed. This spot might be a large shoreline point with some scattered cribs on one lake, while it could be a mid-lake weed bar in another. Larger mid-lake reefs with rocks and weeds seem particularly good for bass, walleyes, and muskies during most seasons, but they're exceptional in the summertime. The only way to know for sure is to fish a variety of promising spots until some contact is made with a fish or two.

This is where the crankbait comes in. Casting a crankbait helps you feel out the configuration of any given mid-lake structure, as well as determine where the best fish-holding cover is. Casting spinners and surface baits does not accomplish this nearly as well. They might take fish after dark, but they do not help you keep tabs on where you are and what's on the bottom in front of you. Crankbaits do all of that as well as catch fish in the process. Crankbaits help in determining precisely what kind of cover the fish came from moments before the fish hits. Take my opening story, for example. I knew that my lure was bumping some deep tall cabbage weeds just a second or two before that big one hit. That told me, for sure, that the preferred cover was cabbage weeds. No doubt about it.

What this enables you to do is learn more about precisely where the fish are positioned. This also provides you with an opportunity to duplicate, and this is the key to future success along with the potential for huge catches. The more you learn about where a big fish comes from, no matter whether it hits at night or during the day, the better your chances to catch more than one. Crankbaits always provide this kind of information. When you're fishing in total darkness having a lure that helps you determine what's out there can really be a big help.

If I had to pick one spot for night fishing that's most apt to produce big fish, I'd opt for a mid-lake bar with good weed growth. If several exist in any given lake, usually the largest one is the best. It matters little whether the lake is 200 acres or 2,000. It also matters little whether the species is largemouth bass, walleyes, or muskies. A large, mid-lake bar with good weed growth is usually the best spot to hit after dark.

When a lake lacks weeds, I then usually just look for the largest shallow shelf. This might be a sand bar on one lake, or a rock pile in another. This shallow shelf might have some brush or cribs on it, or it might not. If it's a flowage or some other kind of artificial reservoir, the shelf will probably have some

Walleyes move into crankin' range after dark on many lakes. Find a large food shelf, and fish it thoroughly after dark with a good quality deep-diving crankbait.

stumps or standing timber on it. Of course, woody cover like this on a shallow shelf is sure to be great cover for all gamefish, night or day.

In the spring, I have had some success casting rock or gravel shorelines at night for walleyes with crankbaits. So have lots of other fishermen across our continent. What self-respecting walleye fisherman hasn't pitched a Rapala along a shoreline after dark for walleyes on some warm spring night? This is a very popular tactic, used successfully by tons of walleye fishermen over the past three decades or more. My only advice in this situation would be not to limit your selection to just a floating minnow bait such as the Rapala. There will be times when the fish are tighter to bottom, demanding a deeper diving lure.

Late fall night crankin' spots are also quite unique. Steep, breaking banks with fall-spawning baitfish such as ciscoes or smelt can be great night crankin' spots for big walleyes and muskies. Some of my greatest late fall catches have come from such spots. This includes an outing that brought in eight muskies only a few days before the annual fall deer season. I also caught my biggest inland lake trout, a 41-incher. Find a steep breaking bank with spawning ciscoes or smelt and you're almost sure to have good night crankin'. A floating deep-diver that can be cast or trolled slowly over a deep, hard bottom is the key to success.

The Best Night Lures

As you already know, I'm partial to crankbaits for night fishing. I've had success with a number of crankbait styles after dark depending on the topography and some other variables. I do like minnow baits for walleyes over shallow flats in the spring. I also like large minnow baits for muskies over really shallow flats no matter what the season. But, if I had to pick one crankbait for nighttime fishing, a floating deep-diver would get my vote. This lure is so versatile, and it gives me that informational option. Plainly put, the floating deep-diver tells me more about what kind of cover I'm casting around.

Jointed deep divers have been particularly good for me on bass and muskies. The jointed bait produces an audible clicking noise as the body parts collide with each other. Just as we talked earlier about how strong this clicking trigger can be in dark water, it has the same effect after dark in clear water. The clicking noise and enticing action is great for big fish after dark. I believe that this clicking action attracts more big fish under the cover of darkness.

Jointed lures normally generate a lot of action at slow speeds, as well as an incredible amount of noise. This all makes them a much easier target for a night predator to home in on. Make that a fat, jointed deep-diver, which improves the lure's silhouette, and you've improved the lure's potential even more. Fat plugs make great night lures. My philosophy has always been to make it easy for the fish to find the bait. A big, fat, jointed lure makes this all possible. Combining the superior slow-speed action of a jointed lure with a bold silhouette, provided by the fatter profile, and big fish are sure to be attracted to it.

My early nighttime fishing success with the jointed Pikie Minnow in the 1970s encouraged me to develop my own jointed crankbait, with many of the same fish-catching characteristics, nearly three decades later. I caught big largemouths, big smallies, and lunker class walleyes after dark on that same bait. The original jointed Pikie Minnow had a lot of great nighttime fishing attributes. It was a fat-bodied, jointed plug with great action, strong clicking noise, and a bold silhouette. All made the old Pikie a good one. Many of today's best nighttime fishing lures have taken some of the Pikie's best features. About the only thing the Pikie lacked was diving depth. The small lip restricted its diving potential. Newer crankers with larger diving lips and a similar body configuration have proven to be even better hybrids.

The Technique

Technique nearly always plays a big role in any kind of fishing, but it's particularly important to the nighttime cranker. The crankbait serves as both a fish-catcher and a boat control tool. The latter, a boat control tool, becomes vital to your overall success. As I've said so many times throughout this book, the crankbait helps you stay on the spot. The crankbait should be considered your second sonar unit. As you make a cast with a crankbait, the goal should always be to "feel" what's going on in front of you. Is the bait making contact with weeds? Is it bumping rocks?

Feel is vital in all forms of crankbait fishing, but it's paramount to the nighttime caster. Night crankin', by its very nature, improves your sense of feel tremendously. The lack of vision increases your awareness automatically whether you know it or not. A crankbait's vibration seems more intense at your rod tip after dark. This is because you're relying on this sense so much more. The key here is to take full advantage of it.

One of the biggest mistakes the novice makes on any typical cast/retrieve presentation after dark is to "over-crank." In other words, the tendency is to crank too fast. Too much speed ruins control. This is really accented when you fish over weeds at night. The inexperienced, nervous cranker plows weeds instead of climbing over them. Plowing through weeds breaks them off and loads them up all around the lure. The result is a lot of wasted casts.

The trick here is to challenge yourself to NEVER have weeds on your bait, but always be making contact with weeds. This is a game you should play anytime you're crankin' weed cover, but it is vital to your success at night. Remember, anytime you have weeds clinging to your lure, you've wasted that cast. You must know when the lure is contacting weeds, and then how to free these weeds from the lure. The combination of weed contact and the movements made to clean weeds from the lure triggers strikes. That's why making contact is important. The fish are near the weed cover. The bumping, rising, and ripping action triggers an almost involuntary reaction from the fish.

Of course, this all takes some practice, but it really comes down to a matter of concentration. Speed control does not mean, fast. It means controlling the speed. The right speed for night crankin' in weed cover is usually a slow to slow/medium retrieve. This slower speed provides you with the ability to react when weed contact is made. Too much speed makes the lure plow before you can react.

Some anglers have the mistaken impression that, if you don't crank these lures fast, you won't generate the necessary speed to trigger a strike. This is a valid consideration, but only to a point. It's important to know that you don't need speed for 30 to 60 feet in order to trigger a fish. You just need it for a foot or two, when it's inside that fish's strike zone. What I'm getting at here is; once you hit weed cover, the next step is to jiggle the bait and allow it to rise upwards. Of course, this is why a floating diver is the preferred bait. Now, once the bait clears the weed tops, a subsequent "rip" of the rod, which drives the lure forward at tremendous speed for only a few feet or so, is all that is needed to trigger the strike.

When you use a crankbait in this manner, tremendous speed is generated at the perfect point, right at the weed top. This area immediately around the weed top is usually right in the fish's strike zone. This is the only place where tremendous speed is necessary. Not surprisingly, the "rip" right after clearing a weed top, produces a lot of strikes. Many fish also hit as you're jiggling the lure to free it from the weeds, as well. However, I've found that the highest percentage of strikes occurs just as the "rip" is being generated. Timing here is usually superb for setting the hook. Both you and the fish react almost simultaneously, which makes for outstanding hooking percentages.

Finally, I nearly always recommend a short cast for night crankin' in cover. The thicker the cover, the shorter the cast. Short casts simply provide you with more control. If you're crankin' clean bottom a long cast is OK. If you're casting a minnow bait along a

Jointed deep-divers have been exceptional night lures for big bass, walleyes, and muskies. The jointed bait produces an audible clicking noise along with a strong vibration that really excites feeding fish in low light.

quite shoreline or flat after dark, a longer cast is recommend. But anytime there's cover, shorten it up.

Night Summary

I saved this chapter for later since I considered it an advanced crankbait technique, as well as being perhaps the deadliest of all big fish crankin' tactics. Nighttime crankin' was also one of my oldest and most

Oversized crankbaits are great for bass and most other gamefish after dark. If you want to up your score on nighttime outings, start using bigger plugs.

cherished secrets for many years. I began night crankin' as a teenage basser way back in the early 1970s. It accounted for some of my best big bass catches in some of my earliest years. I still find it funny that the locals never caught on to my night bass tricks back then. Some of them knew I was night-fishing, but almost no one knew I was catching them on crankbaits.

A few years later, on a vacation to the north, my dad and I turned an unproductive walleye trip around by going out after dark and casting crankbaits. Our traditional daytime live bait tactics were a struggle, and the fish were running small. We happened upon a few nice walleyes while casting Rapalas over a stump field, and it changed the way we looked at walleyes from that point on. Instead of anchoring over a rock hump with a split shot and a minnow, we began aggressively fan-casting stump fields, weed flats, and shallow rock shoals after dark with crankbaits. We caught more and bigger walleyes than ever before. Eventually, we started casting deep-divers for walleyes at other times of the year, over different spots, with the same general results. Crankbaits and night fishing were gaining a credibility with the Bucher family for walleyes and bass that was unmatched.

And then, on one of my first musky trips in June 1972, that same lack of success with traditional musky lures lead me to try a crankbait, and some nighttime fishing. I'll never forget how excited I was when my first 40-inch musky pulverized a big

Heddon Cobra minnow bait, as I cranked it across an offshore weed point. Up to that point, few words were devoted to muskies on crankbaits in any publications, and certainly no one was talking about muskies after dark.

Once I started guiding, a whole new set of rules took over. Now it was time to make certain my clients caught fish consistently. Of course, being consistent at musky fishing was no easy task, but consistency and crankbaits went hand in hand. It didn't take long before we racked up quite the scorecard with big fish caught on crankbaits. Of course, we caught lots of muskies and some big ones on a variety of other lures and tactics, but once I started guiding at night with the crankbait as our main weapon, we began catching big muskies in numbers never before heard of.

Instead of catching an occasional big fish, my clients and I began placing three to five fish a year in the state's top 10. This went on for over a decade. It's been rumored that one of the state's most heralded musky contests, the Vilas County Musky Marathon, established a special "guide's division" in order to keep my big fish out of their listings. Even though I'd placed a number of big fish in that contest before, we (my clients and I) never dominated it until we started night fishing. And the bulk of our night success was with crankbaits. I'm convinced that this domination would have continued if I hadn't retired from the guide business. We had a system: Night fishing with crankbaits. No other system, no other lure, even came close.

Even now, while filming TV episodes, I rely heavily on night fishing with crankbaits to produce big fish when it's all on the line. In June 1998 on my first night excursion of the season, I was rocked by a monster musky strike and the subsequent battle. While the camera was rolling in pitch darkness, I had an incredibly hard strike a few feet into my retrieve. This was an exceptionally powerful fish that wouldn't give an inch. Even with 60 feet of line out, the fish had my rod doubled with drag slippage, and I keep a very tight drag. When the battle finally subsided, another trophy and another Top 10 candidate was being displayed for my television audience. At 49 ½ inches and a 24 ½ inch girth, I had a real brute on my hands. The fish weighed over 35 pounds. Only my second musky of that season, but already another superb trophy. The two common denominators again were night fishing and a crankbait. What can I say?

I can assure you that if you master both night fishing and crankbaits as a tandem, you're going to have some very costly taxidermy bills. No matter what the species, you'll catch 'em consistently after dark, The biggest bass in any system are likely to be taken at night with big crankbaits. Night-fishing also provides one of the best chances for any angler to bag a bruiser walleye of 28 inches or more. Nothing catches big walleyes at night like a crankbait. What night fishing with crankbaits has done for me in the musky world is simply incredible. I know of no better way to consistently bag big trophy class fish from hard-fished waters. Learn your waters intimately, and then fish them hard after dark with a quality crankbait and you're sure to bag the biggest fish in that system.

chapter 20

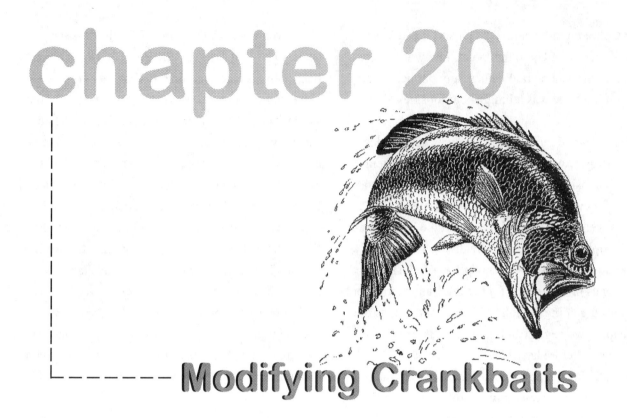

Modifying Crankbaits

As my rod bent for the fifteenth time, I just had to say something. I couldn't keep it a secret any longer. After all, this wasn't some duel between two tournament pros, I was fishing with my dad.

My father certainly was not a patient man to begin with, nor was he an overly polite fellow when he wasn't catching fish. On this day, he hadn't gotten a single strike along the entire weed bed, yet the fish were murdering my bait. To make matters even worse, dad was casting an identical bait. Well, at least he thought so.

"What the heck is wrong with this bait?" he muttered in frustration. "We're throwing the same crankbait at these fish, yet you're tearin' 'em up, and I can't get even get a bump. You've caught walleyes, smallmouths, and northern right alongside me. I'm the first to say you're good, but you ain't that good. What the heck is going on here?"

I finally had to fess up. "It's the hooks, dad. I'm running a larger set of trebles."

He looked at me in total disbelief. "The what?

How can a different set of hooks on the same bait make that much of a difference?" he asked.

As I dipped the landing net on yet another walleye, I exposed my secret. While our lures were technically both #13 Rapalas, mine was much older, and it had one size larger trebles on it. The original hooks had rusted badly over the previous winter, and when I replaced them, these were the only sizes I had to work with. By accident, I had stumbled on to something special. The slightly larger sized trebles made the skinny balsa floater far less buoyant, and also enabled it to run deeper with slightly less side wobble (action). The fact that it was older and had caught tons of fish already probably added to the lure's lack of buoyancy since it no doubt had absorbed a lot of water. In essence, I had created an early suspending version of the Rapala without purposely trying.

Dad's newer model with smaller factory hooks was much more buoyant. It would skim only a few feet below the surface, far above the weed tops. My old-timer, on the other hand, tracked below the line of sight and occasionally even ticked the weed tops. It also stayed down at this slightly deeper depth with a slower retrieve. The older version with the larger set of trebles simply ran closer to the level at which the fish were holding, which was the very tops of the weeds. As insignificantly subtle as this variance may seem to some, it often makes a huge difference when fish aren't in a chasing mood. The closer a lure comes to fish in this situation, the more success you're going to have.

"I still can't believe those bigger hooks would make that big of a difference," Joe Sr. said with obvious disgust. "These fish can't be that picky".

I agreed with him only to make him feel better. The simple fact was that they really were "that picky." To prove the point beyond a doubt, I offered to switch lures. Dad refused at first, but once I set the hook on fish number 16, just two casts later, he was ready to

test my trick. Within minutes, I heard his unmistakable grunt as he set the hook.

"By golly, this bait really is better," he said with a surprise. "I'd never have believed it, if I hadn't seen it happen myself."

Dad ended up taking three more walleyes with that old modified Rapala before we called it a night. I never caught another fish.

This is but one example of how one simple modification on a crankbait can make a world of difference in its productivity. While factory lures, straight out of the box, work exceptionally well the majority of the time, there are those unique situations where applying some ingenuity can spell the difference. Most of the time it's a slight modification, such as the one just described, that makes the biggest impact on a lure's fish-catching potential. Modifications such as

Putting a larger hook on any factory crankbait tightens up the action and decreases buoyancy. It might also increase running depth a bit.

these are almost imperceptible to the naked eye at first glance. I've found that minor changes are usually the best modifications since they do not detract from the lure's original outward design cosmetics, yet they alter its action in a slight, but positive way. With this in mind, let's examine a few of the easiest ways to modify an existing crankbait in order to enhance certain performance characteristics to fit a specific fishing situation.

Changing Hook Sizes & Models

One of the easiest ways to change the running depth, buoyancy, action and even hooking performance of a crankbait without drilling, sawing, or any other cosmetic alterations is to simply change hook sizes. I have to admit that I am always doing just this with my favorite bass and walleye crankbaits in order to make them a bit more versatile. Generally speaking, you'll find that you can easily alter the buoyancy and action of almost any crankbait by simply going up or down in hook size. The thickness or actual weight of one treble hook model over another also has a noticeable bearing. The smaller and more subtle the action is on a specific lure, the more noticeable a hook change will be on the plug's action.

When a more buoyant lure is desired for fishing in and around high-topping submerged cover, such as weeds, switch to a smaller or thinner gauge treble hook. The slight reduction in hook weight is sure to improve buoyancy. An added benefit from the switch to lighter gauge hooks is often additional side wobble, flash, and vibration. This can be a big plus whenever big gamefish are tucked tight to thick shallow cover. The added buoyancy will enable the lure to rise out of snags easier, plus, the superior flash and vibration are sure to trigger more strikes from less active, cover-tight fish.

There are several potential drawbacks to any modification, and "going down" in hook size is not immune to fallout. For one, whenever you go smaller with hook size, you risk creating two new problems: 1) upsetting the tracking, and 2) reducing the ability of the lure to hook fish. Remember, most manufacturers decide on a certain hook size for their lures after some extensive testing. This testing is not only based on a lure's fish-catching potential, but also on it's ability to track straight and true; even at excessive speeds. The weight of hooks beneath a lure creates a keel effect. Without hooks beneath a lure's body, most crankbaits will simply roll out and not wiggle, wobble or track at all. In other words, the hooks on almost every crankbait perform a critical function – balance. Change the hooks on any crankbait and you risk altering the bait's balance.

Luckily, the astute crankbait angler has a bit of an engineering mind, and is able to make the corrections necessary to fine tune almost any crankbait. Checking the crankbait's "track" is first on the list once the hooks are changed; particularly when "going down" in hook size. This is easily done by bending the front line tie left or right in order to straighten a lure that runs off-center. We deal with this issue in much detail in the chapter on tuning crankbaits. But it should be worth noting that many lures become more track sensitive when lighter hooks are used to replace the factory ones.

Instead of "going down" in hook size in order to improve a lure's buoyancy, flash and vibration for shallow cover applications, I often opt to stick with the same factory size, but go to a lighter gauge (weight) treble. In other words, if the particular lure currently carries a pair of #2 trebles, I'll stick with that same size #2, but simply change the style. The idea is to find a hook that is lighter in weight without reducing hook size. The main reason for this is to maintain the lure's ability to hook fish well. Dropping down in hook size can really reduce hooking effectiveness, particularly if the lure has a lot of body mass. Fatter crankbaits require hooks with a wider gap in order to place the hook points outside the restrictive body mass. Otherwise, a fish's mouth is apt to bite down on the large body mass

Minnow baits of all sizes are deadly lures on just about all freshwater gamefish. In addition, they are tremendously versatile baits that work equally well casting over the shallows or being trolled over deep water. they can easily be modified by adding stick-on weights and changing hook sizes in order to alter their action and running depth.

of the lure with no hook points ever actually touching the fish, let alone penetrating deep enough to get the fight started..

With that in mind, you can easily improve the hooking quality of any fat-bodied crankbait by replacing factory hooks with premium, wide-gap versions. Make sure they are very sharp and always keep tabs on any lure's hooking capabilities. Tournament anglers have to be astutely aware of this factor. A lure that attracts a lot of strikes is certainly one worth using, but if it loses a high percentage of fish, it must be modified in order to improve this scorecard. Discarding factory hooks and replacing them with a thin-wire, wide-gap, premium hook will usually solve the problem.

Premium grade hooks, by the way, are almost always the way to go; especially if you're going with light wire trebles. Hook manufacturing has come a long way in the last few years, and no doubt will continue to improve. You can now purchase hooks from manufacturers such as VMC and Gamagatsu that are extremely sharp and made of a superior metal. While these hooks are often too expensive to add to any lure direct from the factory, serious fishermen wouldn't hesitate to add them to their lures in order to upgrade their hooking characteristics even a small amount. Usually, they (premium hooks) do even more than that. They're really that much better.

Anyone who's overly concerned with the aspect of hook strength must consider purchasing the newer premium grade hooks. By utilizing superior technology and materials manufacturers are able to provide an equally strong hook with far less metal surface. The benefits include a sharper hook that will penetrate faster, as well as a lighter weight hook. Faster penetrating hooks that are needle-sharp enable the angler to get a much higher percentage of hook ups on big gamefish when working lures at slower speeds and with lighter tackle. The bigger the fish, the more important fast, deep hook penetration becomes.

Adding a heavier weight hook to a crankbait is also an often-used modification. While reducing hook size has a tendency to improve buoyancy, vibration and side flash, increasing hook size usually does just the opposite. First off, larger heavier hooks decrease buoyancy. This may be desirable in some fishing situations in order to make a lure run slightly deeper, and keep it at that depth. This is precisely what the larger set of trebles did to my old Rapala in the opening stor. It made that old "war horse" run deeper and stay down there with far less speed.

Larger, heavier hooks also improve the keel on almost any crankbait. Any crankbait that gives you tuning trouble can often be cured by simply adding larger hooks. More weight beneath the lure gives it additional ballast. This can be a very desirable feature for the trolling enthusiast. Motor trolling speeds may far exceed those created by any casting presentation. Higher speeds are the ultimate field tests of any crankbaits ability to track true. Anytime you run into an aggravating tuning problem with a crankbait while trolling, consider modifying it with a larger, heavier set of hooks. This usually solves the problem.

Of course, the biggest drawback to heavier gauge hooks is a reduction in action, flash and vibration. While this may not turn out to be a big deal with some lures, it can be critical with others. I saw this recently on a fall Canadian trip for big pike and muskies. My

partner, Mike Novak, and I found most of the fish to be up inside remaining clumps of milfoil weeds, but they were reluctant to come out. None of these fish would chase a high-riding lure such as a spinner bait. The only baits they'd even take a swipe at were jerkbaits. However, because of dark, turbid water combined with cooling air and water temperatures, the fish seemed extra sluggish and held tightly to the cover. Only a perfectly placed cast over the top of a milfoil patch with a minnow bait would produce strikes. And, the only minnow bait they would take produced a noticeably strong rod tip vibration when pulled forward.

Mike and I had purposely rigged heavier gauge treble hooks on most of our big minnow baits to reduce their buoyancy so they could be worked with slower retrieve speeds. We also went with beefier forged hooks so we could muscle the bigger fish out of thick weed cover without fear of a hook bending out. However, this heavy-duty outfitting didn't impress the fish one bit. While our modified minnow baits suspended nicely over the weeds, they produced minimal flash and vibration, and they got caught up in the weeds a lot. But most of all, they simply weren't triggering fish.

While experimenting with various color patterns on the second afternoon, I happened to snap on an old beat up firetiger pattern in an effort to improve the flash I was showing the fish. My first pass with this lure produced a 45-incher that violently roared out of the middle of a milfoil patch to strike the jerking/flashing lure. While unhooking the fish in the net, I noticed that this model still had thin wire trebles. Not wanting to switch at this point, more out of laziness than anything else, I continued using the same lure. Within a short time I caught another muskie, this one 42 inches long, and a huge pike that was every bit as big as the muskie; both on that same lure.

Thinking that it was a color issue, Mike switched to a firetiger pattern, but four hours later he still had no action. We both began to wonder if it wasn't the variance in hook weight, and the additional vibration the lure had with lighter hooks. In an effort to check it

Big minnow baits are exceptional musky producers in cold water. The best way to make them work at a slower retrieve is to decrease the lure's buoyancy. As stick-on weights and or heavier hooks to get the desired results.

out, Mike switched to a minnow bait with lighter wire hooks. I also tried a minnow bait of a different color with the same light wire hooks. Guess what happened? Mike started catching fish, and I continued to trigger strikes with the different color. The answer was definitely the lighter gauge hooks. They reduced the weight underneath the lure, thus improving the bait's flash and vibration. Again, a subtle modification that made a huge difference, and all it really came down to was changing the hooks. Although it may be simple, changing the hooks on your crankbaits can greatly impact your productivity in many instances.

Adding Stick-On Weights

More has been written lately about adding stick-on lead tape to various crankbaits than perhaps any other fishing subject. This is especially true in bass fishing publications. Bass tournament pros and full-time professional bass guides have elevated this particular lure modification almost to an art form. In an effort to present something slightly different to highly pressured fish, or at least make the bait run slightly deeper and hold in place a bit longer, bass anglers are adding weight to various commercial crankbaits.

Those are the three basic reasons for adding weight to crankbaits: 1) to make it run deeper, and 2) to make it hold in place or suspend longer, and 3) to improve its tracking. Any weight added to a crankbait is sure to decrease its buoyancy somewhat and therefore accomplish both of these goals to some extent. The amount of weight added determines just how much the lure's buoyancy will be altered. Small circles or strips of lead tape enable the angler to make the most subtle buoyancy alterations.

Adding any amount of weight to any lure will also alter the lure's action, too; much the same as adding heavier hooks does. The more weight that's added, the less side-to-side wobbling action it will have. The trick here is to add just enough to accomplish the task. Determining the task before adding any weight is very

important. You need to ask yourself, "What am I adding this weight for? What am I trying to accomplish?" Determining precisely where weight should be attached to the lure is also worth noting. In almost every case, weight is best added to the belly side of crankbaits. Adding weight to the underside improves overall ballast with minimal effect on action. This, of course, immediately improves the lure's tracking. Attaching weight to the top of a crankbait is not only more cosmetically detracting, but it can upset the critical balance on some lures, as well. Keeling the crankbait is nearly always a primary concern. You never want to create a tracking problem. Attach weight to the lure's sides and you again mess with cosmetics, and possibly still chance altering the lure's track. Keep weight underneath the lure and you almost can't go wrong.

A "can't miss" formula for adding stick-on weight to crankbaits is to attach the tape near the center balancing point underneath the lure. On most lures this is right in back of the front hook hanger. This is the best way to decrease buoyancy without disturbing the lure's original action. Do this if your task is to simply develop a "suspender" crankbait, one which neither floats nor sinks. Attaching stick-on weight to the underside of a crankbait near the center balancing point can't be beat. The ideal "suspender" hangs perfectly horizontal when paused. Adding weight more towards the tail or head prevents this neutral/horizontal suspension. Some proficient anglers are emphatic that this kind of weighting position is critical since it replicates a natural baitfish more realistically. It is thought that more fish are likely to strike a suspender that hangs in this manner. Perfect "hang time" is thus obtained.
Improved diving performance is also possible through subtle weighting of commercial crankbaits. However, precise weight positioning varies a bit from a "suspender". Again, that's why you must determine why you're weighting the lure. If you could care less about the crankbait's suspending nature, and are just interested in increasing the depth it attains during retrieve, I recommend weighting the lure entirely differently.

One of the best ways to increase a lure's diving potential is to nose-weight the lure. The objective is to force the lure's nose downward at a stronger angle, thus increasing the dig on the diving lip. For example, most floating/diving crankbaits rest horizontally on the water's surface before any retrieve is initiated. As soon as the lure is pulled forward, water pushes against the diving lip surface forcing the tail up and nose down. This diving position is preserved as the lure is continually driven forward. However, if that lure can be made to rest vertically, nose-down on the water's surface, it stands to reason that it will more quickly dig deeper. If the lure is already pointed in the direction you want it to go, any forward movement initiated on this lure will simply move in the direction it's pointed.

Several commercially produced crankbaits are now actually weighted in the manner. Some are even off-shoots of a previously popular unweighted model. They dive significantly deeper than their counterparts and are great performers when additional diving depth is required. Of course, crankbaits weighted in this manner do loose some ability to back out of snags. This is especially true when so much weight is added that the lure either barely floats or even sinks. Therefore, these lures are most useful over clean, hard-bottom spots and are poor choices for weeds or even silty bottoms.

Adding stick-on

weight towards the tail portion of a crankbait has its applications as well. I especially like to add weight towards the tail portions of my minnow baits. A tail-weighted minnow bait automatically casts better. Minnow baits in general tend to cast poorly, although not all minnow baits adhere to this stereotype. Minnow baits that are light in the tail catch the wind unpredictably and blow off course. Gusty winds compound the problem. This can be extremely frustrating when trying to pinpoint your casts to distant targets. If the target happens to be around exposed trees and brush, you'll likely get a lot of tangled, fouled casts. Not a pretty sight. Add weight conservatively to the tail portion of

Low-light walleyes will take many styles of crankbaits. Any time walleyes are working shallow water cover under low-light conditions, they are targets for crankbait presentations.

almost any minnow bait and it's surely going to improve your casting accuracy. The key is to add just enough weight without severely upsetting the lure's action.

Another advantage I've noticed with tail weighting minnow baits leans more towards its ability to attract and trigger fish. Minnow baits that rise "nose up" tend to trigger a lot more fish. Tail-heavy/nose-light minnow baits also react to any jerking action with much more lateral movement. It's always been my contention that creating lateral movement on your lures triggers more strikes. Any following, stalking predator fish simply can't stand lateral movement. The abrupt directional change is key to making the fish strike. Fish muskies for any length of time and you'll discover this secret. 'Wanna trigger a following muskie? Get some abrupt directional change. A tail-weighted minnow bait changes direction from left to right with every jerk and pause.

As long as you can get a tail weighted minnow bait to wiggle, wobble, vibrate and flash to your liking, you'll probably catch more fish on it than any comparable model. Here's where spending a few hours experimenting with adding stick-on weights to your minnow baits at a local swimming pool can pay big dividends down the road. Once again, modifications make all the difference. Fine tune your minnow baits so they rise slightly nose up and you'll have some deadly secret weapons. The difference will be negligible as they rest in your tackle box trays, but tie one of them on and they become a stick of dynamite.

chapter 21

Rattles: Do They Really Work?

I was sure glad my sonar flasher unit had an easy-to-read signal. At this point, it was the only reference I had to keep the boat on the weed edge. Total darkness combined with a moonless night, thick overcast skies, and a misty rain made visibility almost non-existent. The shoreline was no longer visible, and if it wasn't for the small scattering of cabin lights, I'd have had no idea where I was on this lake.

My first inclination was to idle my way back to the landing and head for home, but something told me to stick it out a bit longer. Besides, I knew that big walleyes and some nice muskies were cruising this big weed point after dark, and I had some anxious clients. I figured the super-dark conditions might be just what the doctor ordered. I figured my clients should catch something on this point.

As we began our approach, one of my clients asked what he should use. Of course, I immediately said, "Crankbait."

Now, when I say "crankbait," most musky hunters immediately think – DepthRaider, and that's just exactly what this fellow reached for. He switched on his

head lamp, dug through a tackle box, found a "DR", as many folks call them, and put it to work. His partner did the same. I sipped on a cup of coffee, switched on the trolling motor and instructed them both where to cast. It didn't take more than four or five casts when the fellow fishing from the rear barked "Fish on."

As he battled the fish toward the boat I switched on my headlamp, grabbed the net, and readied for the landing. When the fish finally appeared a few feet from the net, I immediately identified it as a big walleye, but was a bit surprised to see a straight model DR in the fish's mouth instead of a jointed version. "You're using a straight model?" I asked.

"Well Joe," he said. "You did say crankbait, but you didn't specify anything else. I kind of expected you wanted me to try a DepthRaider, but you never said anything about jointed or straight."

I couldn't disagree with him; especially now that he had a trophy walleye.

A few casts later, the same guy hooked another walleye, and then another. On the next spot he caught a 43-inch musky. Then two more walleyes. This was not unexpected, mind you, but I was a bit perplexed as to why the other guy hadn't taken a single fish. I found it even more puzzling after I learned that he'd started with a jointed bait, then quickly switched to a straight model after his partner had taken the second fish. Why hadn't he taken a fish?

As we began casting our third spot of the evening, the same guy set the hook on his sixth fish of the evening, another musky, just over 30 inches. While I was happy for him and his success, I didn't want his partner to feel so left out of the action. So, I suggested a tackle examination right after a few photos and the release of the muskie. Their rods and reels were nearly identical. I then looked at line type and test, since this is often a major factor as we've discussed in-depth in chapter five. If one of these guys had a different weight line on, it would make a difference in maximum running depth; which might have explained the production variance. Both rigs contained the same lines.

I've never been a big believer that lure color had much bearing during night fishing applications, so I was quick to discount the difference between one angler's sucker pattern and the other's night shiner style. However, the night shiner was definitely producing all the action, so I wasn't in disagreement when a color change was mentioned. Since neither

had another straight model night shiner, I opted to save the day, digging in my own tackle box for an old battle-proven model. I suggested snapping the lure on for him since I already had it in my hand. As I fuddled with unsnapping the sucker pattern and attaching the night shiner, I noticed that my client's sucker pattern had no rattles. What tipped me off was how much noisier the night shiner was while I struggled to snap it on.

I immediately suggested that we closely examine the lure that's catching all the fish. Indeed, it had a rattle. Was this the answer? We'd soon find out.

Big, straight-model divers with internal rattles work exceptionally well for muskies in low light conditions. Tom Dietz caught this toothy critter at last light by casting along a deep weed edge.

A few casts into the drift, I felt the boat list a bit and heard a groan as an angler set the hook. This time it was coming from the front of the boat.

"Finally!" the frustrated front angler hollered. "It took all night, but I finally broke the ice. This fish feels like a good one."

The powerful surface thrashing told me right away that this was no walleye. We had a good musky hooked. A full five minutes later, a hefty 45-incher was safely in the net.

The fishing slowed up a lot after that, and we finished with only two more strikes. However, the bow angler, who was fishless prior to the lure switch, caught both of them. In my opinion, this was one of the most clear cut examples of a preference for rattles. Whenever the bow angler is getting severely outfished by the rear one, there's some kind of a lure preference thing going on, or a very obvious difference in the tackle combination. In this case, the preference for rattles was obvious. I've seen similar instances with largemouth bass in muddy reservoir conditions, as well as walleyes in deeply stained lakes. When visibility decreases, rattles become a positive factor.

The subject of rattles in lures has created much debate in the fishing world. Some anglers swear they (rattles) make a big difference, while others claim they have little impact. Even biologists have mixed arguments about how well fish can actually detect the rattling, clicking sound that lures or live creatures make. My observations on the effectiveness of rattling lures fall on both sides of these arguments. What I've found is that it really comes down to an issue of water color and overall visibility. In other words, the less a fish can see, the more that rattles seem to matter. Conversely, the more a fish can see (the clearer the water and the more light available), the less effective rattles seems to be.

Rattling lipless crankbaits are super-productive over thick shallow cover in water with a slight stain. Rattles are nearly always an advantage in these conditions.

Night fishing is one of the most productive applications for crankbaits, especially those with rattles. When night crankin' gets hot, it is common to hook fish on just about ever cast.

I wouldn't hesitate to say that nearly all warm-water gamefish react positively or negatively to rattles according to the water clarity. Cold-water gamefish such as trout and salmon probably have similar responses. As light and visibility within the predatory fish's environment decreases, the less it can rely on sight sensing and the more it must rely on senses of hearing and vibration detection. As light and visibility increase, sight seems to automatically take over as the dominant sense. Being able to hear a prey coming or detect its presence through vibration becomes an almost unused sense. Fish simply don't need their senses of hearing and vibration detection when they can see well. But they really need them when they can't see.

Some anglers claim that loud rattling crankbaits even spook off gamefish in clear water situations. It is suggested that rattles are simply overwhelming in this instance, much like a rock band in a library. There is nothing even remotely natural about a noisy rattling crankbait in any gin-clear water environment. Sight feeding gamefish are more tuned in to movement and flash as triggers. Too much sound does nothing to attract predators here.

On the other hand, dark, dirty, or turbid waters severely limit any fish's ability to see prey for any distance. Sight feeding becomes far less reliable. The prey simply can not be seen beyond a few feet. Gamefish automatically become far more reliant on their lateral line, which functions primarily to detect vibration.

Night feeding and the underwater environment after dark creates a very similar scenario. Pitch black nights offer almost no available light, reducing any possibility of sight feeding. Add any sediment to this water, in the form of algae bloom, run-off, or in-flow stain, and you would think that no gamefish would have a chance to catch prey in these conditions. Yet this is far from true. Many gamefish feed efficiently under the cover of darkness using a combination of all their predatory senses. It is also worth noting here that some gamefish have much more efficient lateral line systems than others, and therefore do much better under low light or turbid water situations. In my experiences, largemouths, walleyes, saugers, smallmouths, and muskies feed exceptionally well in low light. All of these fish can be readily caught in dark, turbid waters, or after dark. Some trout species also seem to do better than others in this regard. Brook trout continue to feed in turbid waters, and are known to be caught after dark. Rainbows and brownies feed strongly after dark, too. Some might argue they're just overly light sensitive since they also seem to bite better on dark overcast days. It may be that they are able to hear better.

Northern pike seem to be very poor low light feeders and rarely feed after dark, unlike their cousins – the musky. Ditto for lake trout. This suggests to me that pike and lakers rely heavily on

Floating divers are great walleye catchers particularly after dark. The ability to bounce bottom and careen off of cover makes them exceptional at triggering fish in low light. The author especially likes rattling crankbaits when the sun goes down.

seeing their prey and have lesser lateral line systems. They are sight feeders primarily. As soon as they loose their ability to see, they simply quit feeding. The only pike I've ever taken at night have come on those bright full moon excursions. This would lend credibility to this sight-feeding theory. I've also seen pike activity drop off on reservoirs across the U.S. and Canada as water clarity decreases. Whenever a section of a reservoir receives a big run-off from rain, or even an erosion of bank sediment from wind or a rising water level, pike activity seems to shut down. Find the clearest section of water on any such situation, and you'll likely find the active pike.

In my opinion, rattles do have their time and place in fishing lures contrary to what some argue. I agree there are definitely those times when a subtle lure sound with no rattles and a more natural look is the way to go, and this is usually in clear water situations with plenty of light available. However, there are just as many conditions where a lure loaded with rattles is bound to be more productive. The most notable are in dark water and night-fishing applications.

I've also believe that there are times when fish prefer smaller rattles over larger ones. Or more rattles over one or two. I've even seen a noticeable fish-catching difference between rattling lures of the same brand. Most notably, I've seen RatLTraps made from various plastics create totally different rattling pitches. The loudest, crispest RatLTraps are chrome models made from ABS plastic. The quietest versions are clear see-through versions made from Lexan or Butyrate. I've seen situations where one was clearly better than the other. I'll be the first to admit when I'm lookin' to wake fish up, I always go for a chrome RatLTrap; then I'll shake the bait to make sure it has that crisp sound I'm looking for. Never underestimate the variances in pitch that are created by building lures with different materials.

The composition of the rattles can also have a bearing on the pitch. Some manufacturers use lead BB's as rattles in their baits, while others go with some kind of steel shot. Lead absorbs more sound and impact, since the material is comparatively soft. This deadens the impact and lowers the rattling pitch. Steel rattles are much harder. Steel shot ricochets off a surface harder and faster. A higher and louder pitch is the result.

Rattle bead or shot size is another factor that influences the sounds created. Smaller beads or shot produce a much higher-pitched rattling sound than larger ones. Smaller rattles have a musical marimba shake to them, while large shot sizes tend to produce a deeper clicking sound. The only way to know which one the fish prefer is to try them both. I've experimented a lot with this size aspect of rattles when developing crankbait prototypes in the past. Just when I think I've discovered a preference for one over the other, I've been shown otherwise on the next fishing outing. For example, there was a time when I was convinced that a deep rhythmic clicking sound produced by adding just one larger lead shot to my DepthRaider crankbaits was superior to all other rattling sounds. I'd caught a lot of fish on this design over the years. But some other experiences I've had since then have weakened this theory.

Certain paint finishes on lures have a tendency to intensify the rattling sound. Chrome lures are usually made from ABS plastic in order to get the best adhesion. The combination of ABS, a harder, impact-resistant plastic, and a metallic chrome finish provides a very crisp, high-pitched rattling sound. When a lure manufacturer wants a clear-bodied lure that will absorb more impact, they're likely to use a softer grade plastic such as Butyrate. This is the same material that many screw driver handles are made from. This material absorbs a blow rather than reflects it. When rattling lures are made from Butyrate lures they tend to produce far less noise.

So where does this all fit into crankbait fishing? Basically, it all comes down to knowing when an angler should fish a rattling crankbait or one without these noise makers. You need to have a selection of both rattling and non-rattling model crankbaits. The choice

Big, jointed divers containing rattles are super producers in dark or stained waters. All gamefish will hit them.

of when to use one over the other should primarily be gauged by water clarity. Generally speaking, stay away from rattling crankbaits in clear water. Go heavy on rattlin' divers in dark water. While this is only a general rule, it's one that has served me well and withstood the test of time on the water.

Rattles can impact your fishing both positively and negatively depending on the conditions. The only way to know which way to go for sure is to try both. Admittedly though, I do tend to lean one way or the other depending upon water clarity and available light. I also tend to lean away from rattles when fishing pressure heightens. It's important to note that all crankbaits create some rattling sound. Hooks anchored loosely off split rings are bound to produce a rattling sound on their own. Attach the hooks directly to a hook hanger without split rings and you decrease this noise a bunch. Whether this is necessary is still being debated.

In general, gin-clear water fish are sight feeders and tend to shy away from bold colors and noisy baits. This is true of crankbaits as well as top-water plugs, jigs, worms and other lures. Less visible, less obvious, low-noise baits are usually better in this situation. Blending in a bit is usually better. A natural subtle action is usually a bigger factor than noise. Rattles do little to the fish catching value of lures in most clear-water situations.

As I've said repeatedly, darken the water and sight feeding efficiency is reduced. Sound-feeding increases. The darker the water becomes the more important sound becomes in helping predators locate the bait. This when more visible, more obvious, high noise lures shine. Blending in is the wrong way to go here. Standing out is the key. A wide heavy vibration that displaces more water is sure to help. Clanging hooks and internal rattles offer the fish more ways to home in. Use a bait that rattles here, and you're probably going to catch more fish. Period.

a crankin'
conclusion

chapter 22

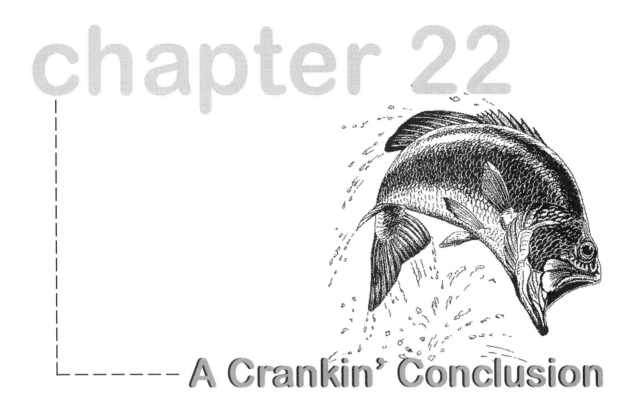

A Crankin' Conclusion

As I put the finishing touches on this book, I just had to relate my latest success story with crankbaits. It was a typically tough October day in search of big pike and muskies. To make matters even worse, we were faced with strong winds from the east, low water, and decaying weeds which all made for a challenging situation. My partner, Mike Novak, and I started out casting bucktail spinners with no success. We then switched to jerkbaits – still no action. We tried all kinds of cover options, but found the best baitfish sign in the few remaining weeds. The thick, shallow weed cover, where we anticipated the fish to be, made it difficult to choose a crankbait, but what did we have to loose? Now was as good a time as any.

The sun was just setting when Mike decided to try one of my hand-made prototype minnow baits. Even though the weeds were thick on this particular spot, and the depth was no more than four feet, Mike was determined to try something different. His first cast, a long one, put the firetiger fake over the top of some of the thickest remaining stands of cabbage. I knew he was going to have some trouble working the bait back

cleanly through those weeds, but who was I to argue or criticize. We hadn't taken a single fish.

Mike vigorously jiggled his rod tip in an effort to free-up the crankbait. Just as I launched another cast the water erupted to my right side, and almost simultaneously I felt Mike set the hook. "That fish just exploded right out of the middle of that weed patch", Mike yelled. "My bait was full of weeds and he still hit it!" I didn't doubt his claim since there was still a stalk of cabbage weeds dangling from the lure as the fish passed by the boat. A few moments later, I slipped the net under our first musky of the trip. It was 35 inches long.

Mike had just taken a musky on his first cast with that minnow bait. As soon as he switched to a crankbait, he caught "the fish of 10,000 casts." After a few quick photos and a release, Mike checked his lure for hook sharpness, and then made another cast. With a big smile on his face and an excited voice, he said "I can't believe it took me this long to put that lure on". But two jerks into his retrieve he had yet another strike. "I can't believe it", Mike exclaimed. "I've got another one!" He sure as heck did. Two muskies on two casts! As my video camera recorded the action, Mike landed another musky, slightly smaller than the last one.

That was enough to convince me to change lures. I quickly searched for my only other hand-made proto-type ShallowRaider, snapped it on, and got to work. Within five minutes or so, I had a strike too, only this time it was a much bigger fish that our previous en-counters. This fish stayed deep, bulldogging for about five minutes without showing itself. Night fall was quickly approaching, the air temp was dropping, and the wind was gusting, but the fish battled on. Just when I thought we'd have to make the ten mile trip back in total darkness, the fish, a fat 45-incher surfaced. A smooth net job, a few quick photos, and a safe release ended our day. Once again, crankbaits saved the trip. By the way, by noon the next day, we had boated three more muskies on that same lure; 35, 41 and 43 inches, and a bonus 40-inch pike.

Another day and another chapter in the success of crankbaits for big gamefish. Crankbaits have surely had an incredible impact on my success as an angler. I owe a lot of my success to crankbaits, and the knowledge I've obtained from using them. This story is but one example in a lifelong quest to learn as much about these lures as possible. In that effort, I've caught a bunch of big fish, including many trophy-class fish of several species. Largemouths over 10 pounds, and smallmouths over six; my biggest walleye, a 12-pounder, all fell for a crankbait. So did my biggest pike, a 48-incher, which is still a line class world record. Of course, crankbaits have also taken some incredible muskies for me, too. A number of these, as you know, have exceeded the ultimate benchmark of 50 inches. My biggest lake trout is also a crankbait fish. What can I say? I've hit a lot of home runs with crankbaits.

Hopefully, if you've learned anything from this book, it's that crankbaits can be fished successfully in a wide variety of ways. I've also tried to impress upon you how important technique is to successful crankbait fishing. The term "crankbait" tends to suggest a mind-less "cast & wind" mentality, yet rarely is such an approach effective. True crankbait fishing involves careful planning, strategy and technique. The right lure must be chosen, and it needs to be matched with the right tackle. Then it must be fished correctly. Miss out on any of these key elements and productivity is sure to drop off substantially.

We now know that speed control is a critical element to crankbait success, and that speed control does not mean fast. It means controlling the speed of the crankbait in order to make it perform to its maxi-mum potential. We also now know that some crankbaits work best with faster retrieves, while others must be worked slowly. Each lure style has its own personality and potential. They are simply tools, designed for specific purposes. Choose the right lure, work it at the right speed and good things happen. To expect things from certain crankbaits, outside their designed purpose, is simply asking too much.

If you did your homework while reading this book, you should now be able to visualize a crankbait's action and running depth by recognizing certain design elements before actually making a cast with it for the first time. In other words, you should be able to look at a tackle shelf full of lures and know approximately how each one will react in the water, what kind of action it will have, and how deep it will run. The dynamics of diving lip shape, size and angle give this all away. Where the line tie is positioned on this diving lip also affects how deep it will run and what its action will probably be. Of course, you now know that, too.

You also now have a good understanding of what makes a crankbait run at a certain depth. No longer will you have to ask the question "how deep does that lure run"? You'll have a good general idea before even fishing, by simply looking at the lure. You'll also know how to make it run deeper by changing to a thinner gauge line and increasing your cast length or trolling line distance. You also know some other tricks to employ in order to make a lure run deeper or shallower depending upon your needs at the time.

Perhaps the most intriguing things we've discussed along the way are the vast differences between various types of crankbaits. No longer will you make the mistake of thinking that all crankbaits are basically the same. Floating divers, lipless cranks, minnow baits, count-down sinkers, and suspenders all have their time and place. There's a noticeable difference between all these various crankbaits in both action and application and you'll be ready to pick the right one for each situation. Of course, on-the-water experience is always the best teacher. Practice is definitely needed in order to really perfect your crankbait fishing.

While few anglers would ever consider fishing a crankbait in weeds, you now know that a crankbait can be deadly in weeds as well as many other forms of cover. The trick here is to choose the right style of crankbait for cover. It's a floating diver. Then you have to maintain speed control so you can manipulate it through the cover. Once you've mastered crankbait fishing in cover such as weeds, wood, and rocks, you step into a different class as an angler. Few competitors would consider pitching crankbaits in spots you would. Of course, that's one of the reasons why crankbaits are so effective in these cover situations.

You now will recognize when a crankbait is out-of-tune, and then know exactly what steps are needed to correct the problem. No longer will you tolerate a crankbait that runs right or left of center. It must track like an arrow. In that process, every crankbait in your box becomes a much better fish-catcher.

I'm sure you'll agree by now that crankbaits are truly phenomenal lures. Their innate ability to catch fish is also unparalleled. The record books are dominated by world record-class fish of all taken on

You've seen this picture before, but it's worth looking at again. To catch bass like this you've got to be versatile.

crankbaits. No other lure even comes close to the productivity of a crankbait in terms of big fish potential. If you're after big fish, crankbaits are sure bets.

I doubt that crankbaits will ever loose their fish-catching productivity. They've been around for nearly a century now, and they still catch as many fish as they did when they first hit the scene. New body shapes, new materials, new diving lip configurations, and much more is likely to come. Some of these innovative concepts may make the lure hold up longer, dive deeper, or wiggle with a slightly different action. But when the chips are down, your old favorites will still catch 'em too.

You're eventually going to develop a short list of "confidence crankbaits" that you know you can rely on to catch fish when things are tough. You'll know more about the workings of these confidence crankers than all other lures. You'll know how deep they run, what

This book is dedicated to the memory of my dad (right). My fishing buddy, and the guy who got me started fishing.

reels work best with them, how fast they should be retrieved, and so on. The more success you have with these confidence crankers, the more cherished they'll become. They'll always have a special place in your tackle box. You'll be crushed if you ever lose one of them.

As I've attempted to show throughout this book, crankbaits have many applications. They are not just a deep, open-water lure as some would believe. They are extremely versatile lures that can catch fish in almost any situation. Even though crankbaits have become famous for their productivity in deeper waters, the that opens this chapter reveals that these lures can be just as deadly in weed-choked shallows. At this point, I am certain that crankbaits will catch fish in almost any situation.

Weather, water temperature, time of day, and water clarity have little bearing on the effectiveness of crankbaits as we've learned throughout the pages of this book. Crankbaits will catch fish right after ice-out in the spring, as well as right before ice-up in the fall. Crankbaits are good during the dog days of mid-

summer, at high noon and near midnight. Clear water is great for crankin', but so is dark, turbid water. Crankbaits are simply the most versatile lures ever designed. They take bass, walleyes, pike, trout, and muskies in almost any conditions. If there's water and gamefish present, crankbaits are sure to catch 'em. They simply have no equal in terms of raw versatility as fish-catchers.

I plan to experiment with various new crankbait concepts in the future. But I'll bet my old favorites will still catch plenty of fish. One thing is sure not to change, knowledge will always be the key to catching more fish consistently. The more you learn about crankbaits and how to fish them, the more fish you're going to catch. Never stop learning everything you can about the fish you pursue as well as the lures you pursue them with. This is the only way I know of to insure your success as an angler. Some like to call fishing success "luck". I think you make your own luck.

Keep crankin'

Joe Bucher